"We have done this because we love liberty
and hate authority."

— Voltairine de Cleyre

The Center for a Stateless Society
presents

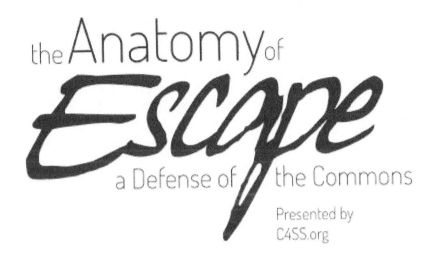

Edited by
JAMES TUTTLE
Financial Coordinator C4SS

Cover designed by
BENJAMIN GODWIN

"*Intellectual property,*" *and the states that enforce it, are the enemies of knowledge, progress, and human life itself. It's time to destroy them.*

— Kevin Carson

Woody Guthrie Public License

"*Anyone found copying and distributing this book without permission will be considered a mighty good friend of ours, because we don't give a durn.*"

The Anatomy of Escape
A Defense of the Commons
Presented by the Center for a Stateless Society

Published by Kindle Direct Publishing
Anno MMXIX

ISBN: 978-172-663-4106

Interior Book Design & Typesetting
by
Alfred DeStefano III
Fourth Mansions Press
fourthmansions.com

The Anatomy of Escape: A Defense of the Commons
Includes bibliographic references
1. Economic – philosophy. 2. Commons. 3. Public Property. 4. Anarchism

Cover Image based on landscape image by Worapol Sittiphaet Landscape #1
Cover design by Benjamin Godwin (benjamingodwin.com)

WE CAN NO LONGER BLIND OURSELVES to the fact that concentrated economic power has become as reckless and ruthless and coercive as concentrated political power.

We can no longer attack subsidies for the poor while supporting even greater subsidies for the rich.

We can no longer speak of protecting freedom in the world by turning the world into protective hamlets. We can no longer oppose tyranny by emulating it.

We cannot speak of individual freedom and free communities, self-reliance and self-responsibility, while honoring the assembly line, promoting urban demolition, and making fetish of commodities. We cannot speak of honest work while honest working people are alienated from the work and treated as mere extensions of their machines.

We cannot attack the abuses of arrogant and bureaucratic labor leaders without attacking the abuses of arrogant and bureaucratic industrial and business leaders.

We cannot speak of a land of liberty and a national-security state in the same breath — we must defend freedom at home if we are ever to have freedom in the world.

We cannot speak of a sweet land of liberty when the very land is soured by greed of those who turn the landscape into real estate, who turn the rivers into open sewers, who see in every living thing nothing but a dollar in the process.

— Karl Hess

OUR GOAL IS NOT TO ASSUME leadership of existing institutions, but rather to render them irrelevant. We don't want to take over the state or change its policies. We want to render its laws unenforceable. We don't want to take over corporations and make them more "socially responsible." We want to build a counter-economy of open-source information, neighborhood garage manufacturing, Permaculture, encrypted currency and mutual banks, leaving the corporations to die on the vine along with the state.

We do not hope to reform the existing order. We intend to serve as its grave-diggers.

— Kevin Carson

The solution is not to seize the state, to seize control of the hierarchies controlling the dominant political and economic institutions, nor to displace the existing ruling class in control of them. So long as these hierarchies exist, they'll simply create new ruling classes to replace the old ones. The only solution is to secede from their rule, to bypass them, to make them obsolete, to build a new society in which they are no longer needed.

— Kevin Carson

Contents

Page

Introduction
Roderick T. Long 1

1 **The Network Economy as New Mutualism**
M. George van der Meer 5

2 **In Defense Of Public Space**
Roderick T. Long 11

3 **A Plea For Public Property**
Roderick T. Long 19

4 **Funding Public Goods: Six Solutions**
Roderick T. Long 35

5 **The Quality Of Publicness**
Dawie Coetzee 45

6 **Communal Property: A Libertarian Analysis**
Kevin Carson 51

7 **Governance, Agency, and Autonomy: Anarchist Themes in the Work of Elinor Ostrom**
Kevin Carson 127

8 **David Graeber's Anarchist Thought: A Survey**
Kevin Carson 175

9   "Public" vs. "Private" Sector
    Kevin Carson 241

10 Geography and Anarchy: A Libertarian Social
    Order as Goal
    Thom Holterman 251

11 Power and Property: A Corollary
    Grant Mincy 269

12 Any (Good) Thing The State Can Do, We Can
    Do Better
    Gary Chartier 347

Authors
    355

C4SS's Mission Statement
    359

Molinari Institute Mission Statement
    361

Alliance of the Libertarian Left Preamble
    363

C4SS's Editorial Policy
    365

Donate Today!
    367

For M. George van der Meer,
thank you for helping light the way.

"Because of its defining flexibility, anarchism is the thing to rise and meet what's next."

INTRODUCTION

Roderick T. Long

Market anarchists favor replacing the state with a fully free market, i.e., one with no restrictions on voluntary production and exchange; all functions of the state are either to be abolished (when they are inherently invasive of people's right to live their lives peacefully) or turned over to free competition (when they are not).

Many market anarchists—especially, though not exclusively, those associated with market anarchism's "right" wing[1]–

---

[1]Speaking generally, and allowing for various exceptions and qualifications: on the "right" wing of market anarchism are the "anarcho-capitalists," who expect the stateless free-market society they advocate to look much like the landscape of contemporary capitalism—large hierarchical corporations, exclusion of workers from ownership and management, etc.—but without the state; while on market anarchism's "left" wing are the "agorists," "mutualists," and "free-market anti-capitalists" who see economic privilege and vast concentrations of wealth as the product of government intervention on behalf of big business, and who expect a radically freed market to be characterized by economic levelling and worker empowerment. The essays in this book come broadly from the left-wing market anarchist position; for a fuller exposition of that position, see Gary Chartier and Charles W. Johnson, eds., *Markets Not Capitalism: Individualist Anarchism Against Bosses, Inequality, Corporate Power, and Structural Poverty* (Minor Compositions, 2011);

tend to envision a fully free market as one in which all resources are privately owned. The essays in this book offer a different perspective: that a stateless free-market society can and should include, alongside private property, a robust role for public property—not, of course, in the sense of *governmental* property, but rather in the sense of property that is owned by the general community rather than by specific individuals or formally organized groups.

The terms "public property," "collective property," and "common property" are often used interchangeably. (Certainly in my own articles, herein included, I rather carelessly did so.) But they are often distinguished as well—though not always in the same way.

As some use these terms, property is *collective* when each member of the relevant group must get permission from all the other members before using it, whereas property is *common* when each member of the relevant group is free to use it without needing to ask permission from anybody. But even this distinction is a bit too blunt, as the *nature of the proposed use* will presumably determine whether permission needs to be asked. May I, a resident of this village, walk across the village green without asking permission from the other villagers? Of course. May I, again without asking permission, bring in a backhoe and start digging up the green in order to lay the foundations for a new shopping mall? Of course not. The nature of the use whereby the property's publicness is established and maintained will presumably determine which new uses are consistent with that original use and so require no additional authorization, and which are an interference with that use and so do need authorization.

A different way in which these terms are sometimes used is to describe "collective" property as open to members of a specific group and "common" property as open to everyone, period; but this seems a matter of degree also. Does "everyone,

---

available online at: http://radgeek.com/gt/2011/10/Markets-Not-Capitalism-2011-Chartier-and-Johnson.pdf

period" really mean every rational being in the universe? In one of the articles included in this volume, I denied the existence of any "limit to the size of the collective to which one can freely give one's property," but can a transfer be said to have succeeded if there is no way, in the natural course of things, for the intended recipient to learn of, accept, or reject the proffered item?

Some defenders of "total privatization" argue that common use creates, not common property rights, but merely easement rights against those who later (legitimately) privatize the property.² But it is unclear how far this distinction is substantive and how far merely terminological; to answer this and other such questions we will need to work out a more detailed theory of the specific contours of common property rights, and of the extent to which those contours are (or are not) appropriately responsive to consequentialist considerations, local traditions and expectations, the specific character of the resource and of its users' relation thereto, etc.

This book is not that theory—and its contributors would probably have a number of disagreements as to what a completed theory should look like. The delineation of the theory of common property under market anarchism is a work in progress. Think of the present volume as a conversation-starter, not a conversation-ender.

For further reading on the subject of public but non-governmental property, I highly recommend the following three articles, all (appropriately enough) freely available online to the public:

> Carol Rose, "The Comedy of the Commons: Custom, Commerce, and Inherently Public Property," *University of Chicago Law Review* 53.3

---

²See, e.g., Hans-Hermann Hoppe, "Of Private, Common, and Public Property and the Rationale for Total Privatization," *Libertarian Papers* 3.1 (2011), pp. 1-13; available online at: http://libertarianpapers.org/articles/2011/lp-3-1.pdf

(Summer 1986), pp. 711-781.[3]

David Schmidtz, "The Institution of Property," *Social Philosophy & Policy* Vol. 11.2 (Summer 1994), pp. 42-62.[4]

Randall Holcombe, "Common Property in Anarcho-Capitalism," *Journal of Libertarian Studies* 19.2 (Spring 2005), pp. 3-29.[5]

---

[3] http://digitalcommons.law.yale.edu/cgi/viewcontent.cgi?article=2827&context=fss_papers

[4] http://www.davidschmidtz.com/sites/default/files/articles/InstitutionProperty2012.pdf

[5] http://mises.org/document/2025/Common-Property-in-AnarchoCapitalism

CHAPTER
ONE

THE NETWORK ECONOMY AS NEW MUTUALISM

M. GEORGE VAN DER MEER

What kinds of economic arrangements does anarchism, as such, want? An old question given new vitality in an age in which networks of autonomous individuals and groups have become more and more relevant and difficult for overlords in capital and in the state to control. In many ways, the new economy of networks, horizontal and decentralized, is the quintessence of the ideas of anarchists such as Benjamin Tucker, who thought that free competition would be "perfect" enough to wipe out profit in exchange, rent on land, and interest on lent credit. That is because monopolization, the source of these kinds of exploitative income, is rendered impossible (or nearly so) by an economy in which a PC and relatively little capital can make each individual her own capitalist business. (See Kevin Carson's *The Homebrew Industrial Revolution*[1] and *The Desktop Regulatory State*[2]). We simply no longer need our overseers. We can employ Josiah Warren's *Cost Principle* as a tool for analyzing the

---
c4ss.org/content/17879
[1] http://homebrewindustrialrevolution.wordpress.com/
[2] http://desktopregulatorystate.wordpress.com/

network economy and the kinds of hopes we may have for it as libertarians.

Tucker in particular constantly reiterated his position that if the Cost Principle (which he regarded as the definitive principle of socialism and which would necessarily mean the absence of usury) could not be realized by libertarian means, by free competition and the demise of privilege, that it was not to be realized at all. In the individualist anarchist free market, people, credit, and resources would move so freely and fluidly, price signals would become so timely and clear, that before long selling goods or services significantly above cost would be rendered impossible. (Few free market libertarians of today share Tucker's antipathy to "usury," as such, but many now share his view of capitalism, placing it in opposition to free markets and competition.) It was thus privilege, restrictions on competition of all kinds, that allowed a capitalist/monopolist class to underpay labor and to overcharge for their products. But new technologies and the networked economy they yield are making the monopolies of old impossible by leaving regulatory and legislative attempts to limit competition powerless.

As Yochai Benkler observes of "the effects of [the] networked information economy on individual autonomy," individuals are more free to operate without the permission of the "powers that be," outside of the proper channels—be they licensing boards, regulatory bodies, or established corporations. The effects on competition will be sweeping; for where once starting a new business, producing a product, etc., required an appeal to tribute-takers in government and in formalized, capitalist institutions, it has today become easier than ever to evade the reaches of those tollways. Similarly, Siva Vaidhyanathan argues that the emergence of the Internet and "the nature of distributed systems" themselves have brought with them their own culture or ideology. He invokes John Dewey's notion of "habits of thought" to suggest that our new peer-to-peer reality has changed the way we think about everything from exchange to personal relationships. And we can perceive the ways that technology informs culture (and vice versa) all around us, back through history. The work of the Center for a Stateless Society's Kevin Carson has demonstrated the effects of a subsidized American car culture on the overall economy, suffusing everything from suburban sprawl to distribution paths for consumer goods. Nothing about the present system was simply a foregone conclusion. Authority has impacted the technological ecosystem at every step of development, suppressed alternatives, and obliged the established economic powers.

Contrast authoritarian capitalism with the decentralized, horizontally-networked and -ordered free market presently materializing, one in which the effective exercise of power through hierarchy is less and less possible. Law professor Butler Shaffer uses the metaphor of "a giant centrifuge" to describe the current trend toward decentralization and away from the pyramidal structures of corporate and government power that we've had to date. With "vertically-structured" institutions in decline, being replaced by networks, society is "spinning increased decision-making authority and control into the hands of individuals." Such was the vision of the individualist anarchists—if *everyone* had the ability to become a capitalist, that is, had equal access to the means of production, then exploitation would cease to be a significant source of individual wealth. Everyone would have to work for his keep, but since no one could exert the power of the state to create "class laws," limiting competition, relatively equal exchange would obtain as the general rule. If the individualists criticized vulgar proponents of "laissez faire" for their inconsistencies, then they also (and even more strenuously) excoriated vulgar socialists for prescribing an absolute equality of material conditions, to be reached through the absolute authority of a central state. Remove coercive privilege, they argued, and whatever result prevailed would necessarily be the most just. Theirs was the ultimate "open source" economy, enabling each individual to enter into any economic endeavor she pleased, to contribute in any way, thereby occupying the margins on which capitalist profits rested. The Internet has thrown open those margins to the benefit of individuals and at the expense of established corporations who have used legislative and regulatory means to keep them closed.

The individualists, from Josiah Warren onward, shared amongst one another an enthusiasm for and desire to undertake experimentations within the economic realm, eschewing uniformity and doctrinaire declarations about what a free economy must be. Experimentation of the kinds they esteemed is of course a threat to the status quo, and thus to the organizations that depend upon and hope to perpetuate it. This is among the chief reasons why the propaganda of largeness, vertical integration, and hierarchy have all but completely overtaken the conversation surrounding efficiency. Anarchists like Benjamin Tucker certainly were not hostile or opposed to largeness *per se*, in and of itself, and neither should we anarchists of today be. Still, Tucker gainsaid the claim that large-scale production for a modern society would require huge accumulations and concentrations of capital. Anticipating the emancipation and empowerment of individuals that we're witnessing today, Tucker wrote, "Processes are expected to become cheaper, more compact, and more easily manageable, until they shall come again within the capacity of individuals and small combinations." He confidently looked forward to a reversal of the centralization and hierarchy he saw in his own day, which has arguably only been compounded in the hundred-plus years since.

With the digitization of the economy generally, and its attending vulnerability and breakdown of monopoly rents, intellectual property has become increasingly important for the monopolist class as a safeguard of those rents. Pitted against the development of the new economy, intellectual property will be a last-ditch effort both for entrenched models in domestic economies and for established, developed nations in the global economy. Expansions of technology have made a post-scarcity world of abundance not only possible, but very likely to come to fruition at some stage in the future. Standing in the way, however, is the capitalist attempt to pen in that technology, which as an abstract thing contained in *ideas* must rely on increasingly draconian intellectual property measures. Scholars such as C. Ford Runge and Edi Defrancesco have done a great service in observing the analogy between the enclosure of common lands and the attempt to subject ideas—specifically "relating to genomics, computer software, and scientific data"—to monopoly ownership standards.

We are now approaching a breaking point, a culmination of long-unfolding trends that will witness the old forces of rigid hierarchy and centrality collide with the dynamism of the networked, freed market. Outcomes, wins and losses, will turn upon the fulcrum of the steps that we take as free, autonomous individuals to leverage and pry ever more open the cracks that we find in the old infrastructure. New currencies (giving life to the mutualistic notions of our anarchist forebears), new organization models, new definitions of liberty and community—all are issuing forth from technological developments of only very recent vintage. Because of its defining flexibility, anarchism is the thing to rise and meet what's next.

CHAPTER
TWO

IN DEFENSE OF PUBLIC SPACE

RODERICK T. LONG

❋ *Nothing to Gain But Our Chains?*

In an important series of articles,[1,2,3,4] Rich Hammer has recently invited us to rethink some of our assumptions about what a libertarian society would be like. We ordinarily think of a libertarian society as one of maximum freedom and maximum privacy: a society where you can do whatever you like (so long as it's peaceful) and no one else can pry into your personal affairs.

Rich suggests otherwise. A libertarian society, he argues, is one in which public space—both physical space and decision space—has been privatized as far as possible. This is desirable, he says, because it is easier to police irresponsible behavior

---

Spring 1996 issue of *Formulations* by the Free Nation Foundation: c4ss.org/content/14724

[1] Richard Hammer, "The Power of Ostracism," in *Formulations*, Vol. II, No. 2 (Winter 1994-95).

[2] Richard Hammer, "Protection from Mass Murderers: Communication of Danger," in *Formulations*, Vol. II, No. 3 (Spring 1995).

[3] Richard Hammer, "'Liberty' is a Bad Name," in *Formulations*, Vol. II, No. 4 (Summer 1995).

[4] Richard Hammer, "Toward Voluntary Courts and Enforcement," in *Formulations*, Vol. III, No. 2 (Winter 1995-96).

in private space than in public space. Since no one can be excluded from public space, no one has any incentive to maintain it properly, and so a "tragedy of the commons" is generated. By contrast, in a world where everything is privately owned, we must abide, wherever we go, by the rules laid down by the owners. Rich envisions a society in which no one is allowed access to the means of cooperation with others unless he submits to a multitude of restrictions: bonding, disarmament, full disclosure of finances, and so forth. Those who do not comply with these rules will find themselves cut off from food, drink, communication, transportation, even the use of restroom facilities.

Rich's arguments are a useful corrective to the popular notion that a libertarian society would be a hopeless chaos. But we may feel some discomfort at how far Rich's vision goes in the direction of the opposite extreme. In a famous quote, the nineteenth-century anarchist Proudhon wrote:

> To be GOVERNED is to be kept in sight, inspected, spied upon, directed, law-driven, numbered, enrolled, indoctrinated, preached at, controlled, estimated, valued, censured, commanded, ...noted, registered, ...taxed, stamped, measured, ...assessed, licensed, authorized, admonished, forbidden, reformed, corrected, punished.[5]

But if to be *free* is also to be inspected, licensed, numbered, stamped, authorized, and so forth, we might wonder whether building a Free Nation is worth the effort.

But is this world of hyper-regulated anarchy the only possible model for a libertarian society? I don't think so. But to see why it is not, I suggest we need to rethink our assumption that a libertarian society must be a society without public space.

---

[5] Pierre-Joseph Proudhon, *General Idea of the Revolution in the Nineteenth Century*, 1851; trans. John B. Robinson (London: Pluto Press, 1989), p. 294. (This quotation is the inspiration for the heading "To be governed..." on *Cato Policy Report*'s back-page horror file.)

✳ Public Property Without Government

When we think of public property, we think of *government* property. But this has not traditionally been the case. Throughout history, legal doctrine has recognized, alongside property owned by the *organized* public (that is, the public as organized into a state and represented by government officials), an additional category of property owned by the *unorganized* public. This was property that the public at large was deemed to have a right of access to, but without any presumption that *government* would be involved in the matter at all. I have learned much about this idea from excellent recent articles by Carol Rose and David Schmidtz:

> Implicit in these older doctrines is the notion that, even if a property should be open to the public, it does not follow that public rights should necessarily vest in an active governmental manager. ...the nineteenth-century common law...recognized...property collectively "owned" and "managed" by society at large....[6]

> Public property is not always a product of rapacious governments or mad ideologues. Sometimes it evolves spontaneously as a way of solving real problems.[7]

I have no interest in defending public property in the sense of property belonging to the *organized* public (i.e., the state). In fact, I do not think government property is public property at all; it is really the private property of an agency calling itself the government. (This agency may claim to be holding the property in trust for the public, but its activities generally belie this.) What I wish to defend is the idea of property rights inhering in the unorganized public.

---

[6] Carol Rose, "The Comedy of the Commons: Custom, Commerce, and Inherently Public Property," p. 720; in *University of Chicago Law Review*, Vol. 53, No. 3 (Summer 1986), pp. 711-781.

[7] David Schmidtz, "The Institution of Property," p. 51; in *Social Philosophy & Policy*, Vol. 11 (1994), pp. 42-62.

❉ *The Economic Argument*

Since the days of Aristotle, the traditional argument against collective ownership of any kind has been the tragedy of the commons: if each additional use depletes or degrades a resource, and yet there is no way of restricting access to the resource, then no one will be motivated to use the resource sparingly, since what one person refrains from, another may take, and so the first person is no better off for having refrained. Hence the need to restrict access by privatizing the commons.

What Rose and Schmidtz point out is that this argument works only to the extent that additional use *diminishes* the value of the resource. But this is not always the case; sometimes, adding more users enhances the value of the resource: the more the merrier. When that is so, there is no point in restricting access; we then have what Rose calls a *comedy* of the commons (i.e., happy ending rather than sad).

Rose's point is clearest when we consider decision space. Think of the libertarian movement as filling a decision space: which libertarian books and articles will be written, which libertarian projects and causes will be promoted, and how, etc. The libertarian movement is a public space; anyone can participate, at any time. And this is all to the good. It would be foolish to restrict access, to make it more difficult for people to participate in the movement, because the movement is not a scarce resource that can be used up; on the contrary, the more additional people start participating, the closer the aims of the movement as a whole will come to being achieved. (Consider how Ayn Rand and Leonard Peikoff have weakened the effectiveness of their own Objectivist movement by trying to make it into their own private property, purging potentially valuable contributors to the cause whenever they resisted the authority of the "owners.")

Intellectual property is another comedy of the commons, I would argue, since one person's use of an idea does not deplete the idea for others, and ordinarily even enhances it. How else, after all, does civilization advance except via some people grabbing other people's ideas and improving on them, to the benefit of society as a whole?

But the clearest case of a comedy of the commons, as Rose and Schmidtz point out, is the market itself. The more people participate in the market, the more everyone benefits. The market is a paradigm of public space. Protectionist laws attempt to turn the market, or portions of it, into *private* property by erecting coercive barriers to access; this sort of "privatization," though, is destructive, and anathema to libertarian ideals.

Of course, these are easy cases of comedies of the commons, because things like markets, ideas, and political movements are not physical, and so are not subject to scarcity. Physical space, though, is always subject to scarcity; so how could there be comedies of the commons *here*? Mustn't any scarce resource inevitably succumb to the tragedy of the commons unless access is restricted?

Not necessarily. There are some cases in which, at least within certain parameters, a physical resource's value is enhanced by increased use. As Rose and Schmidtz point out, this is particularly true when the resource is tied in some way to a *non*-physical comedy-of-the-commons resource, like a market or a town festival; since "the more, the merrier" applies to these non-physical resources, it also applies, to *some* extent, to the physical land on which the market or festival is held, and to the physical roadways leading there. Since everyone benefits from having more people come to the fair, everyone also benefits from making physical access to the fairgrounds free as well.

Of course there are limits. If *too* many people come, the fair will be too crowded to be enjoyable. But this simply shows that some goods have *both* tragedy-of-the-commons and comedy-of-the-commons aspects, and which one predominates will depend on the circumstances. Public property may be the efficient solution in some cases, and private property in others. (Or a bundle of property rights may be split up, with some public, some private.) Most societies have had some common areas, policed by custom only, without overgrazing problems.

* The Ethical Argument

On the libertarian view, we have a right to the fruit of our labor, and we also have a right to what people freely give us. Public property can arise in both these ways. Consider a village near a lake. It is common for the villagers to walk down to the lake to go fishing. In the early days of the community it's hard to get to the lake because of all the bushes and fallen branches in the way. But over time, the way is cleared and a path forms—not through any centrally coordinated effort, but simply as a result of all the individuals walking that way day after day.

The cleared path is the product of labor—not any individual's labor, but all of them together. If one villager decided to take advantage of the now-created path by setting up a gate and charging tolls, he would be violating the collective property right that the villagers together have earned.

Public property can also be the product of gift. In nineteenth-century England, it was common for roads to be built privately and then donated to the public for free use. This was done not out of altruism but because the roadbuilders owned land and businesses alongside the site of the new road, and they knew that having a road there would increase the value of their land and attract more customers to their businesses. Thus, the unorganized public can legitimately come to own land, both through original acquisition (the mixing of labor) and through voluntary transfer.

✽ *Public and Private: Allies, Not Enemies*

Public space has both advantages and disadvantages. On the plus side, unrestricted access means you can do as you please there, without asking permission, so long as you don't violate others' rights. On the minus side, the difficulty of policing public space means there may well be more irresponsible behavior there. A society that permits both public and private spaces—that has public and private roads competing with each other, for example—allows individuals to make the trade-off for themselves. If you want the freedom to drive your motorcycle in the nude, with a howitzer strapped to your back, and you're willing to put up with a greater risk of irresponsible behavior from others, take the public road. If you prefer greater security, and are willing to obey a few more rules and suffer some invasion of privacy to get it, take the private road. If one option becomes too onerous, the other is still available. Private space can become oppressive if there is no public space to compete with it—*and vice versa.*

I envision a world of many individual private spaces, linked by a framework of public spaces. The existence of such a framework may even be a prerequisite for complete control over one's own private space. Suppose a trespasser comes on my land and I want to push him off. If all the land around me is private as well, where can I push him, without violating the rights of my neighbors? But if there is a public walkway nearby, I have somewhere to push him. Thus, the availability of public space may be a moral precondition for the right to freedom from trespassers.

CHAPTER
THREE

A PLEA FOR PUBLIC PROPERTY

RODERICK T. LONG

❋ *Public or Private?*

Libertarians often assume that a free society will be one in which all (or nearly all) property is private. I have previously expressed my dissent from this consensus, arguing that libertarian principles instead support a substantial role for public property.[1] In this article I develop this heretical position further.

Let me specify once again what sort of public property I am defending. To most people, "public property" means "government property," on the (dubious) theory that governments hold their property in trust for the public, and administer such property with an eye to the public interest. As an anarchist, I do not regard government as a legitimate institution, and so do not advocate government property of any sort. But this is not the only kind of public property. As I wrote in my earlier article:

Spring 1996 issue of *Formulations* by the Free Nation Foundation: c4ss.org/content/14721

[1] "In Defense of Public Space," *Formulations*, Vol. III, No. 3 (Spring 1996). Reprinted as Chapter Two of the present text.

> Throughout history, legal doctrine has recognized, alongside property owned by the *organized* public (that is, the public as organized into a state and represented by government officials), an additional category of property owned by the *unorganized* public. This was property that the public at large was deemed to have a right of access to, but without any presumption that *government* would be involved in the matter at all.

It is public property in this sense that I am defending.

I want to stress, however, that in defending public property I do not mean to be criticizing private property. I am a strong proponent of private property. But what I am maintaining is that the very features that make private property valuable are also possessed, in certain contexts, by public property, and so public property can be valuable for the same reasons.

First I shall consider three common libertarian arguments for private property, and I shall try to show that each of these arguments also supports a role for public property. Second, I shall consider several objections I have encountered to my position, and I shall attempt to meet them.

✽ *The Natural-Rights Argument for Private Property*

The standard libertarian natural-rights argument for private property goes back to John Locke's *Second Treatise of Government,* and rests on two basic claims: a *normative* claim about how we should treat other people, and a *descriptive* claim about the boundaries of the person.

The normative claim we may call the Respect Principle. This principle says that it is morally wrong to subject other people to one's own ends without their consent, except as a response to aggression by those others. (There is disagreement as to what deeper moral truths, if any, provide the grounding for this principle, but that question lies beyond my present topic.)

The descriptive claim we may call the Incorporation Principle. This principle says that once I "mix my labor" with an external object—i.e., alter it so as to make it an instrument of my ongoing projects—that object becomes part of me. The case for this principle is that it explains why the matter I'm made of is part of me. After all, I wasn't born with it; living organisms survive through constant replacement of material. The difference between an apple I eat (whose matter becomes part of my cellular composition) and a wooden branch that I carve into a spear (a detachable extension of my hand) is only one of degree.[2]

When we put the Respect Principle and the Incorporation Principle together, the result is that it is wrong to appropriate the products of other people's labor; for if your spear is a part of you, then I cannot subject your spear to my ends without thereby subjecting *you* to my ends. In the words of the nineteenth-century French libertarians Leon Wolowski and Émile Levasseur:

> The producer has left a fragment of his own person in the thing which has thus become valuable, and may hence be regarded as a prolongation of the faculties of man acting upon external nature. As a free being he belongs to himself; now the cause, that is to say, the productive force, is himself; the effect, that is to say, the wealth produced, is still himself. ...Property, made manifest by labor, participates in the rights of the person whose emanation it is; like him, it is inviolable so long as it does not extend so far as to come into collision with another right....[3]

---

[2] For a fuller defense of this claim, see Samuel C. Wheeler III, "Natural Property Rights as Body Rights," in Tibor R. Machan, ed., *The Main Debate: Communism versus Capitalism* (New York: Random House, 1987), pp. 272–289.

[3] Cited in Murray N. Rothbard, *For A New Liberty: The Libertarian Manifesto*, Revised Edition (San Francisco: Fox & Wilkes, 1994), pp. 36–37.

The Incorporation Principle transforms the Respect Principle from a simple right to personal security into a general right to private property.

✲ *How Natural Rights Support Public Property Too*

But this Lockean argument for private property rights can be adapted to support public property rights as well. Lockeans hold that individuals have a property right to the products of their labor (so long as they trespass on no one else's rights in producing them); they also typically hold that individuals have a property right to any goods that they receive by voluntary transfer from their legitimate owners (since to deny such a right would be to interfere with the right of the *givers* to dispose of their property as they choose). But the public at large can acquire property rights in both these ways. To quote once more from "In Defense of Public Space":

> Consider a village near a lake. It is common for the villagers to walk down to the lake to go fishing. In the early days of the community it's hard to get to the lake because of all the bushes and fallen branches in the way. But over time, the way is cleared and a path forms—not through any centrally coordinated effort, but simply as a result of all the individuals walking that way day after day.
>
> The cleared path is the product of labor—not any individual's labor, but of all of them together. If one villager decided to take advantage of the now-created path by setting up a gate and charging tolls, he would be violating the collective property right that the villagers together have earned.
>
> Public property can also be the product of gift. In nineteenth-century England, it was common for roads to be built privately and then donated to the public for free use. This was done not out of altruism but because the roadbuilders owned land and businesses alongside the site of the new road, and they knew

that having a road there would increase the value of their land and attract more customers to their businesses.

Since collectives, like individuals, can mix their labor with unowned resources to make those resources more useful to their purposes, collectives too can claim property rights by homestead. And since collectives, like individuals, can be the beneficiaries of free voluntary transfer, collectives too can claim property rights by bequest.

I should note one important difference between the homesteading case and the bequest case. In the homesteading case, it is presumably not the human race at large, but only the inhabitants of the village, that acquire a collective property right in the cleared path; since it would be difficult for humankind as a whole, or even a substantial portion thereof, to mix its labor with a single resource, and so the homesteading argument places an upper limit on the size of property-owning collectives. But there seems to be no analogous limit to the size of the collective to which one can freely give one's property, so here the recipient might well be the human race as a whole.

I have argued that the Lockean argument does not specify private property as the only justifiable option, but makes a place for public property as well. It should also be noted that in at least one case, the Lockean argument positively forbids private property: namely, the case of intellectual property.

This fact is not always recognized by Lockeans. But consider: suppose Proprius, a defender of protectionist legislation, were to invoke Lockean principles, saying, "Well, surely private property is a good thing, right? So the market for widgets should be my private property; no one else should be allowed to enter that market without my permission. I demand a government-granted monopoly in widget production." No Lockean would take this argument seriously, for a market consists in the freely chosen interactions of individuals—so

Proprius cannot own a market without owning people, and ownership of other people is forbidden by the Respect Principle.

Suppose, however, that Proprius, our would-be monopolist, is also the *inventor* of the widget. Is his plea for exclusive control of the widget market now justified? Many Lockeans would think so, because we have a right to control the products of our labor, and if the product of Proprius's labor is the *idea* of the widget, then no one should be able to use or implement that idea without Proprius's permission.

But the Lockean view is not that we come to own whatever we mix our labor with; rather, we come to own whatever *previously unowned* item we mix our labor with. My plowing a field does not make it mine, if the field was yours to begin with. Likewise, the fact that my labor is the causal origin of the widget-idea in your mind may mean that in *some* sense I have mixed my labor with your mind; but it was your mind to begin with, so you, not I, are the legitimate owner of any improvements I make in it.[4]

✴ The Autonomy Argument for Private Property

A somewhat different libertarian argument for private property focuses on the human need for autonomy: the ability to control one's own life without interference from others. Without private property, I have no place to stand that I can call my own; I have no protected sphere within which I can make decisions unhampered by the will of others. If autonomy (in this sense) is valuable, then we need private property for its realization and protection.

---

[4]For a fuller discussion, see my "The Libertarian Case Against Intellectual Property Rights," *Formulations*, Vol. III, No. 1 (Autumn 1995).

✽ How Autonomy Supports Public Property Too

It is true that private property provides a protected sphere of free decision-making—*for the property's owners*. But what is the position of those who are not property owners (specifically, those who do not own *land*)? A system of exclusively private property certainly does not guarantee *them* a "place to stand." If I am evicted from private plot A, where can I go, except adjoining private plot B, if there is no public highway or parkland connecting the various private spaces? If everywhere I can stand is a place where I have no right to stand without permission, then, it seems, I exist only by the sufferance of the "Lords of the Earth" (in Herbert Spencer's memorable phrase).

Far from providing a sphere of independence, a society in which all property is private thus renders the propertyless completely dependent on those who own property. This strikes me as a dangerous situation, given the human propensity to abuse power when power is available.[5]

It may be argued in response that a libertarian society will be so economically prosperous that those who own no land will easily acquire sufficient resources either to purchase land or to guarantee favorable treatment from existing land owners. This is true enough in the long run, if the society remains a genuinely libertarian one. But in the short run, while the landless are struggling to better their condition, the land owners might be able to exploit them in such a way as to turn the society into something other than a free nation.

---

[5]This is a reason for my reservations about the proprietary-community model for a free nation, in which all land in the nation is held by a central agency and leased to its inhabitants. See my "The Return of Leviathan: Can We Prevent It?" *Formulations*, Vol. III, No. 3 (Spring 1996).

✴ The Rivalry Argument for Private Property

For many libertarians, the most important argument for private property is what Garret Hardin has labeled "the tragedy of the commons" (though the basic idea goes back to Aristotle). Most resources are *rivalrous*—that is to say, the use of the resource by one person diminishes the amount, or the value, of that resource for others. If a rivalrous resource is also public property, meaning that no member of the public may be excluded from its use, there will be no incentive to conserve or improve the resource (why bother to sow what others may freely reap?); on the contrary, the resource will be overused and swiftly exhausted, since the inability to exclude other users makes it risky to defer consumption (why bother to save what others may freely spend?). Hence private property is needed in order to prevent depletion of resources.

✴ How Rivalry Supports Public Property Too

The rivalry argument is quite correct as far as it goes. But how far is that?

First, let's notice that the argument only applies to goods that are in fact rivalrous. So once again it doesn't apply to intellectual property; my use of the idea of the widget doesn't make less available for others. Nor does it make others' widgets less valuable; on the contrary, the more widgets there are, the more uses for widgets are likely to be discovered or developed, and so the value of each widget increases. Ideas are public property, in that no one may be legitimately excluded from their use.

Another example of a largely nonrivalrous good is the Internet. I say *largely* nonrivalrous, because the Internet does have a physical basis, which, though constantly expanding, is finite at any given time, and an increase in users can cause delays for everyone. But this rivalrous aspect is offset by the reverse effect: the value of the Internet to any one user increases as the volume of available information, potential correspondents, etc., increases; so additional users on balance *increase* the value of the good as a whole.

It might be argued that this the-more-the-merrier effect occurs only with goods that are wholly or largely nonphysical, but could never apply to more concrete resources like land. As Carol Rose and David Schmidtz have shown,[6] however, although any physical resource is finite and so inevitably has *some* tragedy-of-the-commons aspects, many resources have "comedy-of-the-commons" aspects as well, and in some cases the latter may outweigh the former, thus making public property more efficient than private property.

For instance (to adapt one of Carol Rose's examples), suppose that a public fair is a comedy-of-the-commons good; the more people who participate, the better (within certain limits, at any rate). Imagine two such fairs, one held on private property and the other on public. The private owner has an incentive to exclude all participants who do not pay him a certain fee; thus the fair is deprived of all the participants who cannot afford the fee. (I am assuming that the purpose of the fair is primarily social rather than commercial, so that impecunious participants would bring as much value to the fair as wealthy ones.) The fair held on public property will thus be more successful than the one held on private property.

Yet, it may be objected, so long as a comedy-of-the-commons good still has *some* rivalrous, tragedy-of-the-commons aspects, it will be depleted, and thus the comedy-of-the-commons benefits will be lost anyway. But this assumes that privatization is the only way to prevent overuse. In fact, however, most societies throughout history have had common areas whose users were successfully restrained by social mores,

---

[6] Carol Rose, "The Comedy of the Commons: Custom, Commerce, and Inherently Public Property," *University of Chicago Law Review*, Vol. 53, No. 3 (Summer 1986), pp. 711–781; David Schmidtz, "The Institution of Property," *Social Philosophy & Policy*, Vol. 11 (1994), pp. 42–62.

peer pressure, and the like.

✽ *Objection One: The Coherence of Public Property*

One common libertarian objection to public property—and particularly, public ownership of land—is that the whole idea makes no sense: a resource cannot be collectively owned unless every part of the resource admits of simultaneous use by all members of the collective. This objection has been forcefully stated by Isabel Paterson:

> Two bodies cannot occupy the same place at the same time. ...Ten men may be legally equal owners of one field, but none of them can get any good of it unless its occupancy and use is allotted among them by measures of time and space. ...If all ten wished to do exactly the same thing at the same time in the same spot, it would be physically impossible.... [G]roup ownership necessarily resolves into management by one person....[7]

Paterson does, however, offer the following qualification to her claim that public property is inherently impossible:

> [I]t is practicable—whether or not it is necessary or advisable—to make roads public property, because the use of a road is to traverse it. Though the user does in fact occupy a given space at a given moment, the duration is negligible, so that there is no need to take time and space into account except by negation, a prohibition: the passenger is not allowed to remain as of right indefinitely on any one spot in the road. The same rule applies to parks and public buildings. The arrangement is sufficiently practicable in those conditions to admit the fiction of "public ownership." To be sure, even in the use of a road, if too many

---

[7]Isabel Paterson, *The God of the Machine* (New Brunswick: Transaction Publishers, 1993), pp. 180–181.

> members of the public try to move along it at once, the rule reverts to first come, first served (allotment in time and space), or the authorities may close the road. The public has not the essential property right of continuous and final occupancy. ...Public property then admits of *use by the public* only in transit, not for production, exchange, consumption, or for security as standing ground.[8]

Note that here Paterson actually points out three ways in which public property can be feasible. First, it may be the case that not enough people are competing for use of the same portion of the property to cause a conflict. Paterson assumes this will only happen in cases where any one user's occupancy of a given area is of minimal duration; but clearly the same result could be achieved when the total volume of users is low enough, and the resource itself is homogeneous enough, that a lengthier occupancy of any particular portion of the resource is no inconvenience to anyone else.

Second and third, in cases where use is becoming rivalrous, Paterson offers two different possible solutions. One solution is to require frequent turnover, so that no one member of the public is allowed to monopolize any portion of the resource for longer than a certain time period; the other solution is to adopt "first come, first served," meaning that those who currently occupy portions of the property may stay there and exclude newcomers. Paterson thinks that both of these options take away from the genuinely "public" nature of the property. But do they?

According to Paterson, the turnover requirement takes away from the publicness of the property because the public then lacks "the essential property right of continuous and final occupancy." But is this true? If no individual *member* of the public has "the essential property right of continuous and final occupancy," it hardly follows that the public as such

---

[8]Paterson, pp. 181–182.

lacks this right; in fact, the turnover requirement is precisely a means of implementing that right.

What about the first-come-first-served rule? Paterson may think that this ends the publicness of the property because it gives individuals the right to exclude others from the particular portions they have claimed. But this falls short of a full private property right. If I have private ownership of a portion of land, then that land remains mine, off limits to others, even when I am away from the land. But if I leave the particular area of a public park that I've been squatting in, I lose all rights to it; in that respect, what I have a "right" to is more like a place in line than it is like freehold property.

Which is preferable, the turnover rule or the first-come-first-served rule? Presumably it depends on the function of the resource in question. In the case of a road, it is in the interest of the owners—the public—that the turnover rule be applied, because a road loses its usefulness if it cannot be traversed. However, the autonomy argument suggests that not all public property should be subject to the turnover rule, so in some cases the first-come-first-served rule is appropriate.

Suppose a conflict arises between two users of the property, one who thinks it should be governed by the turnover rule, and another who thinks it should be governed by the first-come-first-served rule. What happens?

Well, ideally the decision should be made by the owner: the public. But only a unanimous decision could count as the will of the public, and unanimous decisions are hard to come by. (Putting the matter to a vote would reveal only the will of a majority faction of the public.) In that case, the public is in the same situation as an infant, a lunatic, a missing person, or a person in a coma: the public has the right to decide the matter, but is currently incapable of making a coherent decision, and so the decision must be made for them by a court which attempts (presumably in response to a class-action suit) to determine what is in the best interest of the rights-holder.

❋ *Objection Two: Policing Public Property*

As Rich Hammer is fond of pointing out, shopping malls are generally safer than city streets. As Rich notes, this is so for two reasons. First, the owners of the malls have a financial incentive to police their premises so as to avoid losing customers, while government police face much weaker incentives. Second, mall owners can set higher standards for what is permissible behavior on their premises, and can exclude undesirable persons more or less at will, while the police have less power to kick people off the city streets. Does this mean that public property in a libertarian society will be under-policed?

Not necessarily. Consider the incentive issue first. Since the property is public, everyone has an equal right to police it. But some will have stronger motives for policing than others. Consider the case mentioned earlier, of the road built for and donated to the public by those who owned property alongside the road and hoped the road's proximity would raise their property values and bring increased traffic to their businesses. The same incentives that led the owners to build this road would also lead them to police it, since property values will be higher and customers will be more plentiful if the road is safe.

Moreover, the unsafeness of city streets results not only from the fact that they are public but from the fact that the police enjoy a monopoly on protection services. A competitive market in security would probably find some way to offer its customers protection while on public property. For example, public parks might be patrolled by a consortium of insurance companies, if a substantial number of their customers enjoy visiting public parks.

As for the higher-standards issue, it is true that users of public property face a somewhat greater risk from their fellow users than users of private property do. A private mall (particularly in a libertarian society where the right to control access to one's private property is legally protected) can exclude users who simply *appear* to pose a threat to other users, even if they have committed no overt act (or can admit them only if they post a bond, disarm themselves, show proof of insurance or a letter from their pastor, etc.). Public property, by contrast, must be open to anyone whose conduct *so far* is peaceful. By the same token, however, public property allows more freedom. That is why the best option is a society that makes room for both public and private property. Those who place a high value on security, and are willing to put up with some burdensome restrictions in order to get it (call them the Little Old Ladies), will be free to patronize private property, while those who seek self-expression, are averse to restrictions, and are willing to put up with more risk from others (call them the Gun-Toting Pot-Smoking Nudist Bikers), will likewise be free to patronize public property.

✼ *Objection Three: Liability and Public Property*

In a free society, people are liable for harm that they cause. Now suppose I own the road that runs past your house, and I decide to donate that road to the general public. Now it is no longer possible to exclude undesirables from the road. There used to be guards at the toll gate who checked drivers' IDs, but now they are gone, and one day some loony who in the old days would have been excluded takes the public road to your house and massacres your family. Since the loss to your security was caused by my decision, it has been suggested to me (by Rich Hammer) that I should be legally liable for the result. And if this is so, then public property would not be tolerated in a free nation, because the liability costs would simply be too high.

But surely a libertarian legal system will not hold people liable for every harm to which they merely made a causal contribution. The current statist trend of holding gun manufacturers liable for the use of guns by criminals, and so forth, flies in the face of the libertarian principle of personal responsibility. An owner is not obligated to check out the background of everyone he gives or sells property to.

✶ *Objection Four: Reversion of Public Property*

Once property becomes public, how can it ever become private again? In a free-market economy, property tends to be assigned to its highest-valued use, because those who value the property more will purchase it from those who value it less. But if I value Central Park more than the public at large does, how do I go about purchasing it from the public? The dispersed, disorganized, and divided public lacks the ability to consent to the sale.

This is a difficult problem, to which I do not have a full solution. But let me try out a few possibilities.

There are two ways I can lose my claim to property. I can give or sell it, or I can abandon it. The public is not in a position to give or sell its property,[9] but perhaps it is capable of abandoning it.

What counts as the public's having abandoned a piece of property? Well, the easiest case would be if no one has used it for a very long time. (How long? Well, the length of time should presumably be the same as whatever is accepted in the case of abandoning private property.) But what if only a few people have used it? Does that count as the public's

---

[9] At least I don't think so. Someone could argue that the court could act on behalf of the people's interests, authorizing the transfer of ownership from the collective to me, in exchange for the "price" of my doing something judged to be of general benefit to the public. But I am wary of heading too far down that path. For one thing, if the court acquires too much power to administer the property of the "disorganized public," we start to move back toward the "organized public" model of government property, and the whole idea of free access is replaced by access-in-the-interests-of-the-public-as-determined-by-some-official. For another, the value of public property is severely undermined if it can be unpredictably privatized on some judge's say-so.

using it (given that the property has *never* been used by the *entire* public)?

Or suppose I privatize some portion of the property, claiming it for my own use, fencing it in and so forth. Perhaps it then counts as mine so long as no one protests. (How widely do I have to advertise the fact that I've done this?) But again, what if just a few people protest—does that count?

Ultimately these problems will have to be resolved by a libertarian legal system, through evolving common-law precedents. That's fine with me. What I would want to insist on, though, is that *some* role for public property is important for a libertarian society. An all-private system can be oppressive, just as an all-public one can be; but a system that allows networks of private spaces and public spaces to compete against each other offers the greatest scope for individual freedom.

CHAPTER
FOUR

FUNDING PUBLIC GOODS: SIX SOLUTIONS

RODERICK T. LONG

✣ *The Argument for Market Failure*

A *public good*, as economists define the concept, is any good from whose enjoyment non-contributors cannot be excluded. The theory of public goods is of interest to libertarians for two reasons: first, because a great many things we care about—highways, education, law enforcement, fire protection, national defense, etc.—are widely thought to be public goods, or to have public-good characteristics; and second, because the majority of economists are convinced that such public goods cannot be supplied on the free market.

The argument for the inadequacy of markets in this area runs as follows. Suppose there is some good X that 200 people value; but if X is produced, each of those 200 will be able to benefit from it, whether or not they contributed to its production. If you are one of the 200, what is your reaction if you are asked to contribute?

Autumn 1994 issue of *Formulations* by the Free Nation Foundation: c4ss.org/content/21385

According to the orthodox theory of public goods, you reason as follows:

> Either the other 199 are going to raise a sufficient amount of money to fund X, or they aren't. Suppose they do raise enough. Then the good will be funded whether I pay or not, so I might as well not pay, so I can take advantage of the benefits without paying the costs. [This is the Free Rider problem.] On the other hand, suppose they don't raise enough. Then the good won't be funded even if I do contribute, so there's no point in throwing my money away. [This is the Assurance problem.] The chance that my contributing or not will make the decisive difference to X's being funded or not is so minuscule as to be quite properly ignored. So either way, regardless of what others do, it's in my interest not to contribute. So I won't.

And you don't.

The problem is that the other 199 people in the group are reasoning the same way, and so X never gets funded—despite the fact that everyone would be better off—by their own standards—if X *were* funded. It's in everybody's *collective* interest to cooperate, but in everyone's *individual* interest to defect; and since it is individuals, not collectives, who make decisions, the result is that no one cooperates and the public good is never produced. The market system of voluntary cooperation appears to have failed.

* *Solution One: Force*

There is a way of solving this public goods problem: make contribution compulsory. If everyone is forced to contribute, then the public good will be funded, and everyone will be better off—in respect of that public good, that is. They will of course be worse off in another respect: they will no longer be free. Nevertheless, coercive force is widely endorsed as the sole possible solution to the public goods problem. Forced contribution, whether of labor or of property, is certainly the solution of choice in the modern state: taxation, military conscription, eminent domain, and jury empanelment are among the obvious cases.

But is force the only possible solution? By no means. Throughout history, countless so-called "public goods" have been produced through non-coercive means, thus rendering the public-goods problem no more than a bogey from an economist's fantasy. Economists who proclaim, from their ivory towers, that non-coercive solutions to public-goods problems are inconceivable—without ever bothering to examine the empirical facts of private production all around us every day—are in effect demanding that the rest of us be held hostage to their lack of imagination and observation. Perhaps entrepreneurs who stand to make a profit from solving public-goods problems have more incentive to discover solutions than economists whose income is unaffected by their failure to solve such problems!

Leaving governmental coercion aside as both unethical and dangerous, I here offer five other solutions to the funding of public goods. (My list here is not meant to be exhaustive, and I welcome further suggestions.) As I go along I will consider in particular how each solution might apply to what is generally considered the most difficult public-goods problem: national defense.

* Solution Two: Conscience

Public goods can be funded through reliance on custom, morality, and non-material rewards. Many public goods are already so funded; volunteer fire departments are an obvious example. A less obvious example, perhaps, is churches: one can walk into a church, listen to the sermon, ignore the collection plate, and walk out. Indeed, everyone who wants to hear the sermon could free-ride in the same way. Hence the economists ought to predict that no churches would ever be built and no ministers paid; yet somehow this is not the case. A still less obvious example of a public good is tipping: waiters and waitresses provide better service in the hope of getting a tip, so the practice of tipping has the beneficial result of producing better service. (At least I'll assume for the sake of argument that this is true; I don't actually know that countries without the practice of tipping really have worse service.) But why should I leave a tip in a restaurant to which I have no plan to return? I benefit from the tips of other diners, and they benefit from mine; but in this case I could free ride, enjoying the benefits without tipping. Why don't I? The power of custom.

Morality—the conviction that we are obligated to do our part—also plays an important role in overcoming free rider problems. When we consider the millions that are contributed to charity, telethons, etc., there is no reason to doubt that there would be at least as much voluntary support forthcoming for the funding of public goods. Indeed, as Robert Axelrod shows in his book *The Evolution of Cooperation*, both biological and cultural evolution tend to promote the emergence of cooperative dispositions, because those who manifest such dispositions acquire a reputation as a cooperator, and thereby attract other cooperators; as these cooperators flourish by reaping the benefits of increased cooperation, the cooperative impulse is further selected for.

The LiveAid telethon concert generated impressive contributions to feed the starving Ethiopians. Would not people also contribute money to defend their country? (Keep in mind that a military confined to national defense, as opposed to foreign adventuring, would be quite a bit cheaper.) And have not people always volunteered their labor as soldiers in great numbers when their country was attacked? A citizens' militia, manned by volunteers and funded by charity, has been the standard form of national defense throughout human history.

✱ *Solution Three: Delegation*

The third solution is really a variation on the second, but it is distinctive enough to warrant separate mention. Those wishing to solicit contributions to some worthy cause will raise much more money if they devolve responsibility by assigning local people to collect from friends, family, and co-workers. This strategy is employed with great effectiveness by the United Way. Social pressure, and the desire to look good in front of one's peers, are powerful incentives—incentives that might well serve to motivate contributions to the patriotic defense of one's homeland.

✱ *Solution Four: Guarantee*

In his book *The Limits of Government: An Essay on the Public Goods Problem*, David Schmidtz suggests offering money-back guarantees as a way of increasing the incentive to contribute. Remember that a public-goods problem comprises two elements: the Free Rider problem (the temptation to free ride if others contribute enough) and the Assurance problem (the fear that one will end up a sucker if one contributes and others end up not contributing). If those soliciting funds offer to refund contributors' money if insufficient funds are raised to fund the public good, the Assurance problem is defused. The Free Rider problem still remains, of course; but once the incentive to defect has been cut in half, the non-monetary incentives to cooperate may be enough to overwhelm it. War bonds could be offered in this way.

✱ *Solution Five: Privatization*

The problem with funding public goods is that non-contributors are not excluded from enjoying the good. An obvious solution, then, is to try to invent some way of excluding those non-contributors—thus privatizing the public good. For example, although highways are supposed to be a paradigm case of a public good, we all know about toll roads: if you don't pay, you can't drive. At one time in this country fire protection was offered in the same way that insurance is now; firemen only saved houses whose owners had paid their premiums. (This obviously works better if houses are not too close together!) Methods of exclusion may also be discovered as technology progresses; it was once impossible to exclude anyone from viewing television transmissions, but we now have cable TV and broadcast scramblers. In addition, any good that can only be enjoyed in a particular location can be turned into a private good by making the location private property.

It is difficult to apply this solution to national defense; if you defend my fellow citizens from foreign invasion, you *ipso facto* defend me too, whether I contributed or not. There's no way to let enemy missiles through to hit just the houses of non-contributors while leaving those of contributors alone. But there are at least ways of slicing the problem up into more manageable pieces. If we consider defense of the continental United States as a whole, it becomes clear that *local areas* that are net non-contributors can certainly be excluded from that good. So we implement Solution Five by decomposing national defense into a plurality of regional defenses, and then allow the other Solutions to operate within those regions. (Solution Three in particular will naturally work better at the regional than at the national level.)

✱ *Solution Six: Packaging*

One way to fund public goods is to package them with private goods (from which non-contributors *can* be excluded). In nineteenth-century England, private roads were built that were not toll roads: they were completely free, and anyone could use them. Why was it in the road-builders' interest to supply this public good, then? Because the road-builders owned property—a private good—alongside the site of the proposed road, and once the road was built, increased traffic brought increased commerce, and the value of their property was increased. (I learned of this example from Stephen Davies.)

Lighthouses are another example. For decades, standard economic textbooks had loftily explained that lighthouses could never be supplied privately, because ships at sea benefit from the light whether or not they pay. But one day free-market economist Ronald Coase decided to do some research, and discovered that in fact lighthouses in Britain had in the past been supplied privately for many years. True, it was impossible to exclude non-contributors from the light of the lighthouse—but it *was* possible to exclude non-contributors from using the harbor, so the lighthouse fees were simply packaged with the harbor fees. Once again, entrepreneurs who stood to make a profit were motivated to devise innovations undreamed of by pessimistic academic economists.[1]

Broadcast TV is another classic public good: viewers can receive the signals whether or not they pay. If we had never had broadcast TV—if we had started with cable to begin with—economists would no doubt predict the impossibility of broadcast TV (unless financed by tax revenues). But TV broadcasters (and radio broadcasters before them) managed to pay for the broadcasts by packaging them with a private good: advertising. Providers of goods and services value advertising air time—and this definitely *is* a good from which they can be excluded, and for which they are consequently willing to pay. Advertising revenue is then used to fund the broadcasts; a public good for the viewers is funded by being packaged with a private good for the advertisers.

Could the public good of national defense be funded by advertising as well? Perhaps so. How much money would Coca-

---

[1] Coase's article may be found in Tyler Cowen's anthology *Public Goods and Market Failures* (also published under the title *The Theory of Market Failure*).

Cola be willing to donate to national defense, in exchange for the right to advertise:

Coca-Cola

We Defend America!

Quite a bit, I would bet.

Private weapons ownership also represents a kind of packaging, one that operates on its own with no entrepreneurship needed. In a free society, people will have the right to own weapons, and will buy them for the sake of a private good: defense of their own homes and families. But this pursuit of private good brings along with it an important public good: an armed society, formidable to any would-be conqueror, itself represents a powerful deterrent, and thus, to that extent, serves as a means of national defense.

Perhaps another packaging strategy might work as follows. Suppose a group of private protection agencies, individually specializing in domestic law enforcement, were to make binding and enforceable contracts with one another to form a consortium, pooling their resources for the purpose of national defense. These protection agencies could then sell a package of protection services—domestic law enforcement and national defense—and refuse to sell the former to anyone who would not pay for the latter.

At this point, of course, a new entrepreneur in the security field could come along and try to undersell the consortium by charging for domestic law enforcement only. But at this point Solution Six might be combined with Solution Two; just as many people today practice "socially responsible" investing, refusing to invest in companies with bad environmental records or poor employment conditions, many might refuse to deal with any protection agencies other than consortium members.

All these ideas are only armchair speculations, of course. Once again, I expect that entrepreneurs alert for profit opportunities would be a lot more imaginative than I have been here. Thus I am optimistic about the ability of the market to supply even such public goods as national defense.

CHAPTER
FIVE

THE QUALITY OF PUBLICNESS

DAWIE COETZEE

I had been hoping to find time to develop some of the ideas presented in Roderick Long's essays on public space ("A Plea For Public Property"[1] and "In Defense of Public Space"[2]). Now, in the wake of the 2013 Cape Argus Cycle Tour, the route of which ran past the vehicular entrance of the small block of flats where we live, leaving us effectively stranded for the day, I find a moment at last. This is not least because the vociferous nocturnal construction of a temporary pedestrian bridge outside our bedroom window had kept me awake all night, which caused me to sleep all day despite the incessant cries of "slow down!" at the corner. It is appropriate, as this suspension of the publicness of our street quite underlines what I had had brewing on the subject.

If anything I am even more strongly in favour of the preservation of public space, as a precondition to the privacy of private space, than Roderick Long is. As an architect I ever lament the desire of the rich to be architecturally faceless. My impulse is to endow a dwelling with an entrance, a face to the outside world, which for whatever excess of ostentation

---

c4ss.org/content/17697

[1] http://c4ss.org/content/14721; Chapter Three of the present text.
[2] http://c4ss.org/content/14724; Chapter Two of the present text.

I might care to pile on cannot fail by its mere existence to affirm the existence of an outside world, that is, a public realm. There is in the attitude of the wealthy client a shadow of that disrelational insular irrelevance which is to me the failure of Randian Objectivism: not only arrogance but consequent utter pointlessness.

Thus the public sphere is an idea constantly present in the discourse on architecture and urban design as much as in political economy, but in none of these have I encountered a satisfactory understanding of publicness as a quality. Prof. Long's distinction between the organized public and the unorganized public may be roughly restated in other terms, i.e., publicness in origin v. publicness in orientation. We may call a thing public because it belongs to the public and thus in a sense proceeds from the public, or we call a thing public because it is intended for the public. It is generally in the latter class—imperfectly analogous to the "unorganized public"—that I am here interested.

But what, or who, is the public? Are we concerned here with the thing Søren Kierkegaard called "a monstrous nothing"[3]; "a host, more numerous than all the peoples together, but [...] a body which can never be reviewed; it cannot even be represented, because it is an abstraction"? It might be surprising that Kierkegaard's analysis in "The Present Age" might be quite useful in defining what we do "not" mean by "public" for our present purpose. The idea of the public as a fictitious personification of bourgeois values does not help us in understanding the qualities that make for good public space, or good public facilities. I like to think that Kierkegaard might have approved of the alternative conception that would help us in this, as it echoes his Christian embrace of the outcast. For to understand publicness as a quality we must understand the public not as a class, nor even as a specific concrete group of people; nor yet as the universal

---

[3] *A Literary Review* 82-3.

group, "everyone." The public, for our present purpose, is not everyone. The public is *anyone*.

The idea of the public as this undefined but emphatically individual "next person who comes around the corner" is the key to understanding the qualities that are common to all the public spaces and facilities that we have all personally experienced as both good and definitely public. From this conception we can proceed to derive a faintly Ruskinian catalogue of qualities:

1. *Robustness.* It is difficult for something flimsy to be successfully public. Flimsy things need to be policed lest they be broken; and once this relation is allowed the essential indefiniteness of the public is lost. Public things have to be proof against "anyone." This is most graphic in the case of public statuary, which should never be erected for the people's adulation but rather placed at the mercy of "anyone." J. G. Strijdom's[4] eerie floating head[5] should have kept a place in public Pretoria, the better to throw eggs at it.

2. *Blindness.* This rather underlines the quality of robustness with the addition of a certain blunt stupidity. Properly public things tend not to be "smart": the "smart highway" is possibly the perfect antithesis of publicness. The public is fundamentally anonymous and, for that reason, dynamically equal. It has to include the limitations not of everyone but of anyone: in anticipating the tall it must allow for the short; anticipating the thin it must remain suitable for the fat. One size has to fit all—but it really has to fit and fit well. And this is no limitation but the mark of a public facility at its best: affordable to the poorest (ideally free) and simultaneously delightful to the wealthiest. As soon as a facility

---

[4] https://en.wikipedia.org/wiki/J.G._Strijdom
[5] http://fr.academic.ru/pictures/frwiki/83/Strijdom_square.jpg

seeks to identify its custom and conform uniquely to it, it ceases to be public.

3. *Passivity.* Properly public things do not seek one's custom; in so far as they do anything they do it with a pig-headed disregard for anything else, all in the interest of being available to anyone at any time. There are obvious inefficiencies implicit in this—e.g., buses stubbornly sticking to routes and time-tables whether full or empty—which ought to delineate the scope of what might appropriately be endeavoured as a public facility. It also limits the degree of publicness that can be achieved in certain types of facility: it should be obvious that a public street is fundamentally more public than a public library. In the same way a more thoroughgoing publicness can be achieved where facilities are capable of simple, inherent self-correction than where they need external management.

4. *Constancy.* To be properly public, a thing must *always* be public. The indefiniteness of the public has a temporal aspect: it is anyone, at any time. Hence a street, like the pedestrianized part of Parliament Street in Cape Town which is closed with an iron gate at 6 PM, is not properly public even when it is open. Likewise the chain-link gate that closes off the V&A Waterfront at Ebenezer Road at night sees early-morning pedestrians clambering underneath: in being inappropriate to the capabilities of the infirm and the dignity of the elderly it is inappropriate to both the capabilities and the dignity of "anyone," and therefore fails as public space. So, too, Victoria Road outside my garage is $1/365$ less public *all the time* for being closed to me on the day of the Argus Tour. Above all, sporadic publicness implies a power to suspend publicness which is at odds with the notion of it being either "owned" by the "unorganized" public or unowned.

I think most anarchists like the street for its very unownedness, that is, its publicness. There are regions near the borders to vulgar libertarianism and Objectivism where dourer eremitic aspirations are entertained, but to most the street's flavour of stigmergy carries appeal. Where the public realm is disliked it is usually not for a surfeit of publicness but because the public realm has deteriorated to the private domain of the state and its beneficiaries. Where the public realm offends it is where publicness, as above understood, is lacking.

CHAPTER
SIX

COMMUNAL PROPERTY: A LIBERTARIAN ANALYSIS

Kevin Carson

❖ *INTRODUCTION*

The dominant market anarchist view of property takes for granted individual, fee-simple ownership through individual appropriation as the only natural form of property. Although common or collective ownership is grudgingly accepted as a legitimate—if inefficient—form of "voluntary socialism," it's taken for granted that such forms of ownership can only come about through some sort of special contract between preexisting owners of fee-simple individual property. Land can only be appropriated, runs the usually tacit assumption, by individuals.

Right-wing libertarian and Objectivist forums are full of statements that "there's no such thing as collective property," "all property rights are individual," and the like. Ayn Rand argued that it was impossible for European settlers to steal

Center for a Stateless Society Paper No. 13 (Summer/Fall 2011): c4ss.org/content/9805

the land of American Indians, because the latter had no valid property rights:

> Now, I don't care to discuss the alleged complaints American Indians have against this country. I believe, with good reason, the most unsympathetic Hollywood portrayal of Indians and what they did to the white man. They had no right to a country merely because they were born here and then acted like savages. The white man did not conquer this country. And you're a racist if you object, because it means you believe that certain men are entitled to something because of their race. You believe that if someone is born in a magnificent country and doesn't know what to do with it, he still has a property right to it. He does not. Since the Indians did not have the concept of property or property rights—they didn't have a settled society, they had predominantly nomadic tribal "cultures"—they didn't have rights to the land, and there was no reason for anyone to grant them rights that they had not conceived of and were not using. It's wrong to attack a country that respects (or even tries to respect) individual rights. If you do, you're an aggressor and are morally wrong. But if a "country" does not protect rights—if a group of tribesmen are the slaves of their tribal chief—why should you respect the "rights" that they don't have or respect? ...[Y]ou can't claim one should respect the "rights" of Indians, when they had no concept of rights and no respect for rights. But let's suppose they were all beautifully innocent savages—which they certainly were not. What were they fighting for, in opposing the white man on this continent? For their wish to continue a primitive existence; for their "right" to keep part of the earth untouched—to keep everybody out so they could live like animals or cavemen. Any European who brought with him an element of civilization had the right to take over this continent, and it's great that some of them did. The racist Indians

today—those who condemn America—do not respect individual rights.[1]

But as Karl Hess argued in *Libertarian Forum*, libertarian property can take on a wide variety of legitimate forms:

> Libertarianism is a people's movement and a liberation movement. It seeks the sort of open, non-coercive society in which the people, the living, free, distinct people, may voluntarily associate, dis-associate, and, as they see fit, participate in the decisions affecting their lives. This means a truly free market in everything from ideas to idiosyncracies. It means people free collectively to organize the resources of their immediate community or individualistically to organize them; it means the freedom to have a community-based and supported judiciary where wanted, none where not, or private arbitration services where that is seen as most desirable. The same with police. The same with schools, hospitals, factories, farms, laboratories, parks, and pensions. Liberty means the right to shape your own institutions. It opposes the right of those institutions to shape you simply because of accreted power or gerontological status.[2]

Communal ownership of land is a legitimate and plausible model for property rights in a stateless society based on free association.

Roderick Long, in particular, has argued for what he calls "public property"—as opposed to state property: "I have no interest in defending public property in the sense of property belonging to the organized public (i.e., the state). In fact, I do not think government property is public property at all;

---

[1] Ayn Rand, in question and answer session following "Address To the Graduating Class of the United States Military Academy at West Point," New York, March 6, 1974.

[2] Karl Hess, "Letter From Washington: Where Are The Specifics?" *The Libertarian Forum*, June 15, 1969, p. 2.

it is really the private property of an agency calling itself the government."³ Common property, he says, can come about through collective homesteading:

> Consider a village near a lake. It is common for the villagers to walk down to the lake to go fishing. In the early days of the community it's hard to get to the lake because of all the bushes and fallen branches in the way. But over time, the way is cleared and a path forms—not through any centrally coordinated effort, but simply as a result of all the individuals walking that way day after day.
>
> The cleared path is the product of labor—not any individual's labor, but all of them together. If one villager decided to take advantage of the now-created path by setting up a gate and charging tolls, he would be violating the collective property right that the villagers together have earned.⁴

> Since collectives, like individuals, can mix their labor with unowned resources to make those resources more useful to their purposes, collectives too can claim property rights by homestead.⁵

Historically, the overwhelming weight of evidence suggests that the first appropriation of land for agriculture was almost universally by peasant villages working as a social unit.

---

³Roderick T. Long, "In Defense of Public Space," *Formulations* (Free Nation Foundation), Spring 1996. Website offline, accessed via Internet Archive July 6, 2011: http://web.archive.org/web/20090503091359/;http://libertariannation.org/a/f33l2.html; Chapter Two of present text.

⁴Ibid.

⁵Long, "A Plea for Public Property," *Formulations* (Free Nation Foundation), Spring 1998. Website offline, accessed via Internet Archive July 6, 2011: http://web.archive.org/web/20090416204308/; http://libertariannation.org/a/f53l1.html; Chapter Three of present text.

* I. Rise and Persistence of the Village Commune

The village commune was, almost universally, the dominant property model in societies which, so far in human history, came closest to approximating the libertarian ideal of statelessness and voluntary association. At the highest point of human development before the rise of the state, the stateless villages and small market towns that existed in peace without paying tribute to imperial conquerors, the common ownership of land by the peasant commune was almost universal.[6]

Communal ownership of land was the norm in the stateless village societies of the neolithic period, from the Agricultural Revolution until the rise of the first states. The internal pattern of the village commune, wherever it was found, typically approximated the hypothetical case study of traditional tenure practices described by James Scott:

> Let us imagine a community in which families have usufruct rights to parcels of cropland during the main growing season. Only certain crops, however, may be planted, and every seven years the usufruct land is distributed among resident families according to each family's size and its number of able-bodied adults. After the harvest of the main-season crop, all cropland reverts to common land where any family may glean, graze their fowl and livestock, and even plant quickly maturing, dry-season crops. Rights to graze fowl and livestock on pasture-land held in common by the village is extended to all local families, but the number of animals that can be grazed is restricted according to family size, especially in dry years when forage is scarce.... Everyone has the right to gather firewood for normal family needs, and the village blacksmith and baker are given larger allotments. No commercial sale from village woodlands is permitted.
>
> Trees that have been planted and any fruit they may bear are the property of the family who planted

---

[6]Caveats on terminology from P. M. Lawrence via private email.

them, no matter where they are now growing.... Land is set aside for use or leasing out by widows with children and dependents of conscripted males....

After a crop failure leading to a food shortage, many of these arrangements are readjusted. Better-off villagers are expected to assume some responsibility for poorer relatives—by sharing their land, by hiring them, or by simply feeding them. Should the shortage persist, a council composed of heads of families may inventory food supplies and begin daily rationing.[7]

The village commune model traced its origins, in the oldest areas of civilization, back to the beginning of the agricultural revolution, when humans first began to raise crops in permanent village settlements. Before that time, the dominant social grouping was the semi-nomadic hunter-gatherer group. As hunter-gatherers experimented with saving a portion of the grain they'd gathered, they became increasingly tied to permanent settlements.

In the areas where communal tenure reemerged in Dark Age Europe, after the collapse of Roman power, the village commune had its origin in the settlement of barbarian tribes. (Even in Europe, the village commune was actually the reemergence of a social unit which had previously been partly suppressed, first by the Roman Republic in Italy and later by the Empire in its areas of conquest.)

In both cases, the hunter-gatherer group or the clan was a mobile or semi-mobile social unit based on common kinship relations. So the village commune commonly had its origins in a group of settlers who saw themselves as members of the same clan and sharing a common ancestry, who broke the land for a new agricultural settlement by their common efforts. It was not, as the modern town, a group of atomized individuals who simply happened to live in the same geographic area and

---

[7]James Scott, *Seeing Like a State: How Certain Schemes to Improve the Human Condition Have Failed* (New Haven and London: Yale University Press, 1998), pp. 33-34.

had to negotiate the organization of basic public services and utilities in some manner or other. It was an organic social unit of people who saw themselves, in some sense, as related. It was a settlement by "a union between families considered as of common descent and owning a certain territory in common." In fact, in the transition from the clan to the village community, the nucleus of a newly founded village commune was frequently a single joint household or extended family compound, sharing its hearth and livestock in common.[8]

Even after the founding clan split apart into separate patriarchal family households and recognized the private accumulation and hereditary transmission of wealth,

> wealth was conceived exclusively in the shape of *movable* property, including cattle, implements, arms, and the dwelling-house.... As to private property in land, the village community did not, and could not, recognize anything of the kind, and, as a rule, it does not recognize it now.... The clearing of the woods and the breaking of the prairies being mostly done by the communities or, at least, by the joint work of several families—always with the consent of the community—the cleared plots were held by each family for a term of four, twelve, or twenty years, after which term they were treated as parts of the arable land held in common.[9]

And even where a league of separate families together settled a new village, they soon developed a mythology of a common ancestor as a basis for social solidarity.[10] As we shall see below, the atomized groups of landless peasants which Stolypin deported to set up new village colonies in Siberia spontaneously organized the new villages around the *mir*'s

---

[8] Pyotr Kropotkin, *Mutual Aid: A Factor in Evolution* (New York: Doubleday, Page & Company, 1909), pp. 120-121, 123, 123 fn1.

[9] Ibid., pp. 124-125.

[10] Ibid., pp. 125-126.

principle of common ownership (despite Stolypin's vision of individual family farmsteads held in fee simple). The village commune was, therefore, an example of the kind of collective homesteading described above by Roderick Long.

In some variations of the village commune—e.g., in India and in many of the Germanic tribes—Henry Sumner Maine argued, there was a theoretical right for an individual to sever his aliquot share of the common land from the rest and own it individually. But this was almost never done, Maine said, because it was highly impractical.

For one thing, the severance of one's patrimony in the common land from the commune was viewed as akin to divorcing oneself from an organized community and setting up the nucleus of a new community alongside (or within) it, and required some rather involved ceremonial for its legal conclusion. And the individual peasant's subsequent relations with the community, consequently, would take on the complexity and delicacy of relations between two organized societies.[11] So many functions of the agricultural year, like plowing and harvest, were organized in part or in whole collectively, that the transaction costs entailed in organizing cooperative efforts between seceded individuals and the rest of the commune would have been well-nigh prohibitive.

When the great majority of a society considers common ownership as the normal way of doing things, and the normal method of organizing social functions presupposes that background state of affairs, even when there is no legal impediment whatsoever to an individual severing her share of property from the common, there are likely to be very powerful path dependencies that make it costly and impractical to do so. A given social system, even if participation in its institutions is formally completely voluntary and there are no coercive barriers to exit, tends to function like ground cover plants that create an interlocking ecosystem and crowd out

---

[11] Henry Sumner Maine, *Ancient Law* (London: J.M. Dent & Sons Ltd., 1960 [1861]), pp. 159-160.

alternatives, or a forest of one species of trees that exclude other species by overshadowing.[12]

Kropotkin summarized, in sweeping language, the universality of the village commune as a building block of society:

> It is now known, and scarcely contested, that the village community was not a specific feature of the Slavonians, nor even the ancient Teutons. It prevailed in England during both the Saxon and Norman times, and partially survived till the last century; it was at the bottom of the social organization of old Scotland, old Ireland, and old Wales. In France, the communal possession and the communal allotment of arable land by the village folkmote persisted from the first centuries of our era till the times of Turgot, who found the folkmotes "too noisy" and therefore abolished them. It survived Roman rule in Italy, and revived after the fall of the Roman Empire. It was the rule with the Scandinavians, the Slavonians, the Finns (in the *pittaya*, as also, probably, the *kihla-kunta*), the Coures, and the Lives. The village community in India—past and present, Aryan and non-Aryan— is well known through the epoch-making works of Sir Henry Maine; and Elphinstone has described it among the Afghans. We also find it in the Mongolian oulous, the Kabyle thaddart, the Javanese dessa, the Malayan kota or tofa, and under a variety of names in Abyssinia, the Soudan, in the interior of Africa, with natives of both Americas, with all the small and large tribes of the Pacific archipelagos. In short, we do not know one single human race or one single nation which has not had its period of village communities.... It is anterior to serfdom, and even servile submission was powerless to break it. It was a universal phase of

---

[12]For this analogy I am indebted to P. M. Lawrence, an Australian polymath of almost supernatural erudition who has been a frequent email correspondent and commenter under my blog posts and online columns over the years.

evolution, a natural outcome of the clan organization, with all those stems, at least, which have played, or play still, some part in history.[13]

We see a version of this communal ownership in the Jubilee system of Israel, as it was later idealized in the Mosaic Law by the priestly and deuteronomic redactors of Leviticus and Deuteronomy, and had actually existed to a greater or lesser degree in the period of the Judges. The ultimate ownership of land lay with the tribe, clan and family—to whom it reverted in the Jubilee year (every forty-ninth or fiftieth year—there's some scholarly dispute). Sales of land were actually long-term leases, with the price discounted depending on how many years it was until Jubilee. Among the customary by-laws regulating individual and family possessions was the allowance of gleaning. It's likely that the Biblical accounts of a revelation from Mount Sinai performed a function similar to that of the totemic ancestor as a legitimization of communal ownership, legitimizing a Bronze Age society that predated the Torah. At the time of the Judges, even the so-called J and E documents likely existed as nothing but epic poetry preserved in oral form, with the tribes of Israel existing as an amphictyonic league centered on Bethel or Shiloh.

The prophet Isaiah wrote in reference to land "privatization" (i.e., enclosure) in violation of the law of Jubilee by the landed oligarchy, in this passage from the Bible: "Woe unto them who join house to house, who lay field to field, till there is no place, that they may be placed alone in the midst of the earth!" (Isaiah 5:8) An English encloser, Lord Leicester, later said in quite similar language: "It is a melancholy thing to stand alone in one's country. I look around, and not a house is to be seen but mine. I am the giant of Giant Castle, and have eaten up all my neighbours."[14]

---

[13]Kropotkin, *Mutual Aid*, pp. 121-122.

[14]W. E. Tate, *The Enclosure Movement* (New York: Walker and Company, 1967), p. 90.

Henry Sumner Maine, writing in the nineteenth century, pointed to the village communes of India as the most faithful surviving version of what had once been an institution common to all the branches of the Indo-European family.

> The Village Community of India is at once an organised patriarchal society and an assemblage of co-proprietors. The personal relations to each other of the men who compose it are indistinguishably confounded with their proprietary rights, and to the attempts of English functionaries to separate the two may be assigned some of the most formidable miscarriages of Anglo-Indian administration. The Village Community is known to be of immense antiquity. In whatever direction research has been pushed into Indian history, general or local, it has always found the Community in existence at the farthest point of its progress.... Conquests and revolutions seem to have swept over it without disturbing or displacing it, and the most beneficent systems of government in India have always been those which have recognised it as the basis of administration.[15]

Like Kropotkin, Maine saw the village commune's joint ownership of land as rooted in its origin from a group of families sharing common descent. "[T]he simplest form of an Indian Village Community," he wrote, is just such "a body of kindred holding a domain in common..."[16] Although this process of formation of a Village Community from an extended body of kindred comprising several related families "may be regarded as typical," there were many exceptions. Even in villages founded by "a single assemblage of blood-relations," nevertheless "men of alien extraction have always, from time to time, been engrafted on it" and "admitted to the brotherhood." And there were also villages which "appear to have

---

[15] Henry Sumner Maine, *Ancient Law*, p. 153.
[16] Ibid., p. 154.

sprung not from one but from two or more families; and there are some whose composition is known to be entirely artificial...."[17] Even so, all such villages have created a myth of "an original parentage," even when the "assumption of common origin...[is] sometimes notoriously at variance with fact...." The village operated on the fiction of common origin, being *either* an "assemblage of blood relations" *or* "a body of co-proprietors formed on the model of an association of kinsmen."[18]

As Maine's reference to the administration of India suggests, the village commune continued in widespread existence even after the rise of the state, amounting internally to a stateless society with a parasitic layer of kings, priests, bureaucrats, and feudal landlords superimposed on it. The village commune was "under the dominion of comparatively powerful kings" who exacted tribute and conscripted soldiers from it, "but did not otherwise meddle with the cultivating societies."[19] The state's relationship to the governed was through the village as a unit, rather than the exercise of regulatory authority over relations between individuals.

In Russia, Maine saw the enactment of serfdom under the tsars as an imposition upon a preexisting social system: namely, "the ancient organisation of the village."[20]

Where the village commune persisted, the state had little or no direct dealings with individuals. It dealt with the peasantry only collectively, through the commune.

> The premodern and early modern state...dealt more with communities than with individuals when it came to taxes. Some apparently individual taxes, such as the notorious Russian "soul tax," which was collected from all subjects, were actually paid directly by the

---

[17] Ibid., pp. 154-155.
[18] Ibid., pp. 155-156.
[19] Henry Sumner Maine, *Village-Communities in the East and West*, Third Edition (New York: Henry Holt and Company, 1890), pp. 159-160.
[20] Maine, *Ancient Law*, p. 157.

communities or indirectly through the nobles whose subjects they were. Failure to deliver the required sum usually led to collective punishment. The only agents of taxation who regularly reached to the level of the household and its cultivated fields were the local nobility and clergy in the course of collecting feudal dues and the religious tithe. For its part, the state had neither the administrative tools nor the information to penetrate to this level.

In such cases the commune functioned internally much as it had before the rise of the state, allotting land and mediating disputes among the families, with the additional functions of handling relations with the state collectively when a member of the commune was charged with violating one of the state's laws and assessing each family's share of taxes imposed on the village by the state.

The central political conflict in the Roman Republic, as recounted in Livy, was the patricians' attempt to appropriate and enclose—"privatize"—common lands to which all members of the community had legal rights of access.

The open-field system of England, which was gradually eroded by enclosures of arable land (mainly for sheep pasturage) from the late Middle Ages on, was another version of the same early Teutonic communal property system—the Arable Mark and Common Mark—whose survivals von Maurer noted in Germany.

It was a later evolution of the system Tacitus had observed among the Germanic tribes. The system Tacitus remarked on was used by the Teutons when they were semi-nomadic and had access to extensive land inputs. It was an open-field system with interstripping of family plots, but with only a single field. When the soil was exhausted, the community moved on and broke fresh ground. This—the system likely first used at the time of the agricultural revolution—could only work with low population densities, obviously. The first adaptation as the tribes settled down and the amount of vacant land declined was a primitive two-field system, with half the arable land remaining fallow each year. By the time the low German descendants of Tacitus's subjects were observed in England, they had progressed to the full-blown three- or four-field system.[21]

The Arable Mark, and its English open-field counterpart, was a three-field system with interstripping of family plots in each field and a periodic redivision of plots between families. The Common Mark consisted of common waste, woodlot, and pasture, of which each family was entitled to some defined share of use.[22] Here's how William Marshall described the open field system in 1804:

> In this place it is sufficient to premise that a very few centuries ago, nearly the whole of the lands of England lay in an open, and more or less in a commonable state.... [T]he following statement may serve to convey a general idea of the whole of what may be termed Common-field Townships, throughout England.
>
> Under this ingenious mode of organization, each parish or township was considered as one common farm; though the tenantry were numerous.
>
> Round the village, in which the tenants reside, lay a few small inclosures, or grass yards; for rearing calves, and as baiting and nursery grounds for other farm stock. This was the common farmstead, or homestall....
>
> Round the homestall, lay a suit of arable fields; including the deepest and soundest of the lower grounds, situated out of water's way; for raising corn and pulse; as well as to produce fodder and litter for cattle and horses in the winter season.
>
> And, in the lowest situation..., shooting up among the arable lands, lay an extent of meadow grounds...,

---

[21]Tate, *The Enclosure Movement*, pp. 40-41.
[22]Maine, *Village-Communities*, pp. 78-87.

to afford a supply of hay, for cows and working stock, in the winter and spring months.

On the outskirts of the arable lands, where the soil is adapted to the pasturage of cattle, or...less adapted to cultivation..., one or more stinted pastures, or hams, were laid out for milking cows, working cattle, or other stock which required superior pasturage in summer.

While the bleakest, worst-soiled, and most distant lands of the township, were left in their native wild state; for timber and fuel; and for a common pasture....

The appropriated lands of each township were laid out with equal good sense and propriety. That each occupier might have his proportionate share of lands of different qualities, and lying in different situations, the arable lands, more particularly, were divided into numerous parcels....

And that the whole might be subjected to the same plan of management, and be conducted as one farm, the arable lands were moreover divided into compartments, or "fields," of nearly equal size, and generally three in number, to receive, in constant rotation, the triennial succession of fallow, wheat (or rye) and spring crops (as barley, oats, beans and peas)....[23]

The open-field system, according to J. L. and Barbara Hammond, was "more ancient than the manorial order.... The manorial element...is superimposed on the communal...: the medieval village is a free village gradually feudalised." As late as 1685, an estimated 85% of the surviving arable land that had not been converted to pasturage was organized on the open-field model.[24] The Russian *mir* or *obshchina*

---

[23]William Marshall, *Elementary and Practical Treatise on Landed Property*, quoted in Maine, *Village-Communities*, pp. 90-93.

[24]J. L. and Barbara Hammond, *The Village Labourer: 1760-1832* (London: Longmans, Green, and Co., 1913), pp. 26-27.

was essentially a variant of the same primeval open-field system that prevailed in Western Europe, but with a state far more despotic than the Western European feudal structure superimposed on it.

Marx's view of the uniqueness of the "Asiatic mode of production," and of the backwardness that resulted from the absence of private ownership of land and the predominance of collective village ownership with the state as landlord, probably reflected the limited awareness of the time as to the extent to which the open-field system has persisted in the Middle Ages. The chief difference between the "Asiatic mode" and the open-field system of Western Europe was that in the former case a despotic central state was superimposed as a parasitic layer atop the communal peasant society, whereas in the latter case it was a pattern of feudal organization that overlay the peasant commune.

Marx's Asiatic mode in India was essentially a variant of the open-field system, but—as with the Russian *mir*—with a despotic imperial state rather than a feudal system superimposed on it. As described by Maine:

> If very general language were employed, the description of the Teutonic or Scandinavian village-communities might actually serve as a description of the same institution in India. There is the arable mark, divided into separate lots but cultivated according to minute customary rules binding on all. Wherever the climate admits of the finer grass crops, there are the reserved meadows, lying generally on the verge of the arable mark. There is the waste or common land, out of which the arable mark has been cut, enjoyed as pasture by all the community *pro indiviso*. There is the village, consisting of habitations each ruled by a despotic pater-familias. And there is constantly a council of government to determine disputes as to custom.[25]

---

[25] Maine, *Village-Communities*, pp. 107-108.

The "despotic pater-familias"—apparently a common Indo-European institution, and also noted among the archaic Latins—is obviously something to which libertarians will have moral objections. But a more democratic system of governance within the family or household would in no way affect communal tenure.

❋ *II. Destruction of the Peasant Commune by the State.*

It was only with the rise of the modern state, toward the end of the Middle Ages, that governments began to take an interest in regulating the lives of individuals. The modern centralized state was confronted with the problem of opacity, and became preoccupied with, in James Scott's language, an "attempt to make society legible, to arrange the population in ways that simplified the classic state functions of taxation, conscription, and prevention of rebellion."[26] Although the state has always had such concerns to a greater or lesser extent, it was only the modern state—at least since Roman times—that actually sought to touch individuals in their daily lives.

> Legibility is a condition of manipulation. Any substantial state intervention in society—to vaccinate a population, produce goods, mobilize labor, tax people and their property, conduct literacy campaigns, conscript soldiers, enforce sanitation standards, catch criminals, start universal schooling—requires the invention of units that are visible.... Whatever the units being manipulated, they must be organized in a manner that permits them to be identified, observed, recorded, counted, aggregated, and monitored. The degree of knowledge required would have to be roughly commensurate with the depth of the intervention. In other words, one might say that the greater

[26]Scott, *Seeing Like a State*, p. 24.

the manipulation envisaged, the greater the legibility required to effect it.

It was precisely this phenomenon, which had reached full tide by the middle of the nineteenth century, that Proudhon had in mind when he declared, "To be ruled is to be kept an eye on, inspected, spied on, regulated, indoctrinated, sermonized, listed and checked off, estimated, appraised, censured, ordered about.... To be ruled is at every operation, transaction, movement, to be noted, registered, counted, priced, admonished, prevented, reformed, redressed, corrected."

From another perspective, what Proudhon was deploring was in fact the great achievement of modern statecraft. How hard-won and tenuous this achievement was is worth emphasizing. Most states, to speak broadly, are "younger" than the societies that they purport to administer. States therefore confront patterns of settlement, social relations, and production, not to mention a natural environment, that have evolved largely independent of state plans. The result is typically a diversity, complexity, and unrepeatability of social forms that are relatively opaque to the state, often purposefully so....

If the state's goals are minimal, it may not need to know much about the society.... If, however, the state is ambitious—if it wants to extract as much grain and manpower as it can, short of provoking a famine or a rebellion, if it wants to create a literate, skilled, and healthy population, if it wants everyone to speak the same language or worship the same god—then it will have to become both far more knowledgeable and far more intrusive.[27]

The imperative of rendering the opaque legible results, in the specific case of property rules in land, in hostility toward

---

[27]Ibid., pp. 183-184.

communal forms of property regulated as a purely internal matter by a village according to local custom:

> ...open commons landholding...is less legible and taxable than closed commons landholding, which in turn is less legible than private freeholding, which is less legible than state ownership.... It is no coincidence that the more legible or appropriable form can more readily be converted into a source of rent—either as private property or as the monopoly rent of the state.[28]

Fee-simple "privatization," and more recently Soviet-style "collectivization" (i.e., *de facto* state ownership), are both methods by which the state has destroyed the village commune and overcome the problem (from the state's perspective) of opacity within it. In both cases the village commune, while quite legible horizontally from the perspective of its inhabitants, was opaque to the state.

The fee-simple model of private property, wherever it has existed, has almost always been a creature of the state.

> In the case of common property farmland, the imposition of freehold property was clarifying not so much for the local inhabitants—the customary structure of rights had always been clear enough to them—as it was for the tax official and the land speculator. The cadastral map added documentary intelligence to state power and thus provided the basis for the synoptic view of the state and a supralocal market in land.[29]
>
> Freehold title and standard land measurement were to central taxation and the real-estate market what central bank currency was to the marketplace.[30]

---

[28] Ibid., pp. 219-220.
[29] Ibid., p. 39.
[30] Ibid., p. 48.

Replacing a society in which most ordinary people have access to the land on a customary basis, with a society in which most of those same people must rent or purchase land in order to cultivate it, has the virtue—from the perspective of the state and the ruling economic class—of forcing the peasantry into the cash economy.

> Commoditization in general, by denominating all goods and services according to a common currency, makes for what Tilly has called the "visibility [of] a commercial economy." He writes, "In an economy where only a small share of goods and services are bought and sold, a number of conditions prevail: collectors of revenue are unable to observe or evaluate resources with any accuracy, [and] many people have claims on any particular resource (*Coercion, Capital, and European States*, pp. 89, 85).[31]

In addition, forcing peasants and laborers into the cash economy means they must have a source of cash income to participate in it, which means an expansion of the wage labor market.

Scott's functional explanation of individual fee simple ownership sounds remarkably like Foucault's description of the "individualism" entailed in "panopticism."

> The fiscal or administrative goal toward which all modern states aspire is to measure, codify, and simplify land tenure in much the same way as scientific forestry reconceived the forest. Accommodating the luxuriant variety of customary land tenure was simply inconceivable. The historic solution, at least for the liberal state, has typically been the heroic simplification of individual freehold tenure. Land is owned by a legal individual who possesses wide powers of use, inheritance, or sale and whose ownership is represented by a uniform deed of title enforced through

---

[31] Ibid., pp. 367-368 no. 94.

the judicial and police institutions of the state.... In an agrarian setting, the administrative landscape is blanketed with a uniform grid of homogeneous land, each parcel of which has a legal person as owner and hence taxpayer. How much easier it then becomes to assess such property and its owner on the basis of its acreage, its soil class, the crops it normally bears, and its assumed yield than to untangle the thicket of common property and mixed forms of tenure.[32]

✣ The Enclosures in England

Fairly early in Medieval times, there had been a modest amount of land ownership in severalty. Lords of manors, who had originally interstripped their domains with the rest of the holdings in the open fields, had early on consolidated them into closes. As the village expanded the area under cultivation into the waste, newly broken ground was usually incorporated into existing open fields. But some families developed waste land independently and enclosed it as private holdings. Nevertheless, a decided majority of land was held communally in the open fields.[33]

There were early complaints by tenants in the thirteenth century of lords enclosing parts of common lands without consent, and reducing villagers' rights of pasture. The Statute of Merton in 1235 recognized the paramount authority of the lord of the manor over the waste, and authorized lords to enclose the commons at their own discretion, so long as they left a "sufficiency" of land to meet the commoning needs of the free tenants (although the burden of proof fell on the lords).[34]

The first large-scale assault on the village commune was the Tudor seizure of monastic lands—entailing around a fifth of the arable land in England—followed by the distribution of

---

[32]Ibid., p. 36.
[33]Tate, *The Enclosure Movement*, p. 59.
[34]Ibid., p. 60.

it to royal favorites among the nobility. The subsequent Tudor era was also characterized by large-scale enclosure of open fields for sheep pasturage for the lucrative textile markets.

The estates seized with the suppression of the monasteries, and those seized of which the Church was feudal proprietor, "were to a large extent given away to rapacious feudal favourites, or sold at a nominal price to speculating farmers and citizens, who drove out, *en masse*, the hereditary sub-tenants and threw their holdings into one."[35]

The king's men to whom the monastic lands were distributed engaged in wholesale "[r]ack-renting, evictions, and... conversions of arable to pasture." The new landlords were less than sympathetic to complaints from their tenants:

> "Do ye not know," said the grantee of one of the Sussex manors of the monastery of Sion, in answer to some peasants who protested at the seizure of their commons, "that the King's grace hath put down all the houses of monks, friars, and nuns? Therefore is the time come that we gentlemen will pull down the houses of such poor knaves as ye be."[36]

The dissolution of the monasteries dispossessed some 50,000 tenants, and the ensuing enclosures for pasturage through the early seventeenth century involved around half a million acres (almost a thousand square miles) and 30-40,000 tenants. Maurice Dobb argues that this might have represented over ten percent of "all middling and small landholders and 10 and 20 per cent. of those employed at wages...; in which case the labour reserves thereby created would have been of comparable dimensions to that which existed in all but the

---

[35] Karl Marx and Friedrich Engels, *Capital* Vol. I, Vol. 35 of *Marx and Engels Collected Works* (New York: International Publishers, 1996), p. 711.

[36] R. H. Tawney, *Religion and the Rise of Capitalism* (New York: Harcourt, Brace, and Company, Inc., 1926), p. 120.

worst months of the economic crisis of the 1930s."[37]

Tenants not subject to enclosure under the Tudors were instead victimized by rack-renting and arbitrary fines, which frequently resulted in their being driven off the land—"land," in Marx's words, to which the peasantry "had the same feudal rights as the lord himself"—when unable to pay them.[38]

Nevertheless the land that remained under peasant control, though much diminished in extent, persisted under the open-field system. And many of the "vagabonds" dispossessed by the Tudor expropriations found a safety net in the common lands, migrating into "such open-field villages as would allow them to squat precariously on the edge of common or waste."[39]

The pace of enclosure slowed considerably under James I and Charles I. The Stuarts, up until the Civil War, sporadically attempted—with only mixed success at best—to counter the depopulation and impoverishment of the countryside. The availability of access to the common lands in open-field villages, and the proliferation of unauthorized cottagers squatting on the common, was a thorn in the side to landlords who could not obtain sufficient wage labor at low enough wages so long as alternative means of subsistence existed. One seventeenth-century pamphleteer complained of "upstart intruders" and "loyterers," inhabitants of "unlawful cottages erected contrary to law" wherever "the fields lie open and are used in common...." The result was that such people "will not usually be got to work unless they may have such excessive wages as they themselves desire."[40]

With the deposition of Charles I and the triumph of the Presbyterian party in Parliament, the gentry faced consider-

---

[37] Maurice Dobb, *Studies in the Development of Capitalism* (New York: International Publishers, 1947), pp. 224-225, 224-225n.

[38] Immanuel Wallerstein, *The Modern World System*, Part I (New York: Academic Press, 1974), p. 251n; Marx quote is from *Capital* Vol. I, p. 709.

[39] Dobb, *Studies in the Development of Capitalism*, p. 226.

[40] Ibid.

ably less in the way of obstacles to its rapacity.

The so-called land reform of 1646 (which was confirmed by the Convention Parliament in 1660) abolished feudal tenures. It abolished the Court of Wards, and with it the death duties, and "[gave] landowners, whose rights in their estates had hitherto been limited, an absolute power to do what they would with their own, including the right to settle the inheritance of all their lands by will." It converted all military tenures into freehold.[41]

> ...[F]eudal tenures were abolished upwards only, not downwards.... Copyholders obtained no absolute property rights in their holdings, remaining in abject dependence on their landlords, liable to arbitrary death duties which could be used as a means of evicting the recalcitrant. The effect was completed by an act of 1677 which ensured that the property of small freeholders should be no less insecure than that of copyholders, unless supported by written legal title.[42]

Parliament rejected two bills which would limit the entry fees for tenants in copyhold, and rein in enclosures, on the grounds that they would "destroy property."[43] Landlords gained absolute ownership of their estates against previous obligations to the monarchy and aristocracy, but the peasantry secured no corresponding guarantee in the royal courts of their own customary property rights against the landlord. This essentially eliminated all legal barriers to rack-renting, eviction and enclosure.[44] Marx described the "act of usurpation" which the landed proprietors "vindicated for themselves the rights of

---

[41] Christopher Hill, *The Century of Revolution: 1603-1714* (New York: W. W. Norton & Co., Inc., 1961), p. 148.

[42] Christopher Hill, *Reformation to Industrial Revolution: A Social and Economic History of Britain 1530-1780* (London: Weidenfeld & Nicholson, 1967), pp. 115-116.

[43] Hill, *Century of Revolution*, p. 149.

[44] Hill, *Reformation to Industrial Revolution*, pp. 115-116.

modern private property in estates to which they had only a feudal title...."[45]

Royalist land expropriated during the Interregnum was typically purchased by men on the make, "anxious to secure quick returns. Those of their tenants who could not produce written evidence of their titles were liable to eviction."[46] Tenants of these new landlords complained that they "wrest from the poor Tenants all former Immunities and Freedoms they formerly enjoyed...."[47]

None of this passed without opposition, of course. Although Chesterton called the Civil War the "Rebellion of the Rich," it was in fact contested terrain. Although republican, egalitarian, and libertarian rhetoric may have been used by the Parliamentary side to whitewash what were actually rather venal purposes, the rhetoric filtered downward and was taken up seriously by the laboring classes. During the Civil War, popular resistance in the countryside often checked the enclosure of commons and waste. Some of the Leveller writers sought an alliance with the countryside and called for the tearing down of enclosures. In 1649 William Everard ("a cashiered army officer 'who termeth himself a prophett'"[48]), Gerrard Winstanley, and their followers broke down enclosures and attempted to cultivate the waste land communally—for which they earned the name "Diggers." But the left wing of the republican forces never secured a broad alliance with the peasantry, or managed to instigate a full-scale uprising in the countryside, and the restoration of central authority put an end to what resistance there was and gave the landlords a free hand. If anything, the Diggers' travelling missionaries in the countryside hardened local landowners against any proposal that smacked even of modest land reform.[49]

---

[45]Marx and Engels, *Capital* Vol. I, p. 713.
[46]Hill, *The Century of Revolution*, p. 147.
[47]Dobb, *Studies in the Development of Capitalism*, p. 172.
[48]Tate, *The Enclosure Movement*, p. 148.
[49]Ibid., p. 149.

During the Glorious Revolution in 1688-1689, the great landlords took advantage of the power vacuum left by James II's departure to seize Crown lands on a large scale, either by acting quasi-legally through the state by giving them away or selling them at sweetheart prices, or "even annexed to private estates by direct seizure."[50]

The Whig Parliament under William and Mary also passed Game Laws in order to further restrict independent subsistence by the laboring classes. Hunting, for the rural population, had traditionally been a supplementary source of food. The enclosure of common forests and abrogation of access rights put an end to this. As the 1692 law stated in its preamble, it was intended to remedy the "great mischief" by which "inferior tradesmen, apprentices, and other dissolute persons neglect their trades and employments" in favor of hunting and fishing.[51]

The enclosure of open fields under the Tudors (and on a smaller scale under the Stuarts) had taken place largely "by means of individual acts of violence against which legislation, for a hundred and fifty years, fought in vain...." With the Parliamentary Enclosures of the eighteenth century, in contrast, "the law itself becomes now an instrument of the theft of the people's land...." In practical terms, Parliamentary Acts of Enclosure amounted to a "parliamentary coup d'état," through "decrees by which the landlords grant themselves the people's land as private property...."[52] "From the beginning of the eighteenth century the reins are thrown to the enclosure movement, and the policy of enclosure is emancipated from all these checks and afterthoughts."[53]

Just as with Stolypin's and Stalin's policies toward the

---

[50] Marx and Engels, *Capital* Vol. I, p. 714.
[51] Michael Perelman, *Classical Political Economy: Primitive Accumulation and the Social Division of Labour* (Totowa, N.J.: Rowman & Allanheld; London: F. Pinter, 1984, c. 1983), pp. 48-49.
[52] Marx and Engels, *Capital* Vol. I, p. 715.
[53] J. L. and Barbara Hammond, *Village Labourer*, p. 35.

mir, and the destruction of the Indian village communes by the British Permanent Settlement, in Britain "[t]he agricultural community...was taken to pieces in the eighteenth century and reconstructed in the manner in which a dictator reconstructs a free government...."[54]

The goal, as in the other cases, was legibility—"the simplifying appetites of the landlords"[55]—not only for purposes of central taxation, but perhaps more importantly for the ease of the landed classes in extracting a surplus from rural labor.

The landlords saw themselves as the backbone of the British way of life, and the imposition of more effective control on village society as a general benefit to the peace and order of society. Given their assumption that "order would be resolved into its original chaos, if they ceased to control the lives and destinies of their neighbours," they concluded "that this old peasant community, with its troublesome rights, was a public encumbrance."[56] The customary rights of the peasantry hindered the landlord's power to unilaterally introduce new farming techniques.[57] The goal of the "governing class," in language that might just as easily have described Stalin's motives in collectivization, was "extinguishing the old village life and all the relationships and interests attached to it, with unsparing and unhesitating hand."[58]

But the extraction of a larger surplus from the agricultural labor force was also very much a conscious—and explicitly avowed—part of their motivation. The landed classes bore a powerful animus against the common lands because they rendered the rural population less dependent on wage labor, so that rural laborers were uninterested in accepting as much work from the landlords as the latter saw fit to offer.

---

[54]Ibid., p. 35.
[55]Ibid., p. 40.
[56]Ibid., p. 35.
[57]Ibid., pp. 36-37.
[58]Ibid., p. 97.

A pamphleteer in 1739 argued that "the only way to make the lower orders temperate and industrious...was 'to lay them under the necessity of labouring all the time they can spare from rest and sleep, in order to procure the common necessities of life.'"[59]

A 1770 tract called "Essay on Trade and Commerce" warned that "[t]he labouring people should never think themselves independent of their superiors.... The cure will not be perfect, till our manufacturing poor are contented to labour six days for the same sum which they now earn in four days."[60]

Arbuthnot, in 1773, denounced commons as "a plea for their idleness; for, some few excepted, if you offer them work, they will tell you, that they must go to look up their sheep, cut furzes, get their cow out of the pound, or perhaps, say they must take their horse to be shod, that he may carry them to a horse-race or cricket match."[61]

John Billingsley, in his 1795 *Report on Somerset* to the Board of Agriculture, wrote of the pernicious effect of the common on a peasant's character:

> In sauntering after his cattle, he acquires a habit of indolence. Quarter, half, and occasionally whole days are imperceptibly lost. Day labour becomes disgusting; the aversion increases by indulgence; and at length the sale of a half-fed calf, or hog, furnishes the means of adding intemperance to idleness.[62]

Bishton, in his 1794 *Report on Shropshire*, was among the most honest in stating the goals of Enclosure. "The use of common land by labourers operates upon the mind as a sort of independence." The result of their enclosure would be that "the labourers will work every day in the year, their children will be put out to labour early, ...and that subordination of

---

[59]Hill, *Reformation to Industrial Revolution*, p. 225.
[60]Marx and Engels, *Capital* Vol. I, p. 231.
[61]J. L. and Barbara Hammond, *Village Labourer*, p. 37.
[62]Ibid., p. 37.

the lower ranks of society which in the present times is so much wanted, would be thereby considerably secured."[63]

John Clark of Herefordshire wrote in 1807 that farmers in his county were "often at a loss for labourers: the inclosure of the wastes would increase the number of hands for labour, by removing the means of subsisting in idleness."[64]

The 1807 Gloucestershire Survey warned that "the greatest of evils to agriculture would be to place the labourer in a state of independence," and another writer of that time wrote that "Farmers...require constant labourers—men who have no other means of support than their daily labour...."[65]

Of course such motives were frequently expressed in the form of concern for the laborers' own welfare, lest being able to feed oneself too easily lead to irreparable spiritual damage from idleness and dissolution. The words of Cool Hand Luke come to mind: "You shouldn't be so good to me, Cap'n."

The Hammonds estimated the total land enclosed between a sixth and a fifth of the remaining unenclosed arable land (i.e., that not already enclosed before 1700).[66] According to the higher estimate of E. J. Hobsbawm and George Rude, "something like one quarter of the cultivated acreage from open field, common land, meadow or waste" were transformed into private fields between 1750 and 1850.[67] And Maurice Dobb's figure was a quarter to a half of the land in the fourteen counties most affected by Enclosure.[68] W. E. Tate estimates the total land enclosed in the eighteenth and nineteenth century at seven million acres, or an area over a hundred miles square—the equivalent of eight English counties.[69] About two-thirds of the four thousand Private Acts of Enclosure

---

[63]Ibid., p. 38.
[64]Neeson, *Commoners*, p. 28.
[65]Dobb, *Studies in the Development of Capitalism*, p. 222.
[66]J. L. and Barbara Hammond, *Village Labourer*, p. 42.
[67]E. J. Hobsbawm and George Rude, *Captain Swing* (New York: W. W. Norton & Company Inc., 1968), p. 27.
[68]Dobb, *Studies in the Development of Capitalism*, p. 227.
[69]Tate, *The Enclosure Movement*, p. 88.

involved "open fields belonging to cottagers," and the other third involved "common woodland and heath."[70]

✣ France: War on the Commons by Monarchy, Republic, and Empire

As in England, the plunder of the common lands in France began in early modern times. By the late-eighteenth century, on the eve of the Revolution, "the nobles and the clergy had already taken possession of immense tracts of land—one-half of the cultivated area, according to certain estimates—mostly to let it go out of culture."[71] One of the last acts of the monarchy, confirmed two years later by the Constituent Assembly, was to replace the village folkmotes with elected councils of a mayor and three to six syndics "chosen from among the wealthier peasants."[72] In 1792 the Convention, in the face of peasant insurrection in the countryside, returned the enclosed lands to the communes, but

> ordered at the same time that they should be divided in equal parts among the wealthier peasants only—a measure which provoked new insurrections and was abrogated next year, in 1793, when the order came to divide the communal lands among all commoners, rich and poor alike, "active" and "inactive."

This policy, typical of measures by "liberal" states to impose fee-simple ownership on peasant communes, was honored mainly in the breach by the peasantry. In most cases the villagers kept undivided whatever land they manged to retake possession of.

The common lands, subsequently, were repeatedly confiscated—declared to be state domains—and used as collateral for state war loans, and then returned to the communes, from

---

[70]"Development as Enclosure: The Establishment of the Global Economy," *The Ecologist* (July/August 1992), p. 133.

[71]Kropotkin, *Mutual Aid*, pp. 230-231.

[72]Ibid., p. 230.

1794 through 1813. But each time the total acreage returned to the peasantry was further diminished in quantity, with the portion of land restored of disproportionately poor quality.[73]

A similar process continued after the Wars, with three laws passed from 1837 to the reign of Napoleon III "to induce the village communities to divide their estates." Each time the laws were repealed in the face of opposition in the countryside, but (as during the Napoleonic Wars) "something was snapped up each time." Napoleon III, finally, "under the pretext of encouraging perfected methods of agriculture, granted large estates out of the communal lands to some of his favorites."[74]

* *The Permanent Settlement in India*

According to James Scott, the permanent settlement in India

> created a new class who, because they paid the taxes on the land, became full owners with rights of inheritance and sale where none had existed earlier. At the same time, literally millions of cultivators, tenants, and laborers lost their customary rights of access to the land and its products.[75]

As Henry Maine described it, the pernicious effects of the Settlement resulted from the need—in Scott's terminology—to render the native property landscape legible to the taxing authorities.

> Let us suppose a province annexed for the first time to the British Indian Empire. The first civil act of the new government is always to effect a settlement of the land revenue; that is, to determine the amount of that relatively large share of the produce of the soil, or its value, which is demanded by the sovereign in all Oriental States, and out of which all the main

---

[73] Ibid., pp. 231-232.
[74] Ibid., pp. 232-233, 232n.
[75] Scott, *Seeing Like a State*, p. 48.

expenses of government are defrayed. Among the many questions upon which a decision must be had, the one of the most practical importance is, "Who shall be settled with?"—with whom shall the settlement be made? What persons, what bodies, what groups, shall be held responsible to the British Government for its land revenue? What practically has to be determined is the unit of society for agrarian purposes; and you find that, in determining it, you determine everything, and give its character finally to the entire political and social constitution of the province. You are at once compelled to confer on the selected class powers co-extensive with its duties to the sovereign. Not that the assumption is ever made that new proprietary powers are conferred on it, but what are supposed to be its rights in relation to all other classes are defined.... I will not ask you to remember the technical names of the various classes of persons "settled with" in different parts of India—Zemindars, Talukdars, Lumberdars...— but I dwell on the fact that the various interests in the soil which these names symbolise are seen to grow at the expense of all the others. Do you, on entering on the settlement of a new province, find that a peasant proprietary has been displaced by an oligarchy of vigorous usurpers, and do you think it expedient to take the government dues from the once oppressed yeomen? The result is the immediate decline...of the class above them.... Such was the land settlement of Oudh, which was shattered to pieces by the Sepoy mutiny of 1857.... Do you, reversing this policy, arrange that the superior holder shall be answerable to Government? You shall find that you have created a landed aristocracy which has no parallel in wealth or power except the proprietors of English soil. Of this nature is the more modern settlement of the province of Oudh, only recently consummated; and such will ultimately be the position of the Talukdars, or Barons, among whom its soil has been divided.[76]

Neither course was really adequate, according to Maine. For most of India, the records of the time suggested "that no ownership of Indian land was discoverable, except that of the village-communities, subject to the dominion of the State."[77]

The most famous Settlement was that of Lord Cornwallis in Lower Bengal, which Maine described as "an attempt to create a landed-proprietary like that of this country [Great Britain]" by "conferring estates in fee simple on the natural aristocracy of certain parts of India...."[78] In reaction against the pernicious effects of this, the English administration experimented with the opposite approach in an area of southern India centering on Madras: "to recognize nothing between itself and the immediate cultivators of the soil; and from them [to take] directly its share of the produce. The effect of this was to create a peasant proprietary." Although the effects on productivity were far more favorable than those from Cornwallis's Settlement, it was a radical departure from the customary system.[79]

But as Maine suggested above, the primary tendency of the English settlement policy over time was toward the creation of a landed aristocracy from those on whom the payment of taxes was settled—"by registering all the owners of superior rights as landowners, their conception of ownership being taken from their own country...."[80] Their motive was simply to find the class in each province which mostly approximated "ownership" in English terms: "the class to be 'settled with' was the class best entitled to be regarded as having rights of property in the soil." But the English commonly made this judgment on the implicit assumptions of English fee simple ownership, and without regard to the

---
[76]Maine, *Village-Communities*, pp. 149-151.
[77]Ibid., p. 154.
[78]Ibid., p. 105.
[79]Ibid., pp. 105-106.
[80]Ibid., p. 157.

specific kinds of "ownership" the class in question had under native customary law. The practical effect was to take a class whose rights of ownership were significantly restricted by custom, and to transform it into a class of landlords with an uncontrolled right of dominion, or fee simple ownership, in the land—with an at-will tenantry subject to unlimited evictions and rack-rent in a country where such things had previously been almost unknown.[81]

In the case of Lord Cornwallis in Bengal—a province where the village system had already "fallen to pieces of itself" and there was nothing that could be regarded as a real landlord class—instead of following what Maine considered the obvious course of creating a "peasant proprietary" Cornwallis "turned it into a country of great estates and was compelled to take his landlords from the tax-gatherers of his worthless predecessors."[82]

There were other forces besides the Settlement working to undermine the property rules of the village commune. Maine gives the example, in Bengal—the province in his own time in which the invasion of English law and the weakening of native customs of common ownership were most advanced—of English testamentary law undermining the collective property of families. A growing number of native plutocrats, like Maine's example of "a Brahmin of high lineage," were using the testamentary power under English law to circumvent Indian custom and determine the line of succession and disinherit some in favor of others—a practice entirely repugnant to native custom, by which individual rights to the collective property of a family are beyond the power even of a family patriarch to alter. Free testamentary succession, to the prejudice of traditional common property rights of the family and village, exercised great destructive power over native property rules.[83]

---

[81] Ibid., pp. 152-153, 185-186.
[82] Ibid., p. 154.
[83] Ibid., pp. 40-42.

✱ *The Destruction of the Mir in Russia*

In Russia, the *mir* was subjected to a one-two punch, first under Stolypin and then under Stalin.

Stolypin's so-called "reforms" were aimed at rendering the peasantry more legible and taxable, as well as making it possible to permanently alienate individual holdings by sale or as debt collateral, by imposing fee simple private ownership on them—with the additional benefit, from his perspective, of turning the rural population into conservative property owners.

> The dream of state officials and agrarian reformers, at least since emancipation, was to transform the open-field system into a series of consolidated, independent farmsteads on what they took to be the western European model. They were driven by the desire to break the hold of the community over the individual household and to move from collective taxation of the whole community to a tax on individual landholders....
>
> ...It was abundantly clear that the prejudicial attitude toward interstripping was based as much on the autonomy of the Russian village, its illegibility to outsiders, and prevailing dogma about scientific agriculture as it was on hard evidence.[84]

Stolypin's attempted revolution from above met with incomplete success. In most villages a majority of peasants ignored the new property lines laid out from St. Petersburg and continued to practice interstripping and allot their land within the *mir*.[85] And even in the new villages, composed of the "surplus rural population" which Stolypin settled in Siberia, the colonists frequently disregarded Stolypin's plan for new

[84]Scott, *Seeing Like a State*, pp. 41-43.
[85]Ibid., p. 44.

model villages with independent family farmsteads in freehold and instead settled the land as a group, with common property.[86]

After the Revolution, the peasantry initiated a unilateral land reform that included fully restoring the *mir* as it had existed before the Stolypin program.

> In fact, after the collapse of the offensive into Austria during the war and the subsequent mass desertions, much of the land of the gentry and church, as well as "crown land," had been absorbed by the peasantry. Rich peasants cultivating independent farmsteads (the "separators" of the Stolypin reforms) were typically forced back into the village allotments, and rural society was in effect radically compressed. The very rich had been dispossessed, and many of the very poor became smallholders for the first time in their lives. According to one set of figures, the number of landless rural laborers in Russia dropped by half, and the average peasant holding increased by 20 percent (in the Ukraine, by 100 percent). A total of 248 million acres was confiscated, almost always by local initiative, from large and small landlords and added to peasant holdings, which now averaged about 70 acres per household.[87]

Although many libertarians will no doubt regard the seizure of the separators' land as theft, it should be considered at the very least a contested issue. If the *mir*'s collective property in the land, dating time out of mind, is regarded as a legitimate property right, then it follows that Stolypin's imposed division and alienation of parts of the *mir*'s property through fee-simple ownership was theft from the *mir*, and that reincorporating the separators' farmsteads was a simple act of restoration.

---

[86]Ibid., p. 366 n. 78.
[87]Ibid., p. 205.

The newly reinvigorated village communes which the Soviet state confronted were almost entirely opaque to it, and their output far less appropriable.

> From the perspective of a tax official or a military procurement unit, the situation was nearly unfathomable. The land-tenure status in each village had changed dramatically. Prior landholding records, if they existed at all, were entirely unreliable as a guide to current land claims. Each village was unique in many respects, and, even if it could in principle have been "mapped," the population's mobility and military turmoil of the period all but guaranteed that the map would have been made obsolete in six months or sooner. The combination, then, of smallholdings, communal tenure, and constant change, both spatial and temporal, operated as an impenetrable barrier to any finely attuned tax system.
>
> Two additional consequences of the revolution in the countryside compounded the difficulties of state officials. Before 1917, large peasant farms and landlord enterprises had produced nearly three-fourths of the grain marketed for domestic use and export. It was this sector of the rural economy that had fed the cities. Now it was gone. The bulk of the remaining cultivators were consuming a much larger share of their own yield. They would not surrender this grain without a fight. The new, more egalitarian distribution of land meant that extracting anything like the czarist "take" in grain would bring the Bolsheviks in conflict with the subsistence needs of small and middle peasants.
>
> The second and perhaps decisive consequence of the revolution was that it had greatly enhanced the determination and capacity of the peasant communities to resist the state. Every revolution creates a temporary power vacuum when the power of the ancient regime has been destroyed but the revolutionary

> regime has not yet asserted itself throughout the territory. Inasmuch as the Bolsheviks were largely urban and found themselves fighting an extended civil war, the power vacuum in much of the countryside was unusually pronounced. It was the first time...that the villages, although in straitened circumstances, were free to organize their own affairs. As we have seen, the villagers typically forced out or burned out the gentry, seized the land (including rights to common land and forests), and forced the separators back into the communes. The villages tended to behave as autonomous republics, well disposed to the Reds as long as they confirmed the local "revolution," but strongly resistant to forced levies of grain, livestock, or men from any quarter.[88]

The problem of opacity was intensified by the destruction of even the limited knowledge of the local terrain possessed by the tsarist network of local officials and gentry, who had managed tax collection before the Revolution. The village soviets, which were supposed to carry out this function, were typically made up of people whose first loyalty was to the village rather than the Soviet state.[89] As it had done to the tsarist state before the Stolypin program, the village commune deliberately set out to obfuscate the internal economic conditions of the village and render it opaque to the Soviet state. Even before the Revolution, the peasant communes had been able to underreport the amount of arable land by about fifteen percent. After the Revolution, they concealed the extent of land seized from the gentry and landlords.

The amount and distribution of land, of course, was quite legible horizontally, to the peasants within the village commune. "Village committees did...keep records for allocating allotment land, organizing communal plow teams, fixing grazing schedules, and so on, but none of these records was made

---
[88] Ibid., pp. 205-206.
[89] Ibid., p. 207.

available...to officials...."⁹⁰ Under the reinvigorated communes after the Revolution, the village *mir* supervised something like the interstripping and periodic redivisions which had prevailed under the full-blown open field system.

Stalin's industrial program, with its need for increased delivery of food from the countryside, ran up against the reduced appropriability of agricultural output as a serious obstacle. The state's official procurement prices for grain were one-fifth the market price, which meant the peasants were hardly eager to part with it on such terms. The state resorted to forced seizure, along the lines of military requisitions during the Civil War, but its seizures were generally as ineffective as during the war for the same reason: the village communes were pretty effective at concealing how much grain there actually was. It was primarily the desire to overcome this peasant withholding of grain that motivated Stalin's program for forced, total collectivization.

> It was in the context of this war over grain, and not as a carefully planned policy initiative, that the decision to force "total" (*sploshnaia*) collectivization in 1929. Scholars who agree on little else are in accord on this point: the overriding purpose of collectivization was to ensure the seizure of grain.⁹¹

In the debates leading up to forced collectivization, its advocates (e.g., Yevgeny Preobrazhensky) explicitly promoted it as a form of "primitive socialist accumulation" directly to the primitive accumulation Marx described as a prerequisite for the industrial revolution. As large a surplus as possible was to be extracted from the countryside in order to support industrialization in the cities.

The main goal of state collectivization was to make the *terra incognita* of customary village property rules legible from

---

⁹⁰Ibid., p. 207
⁹¹Ibid., p. 210.

above and enable the state to exact a maximum rate of tribute. As envisioned, it was a classic example of a state attempt to impose legibility: it involved consolidating the rural economy into gigantic, centrally controlled units with clear chains of command, proletarianizing the peasantry, and imposing Taylorist work rules on the production process. Among other things, this included a large-scale rural division of labor with each *kolkhoz* specializing in some monoculture crop and the individual village ceasing to be a diversified economic unit. The collective farms were envisioned as enormous assembly lines, automatically churning out state orders like one of Henry Ford's auto factories. The collective farms' lines of command cut across village boundaries, with either enormous *kolkhozes* that incorporated numerous villages, or smaller ones whose boundaries were drawn without regard to existing villages.[92] Unlike the village soviets, which had quickly been coopted by the *mir*, the new "huge collectives" bypassed the traditional village social structures and were governed by "a board consisting of cadres and specialist," with the separate sections of the *kolkhoz* under the control of its own state-appointed manager.[93]

And if collectivization was a miserable failure in terms of total output and efficiency of production, it was for the most part a success at achieving its stated goals—even at the cost of mass starvation in the countryside—of increasing the efficiency of extraction and obtaining sufficient food to support Stalin's urban industrialization program.

> The great achievement, if one can call it that, of the Soviet state in the agricultural sector was to take a social and economic terrain singularly unfavorable to appropriation and control and to create institutional forms and production units far better adapted to monitoring, managing, appropriating, and

---

[92]Ibid., pp. 211-212.
[93]Ibid., p. 214.

controlling from above.... Confronting a tumultuous, footloose and "headless" (acephalous) rural society which was hard to control and which had few political assets, the Bolsheviks, like the scientific foresters, set about redesigning their environment with a few simple goals in mind. They created, in place of what they had inherited, a new landscape of large, hierarchical, state-managed farms whose cropping patterns and procurement quotas were centrally mandated and whose population was, by law, immobile. The system thus devised served for nearly sixty years as a mechanism for procurement and control at a massive cost in stagnation, waste, demoralization, and ecological failure.[94]

The Soviet state collectivization program amounted to a reimposition of serfdom. From the peasant perspective, during the previous Civil War, "the fledgling Bolshevik state, arriving as it often did in the form of military plunder, must have been experienced...as a reconquest of the countryside by the state—as a brand of colonization that threatened their newly won autonomy."[95] But after the brief lull of the New Economic Policy, the peasants experienced reconquest and plunder in earnest. The peasants commonly compared the new collective farm regime to serfdom, with the obligation to work the *kolkhoz*'s fields at nominal wages under the orders of a state manager as a revived form of *barschina* (feudal labor dues). Like their enserfed great-grandparents, the peasants were required to perform annual draft labor repairing roads. *Kolkhoz* officials, like the old landlords, used peasant labor for their own private purposes, and had the power—in fact if not in law—"to insult, beat, or deport" peasants for disobedience. The internal passport system effectively made it illegal, as under serfdom, for the peasant to flee the countryside.[96]

---

[94]Ibid., p. 203.
[95]Ibid., p. 206.
[96]Ibid., p. 213.

Naturally, the peasants saw their work for the *kolkhoz*—like their labor obligations to the old landlord—as something to be done as perfunctorily as possible so they could get back to working their own kitchen gardens.

In sum, Scott writes, "collectivization was at least as notable for what it destroyed as for what it built."

> The initial intent of collectivization was not just to crush the resistance of well-to-do peasants and grab their land; it was also to dismantle the social unit through which that resistance was expressed: the mir. The peasant commune had typically been the vehicle for organizing land seizures during the revolution, for orchestrating land use and grazing, for managing local affairs generally, and for opposing procurements.
>
> The kolkhoz was not...just window dressing hiding a traditional commune. Almost everything had changed. All the focal points for an autonomous public life had been eliminated. The tavern, rural fairs and markets, the church, and the local mill disappeared; in their places stood the kolkhoz office, the public meeting room, and the school.[97]
>
> ...In place of a peasant economy whose harvests, income, and profits were well-nigh indecipherable, it had created units that were ideal for simple and direct appropriation. In place of a variety of social units with their own unique histories and practices, it had created homologous units of accounting that could all be fitted into a national administrative grid.[98]

If anything, collectivization can be compared to Enclosure insofar as a landed peasantry working its own allotments and appropriating a significant share of its full product was transformed into a rural proletariat working the land under the supervision of a hired overseer representing an absentee owner.

---

[97]Ibid., pp. 213-214.
[98]Ibid., p. 217.

* British Land Policy in Africa

British land policy in East Africa centered on "dispossessing indigenous communities of the greater part of their traditional territories": claiming uncultivated or common lands, forests, and grazing lands as property of the colonial administration, and abrogating traditional rights of assess—not to mention head taxes to compel subsistence cultivators to enter the money economy.

> Throughout the colonies, it became standard practice to declare all "uncultivated" land to be the property of the colonial administration. At a stroke, local communities were denied legal title to lands they had traditionally set aside as fallow and to the forests, grazing lands and streams they relied upon for hunting, gathering, fishing and herding.
>
> Where, as was frequently the case, the colonial authorities found that the lands they sought to exploit were already "cultivated", the problem was remedied by restricting the indigenous population to tracts of low quality land deemed unsuitable for European settlement. In Kenya, such "reserves" were "structured to allow the Europeans, who accounted for less than one per cent of the population, to have full access to the agriculturally rich uplands that constituted 20 per cent of the country. In Southern Rhodesia, white colonists, who constituted just five per cent of the population, became the new owners of two-thirds of the land....
>
> Once secured, the commons appropriated by the colonial administration were typically leased out to commercial concerns for plantations, mining and logging, or sold to white settlers.[99]

---

[99] "Development as Enclosure: The Establishment of the Global Economy," *The Ecologist* (July/August 1992), p. 134.

✳ III. The Question of Efficiency

A good many of the criticisms raised of the alleged inefficiency of the open field system and common pasturage turn out, on examination, to be spurious. These include most of the objections raised by Chambers and Mingay, and commonly cited by apologists for the Enclosures—which we will examine in the appendix. But one of the more credible problems, raised by Henry Sumner Maine, was that of reclamation of waste land when expansion of the cultivated area was an urgent necessity. And from the failure to expand cultivation into the waste areas there followed a related set of social distortions within the village.

Although village communes "in one stage" had been democratically governed, they tended over time to become "oligarchies"—as Maine had observed in particular of the Indian villages at the time of Settlement. The relative democracy of the village commune resulted from a comparatively higher "capacity for absorption of strangers" in earlier times, "when men were of more value than land." The villages then, owing to "the extreme value of new labour," were more willing to welcome and amalgamate with outsiders, admitting them to the privileges of the village brotherhood with equal rights of access to the land. But as increased population ran up against the existing extent of cultivation, land became more valuable than people, and the result was social stratification based on the more prestigious families' control of access to land and the increasing deference required to secure access rights. At the same time, the villages tended to become "close corporations," welcoming outsiders only as tenants (thus creating the same problem of a two-tier workforce that has plagued modern cooperatives and kibbutzim when they've hired non-members as wage laborers). Of course all this resulted in a conflict of interest, in which it served the interests of the dominant families in the village to be slow and grudging in allowing the expansion of arable land into the waste.

The one advantage of the form taken by Cornwallis's Settlement in Bengal, Main argued, was that it overcame the problem of developing the waste land. The British, by erecting the Zemindars into a class of fee-simple landlords, freed them from all customary limitations on "their power over subordinate holders" as well as putting the wastes under their dominion at their full disposal. The Zemindars brought these wastes, freed from the villages' customary controls over access, into cultivation by the colony villages of landless peasants they settled there. In countries with large amounts of uncultivated waste and insufficient cultivation to feed the population, Maine argued, fee simple ownership by a landlord was a way to overcome traditional restrictions on waste reclamation and expand the area under cultivation.[100]

It seems to me, however, that the root of this problem was not the want of a dictatorial power to overcome customary restrictions and bring the waste under cultivation. It lay in the village commune's illegitimate and unlibertarian power to control access to uncultivated waste. The arable lands of the village, its pastures and meadows, its woodlots from which its members are in the habit of gathering timber and firewood, were all collectively homesteaded by admixture of the village's labor with the soil—as described by Roderick Long above. But land can only be homesteaded collectively by actual development in common—not simply by making claims to unused land. Having not homesteaded the uncultivated waste, the village has no right to restrict either landless outsiders, or its own comparatively subordinate members, from colonizing a new village on the waste land.

❋ *Conclusion*

Kropotkin, in *Mutual Aid*, mocked those who defended the process of enclosure and private appropriation of the com-

---

[100]Maine, *Village-Communities*, pp. 163-166, 178-179.

munes as "a natural death...in virtue of economical laws." It was, he wrote, "as grim a joke as to speak of the natural death of soldiers slaughtered on a battlefield."

> The fact was simply this: The village communities had lived for over a thousand years; and where and when the peasants were not ruined by wars and exactions they steadily improved their methods of culture. But as the value of land was increasing, in consequence of the growth of industries, and the nobility had acquired, under the State organization, a power which it never had had under the feudal system, it took possession of the best parts of the communal lands, and did its best to destroy the communal institutions.[101]

If there is any one lesson to be gained from all this, it is a warning against the common tendency for libertarians to conflate the private-state dichotomy with the individual/common dichotomy.

✻ *Appendix: The Debates on Enclosure*

Starting in the 1960s, there was a reaction—centered on *The Agricultural Revolution* and other work by J. D. Chambers and G. E. Mingay—against the dominant radical critique of Enclosure inherited from Marx's account of primitive accumulation in volume one of *Capital* and leftist writers like J. L. and Barbara Hammond or E. P. Thompson. Since then, it's been standard practice for anyone on the Right grasping for a defense of the "property rights" of the landed classes to fall back on Chambers as having "disproved" the radical historians.

It's quite similar to claims that Jeavons, Menger, Bohm-Bawerk, Mises, or some other thinker(s) from the marginalist-subjectivist tradition "disproved" Ricardian classical political

---

[101] Kropotkin, *Mutual Aid*, p. 236.

economy—claims typically coming from people whose understanding of both the classical political economists and the marginalists is entirely second-hand, and who have little or no understanding of the actual points at issue between them.

A good recent example is Thomas Woods of the Ludwig von Mises Institute, who dismissed as "socialist" any arguments that the Industrial Revolution and wage system were shaped in any way, and particularly made more exploitative than they otherwise would have been, by the Enclosures.

> This was a central socialist theme: the people must not be viewed as having chosen to abandon the land for the factory, having made a rational assessment of what was best for them. They must have been tricked or forced into it.... [I]t is how nearly all social-democratic historians, until the weight of the evidence began to overwhelm them, tried to portray matters....
>
> Whether the process of enclosure satisfies libertarian standards of justice is not the issue before us here, although much injustice is probably concealed beneath many modern scholars' assurances that the process (which, although it sought substantial consensus, stopped short of unanimity) made agriculture more efficient.... The question, rather, is whether the process was responsible for systematic dispossession, the depopulation of the countryside, or rural poverty. It caused none of these outcomes.

In Woods's version of things, the older left-wing history was "propaganda," in contrast to "modern research."[102] Woods's overwhelming "weight of the evidence," otherwise known as "the past 50 years of scholarship," turns out to refer almost entirely to the work of Mingay. For Woods, apparently, historiography stopped with the groundbreaking scholarship

---

[102]Tom Woods, "Propaganda, Meet Modern Research," *Tom Woods*, July 18, 2011. http://www.tomwoods.com/blog/anti-capitalist-propaganda-meet-modern-research/

of Mingay. He displays no awareness whatsoever that the "revisionism" of Mingay has since become the new orthodoxy, or that subsequent critics like J. M. Neeson have administered the equivalent of a curb-stomping to Mingay's reading of the history of Enclosure.

Chambers and Mingay, in *The Agricultural Revolution*, argued that only a minority of the rural population held commoning rights, that they were only marginally important to the rural population, that they were of little benefit to most, that the stock fed on commons was poorly fed and disease-ridden, and that the English landed peasantry had already disappeared by 1750.[103]

Very little of this stands up to close examination. For example, the extent of common rights was seriously undercounted in official records, according to J. M. Neeson, because they did not include rights under the custom of the manor:

> The number of common-right cottages counted by enclosure commissioners or lords of manors at enclosure gives us an estimate of the number of common-right *cottagers*, but it is almost certainly an underestimate. For only narrowly defined legal right was acknowledged at enclosure; more widely enjoyed customary right was sometimes ignored.

Customary rights based on residence alone, rather than ownership of cottages with common rights attached, went unrecognized by Enclosure commissioners.[104] Chambers and Mingay conceded as much in principle, although arguing in other passages that Enclosure commissions sometimes recognized customary right.

> The legal owners of common rights were always compensated by the commissioners with an allotment

---

[103] J. D. Chambers and G. E. Mingay, *The Agricultural Revolution 1750-1880* (New York: Schocken Books, 1966).

[104] Neeson, *Commoners*, p. 77.

of land. (The *occupiers* of common right cottages, it should be noticed, who enjoyed common rights by virtue of their tenancy of the cottage, received no compensation because they were not, of course, the owners of the rights. This was a perfectly proper distinction between owner and tenant, and involved no fraud or disregard for cottagers on the part of the commissioners.)[105]

Also unrecognized were common rights claims for cottage commons which were unstocked at the time of Enclosure, even when the holder of common rights periodically used them depending on his fluctuating economic circumstances.[106]

The extent of common rights is also undercounted by historians because cottage rights of common were divisible, and sometimes a number of cottagers might split a single cottage right of common, with some individual households holding half or a quarter suit-house cottage rights.[107]

In total, around half of the population on the eve of Parliamentary Enclosure were commoners with "rights of pasture attached to land they worked or to cottages they occupied." In addition, there were landless commoners who supplemented income from wage labor or self-employment as artisans with a small right of pasturage, widows with children to support, and squatters on the waste.[108] Arguably such customary common rights were economically more significant to landless and land-poor peasants than to those with formal title to land in the open fields. And in some parishes common rights were attached to occupancy rather than ownership of a cottage, with a large number of commoners despite the concentration of land ownership.[109]

---

[105]Chambers and Mingay, *The Agricultural Revolution*, p. 97.
[106]Neeson, *Commoners*, p. 78.
[107]Ibid., p. 63.
[108]Ibid., p. 64.
[109]Ibid., p. 75.

So in many villages that were supposedly devoid of a peasantry in Chambers and Mingay's terms, there was in fact still a sizable "landless" rural population with rights to the land.

Chambers and Mingay minimized the economic significance of the supposedly minimal common rights of cottagers and squatters. But even small holdings, which were held by a large portion of the rural population, were a source of considerable independence. Occupancy of an acre or even just a few furlong strips in an open field, coupled with a kitchen garden and common right to graze a few sheep, according to Neeson, could be a "great advantage." With only one to three acres, a family could raise sufficient potatoes, or wheat, barley, and rye—"bread corn"—to subsist "in years of dearth." The landless normally had customary right to pasture pigs on the common, as well. Pigs on the forests and waste and geese in the fen pastures were frequently sold to farmers who fattened them for the table—hence the decline in roast goose and goose down after Enclosure. And a cottage on the border of the waste rendered a laborer "independent of the farmers and many of the country gentlemen."[110]

> The value of the common [according to critics] was no more than wood for the fire. Evidently critics did not know that a waste might provide much more than fuel. Sauntering after a grazing cow, snaring rabbits and birds, fishing, looking for wood, watercress, nuts or spring flowers, gathering teazles, rushes, mushrooms or berries, and cutting peat and turves were all part of a commoning economy and a commoning way of life invisible to outsiders.[111]

Taking it a step further, even for those without common-right cottages, land rights, or pasture rights of any kind, the right to extract fuel, food, and materials from common waste

---

[110]Ibid., pp. 35, 65-67, 312.
[111]Ibid., p. 40.

provided a "variety of useful products."[112] Common waste was a source of hazelnuts, mushrooms, truffles, herbs, salad greens, crabapples, and small game like fowl and rabbits.[113] The right to cut wood in forests, wastes, and private woods enabled families in some areas to cut a year's worth of fuel in a week—fuel which, after Enclosure, would cost four or five weeks' wages for an agricultural laborer.[114] Not only was gleaning unharvested grain a significant source of subsistence for the poorest (at least enough to provide flour till Christmas),[115] but the right to glean wool caught on thorn bushes and the old winter fleece that dropped off in summer was a significant source of fiber for spinning. A contemporary observer estimated around one half of wool from common-field flocks was gathered in this way, rather than by shearing.[116]

Such rights also gave the landless "the means of exchange with other commoners and so made them part of the network of exchange from which mutuality grew. Even for the landless, rights such as gleaning and access to the common waste provided some margin of subsistence and helped knit the village together as a social and economic unit.[117]

The social and economic unit thus knit together included a significant social safety net, of the sort Kropotkin described in *Mutual Aid*. According to Neeson, seasonal shared labor like gathering rushes, harvesting and gleaning, peating, berrying, etc., and the small exchange economy in which even landless commoners participated—"blackberries, dandelion wine, jam, or labour in carrying home wood or reeds"—both created connections between families and "bonds of obligation." Poor families after Enclosure, with no access to the common waste, were unable to obtain the material for participating in this

---

[112]Ibid., p. 158.
[113]Ibid., pp. 169-170.
[114]Ibid., p. 165.
[115]Ibid., p. 313.
[116]Ibid., pp. 168-169.
[117]Ibid., p. 158.

gifting economy from their meager wages, and so could no longer build the ties of mutual obligation and good will with other families which had previously served as a safety net.[118]

One might read all this material in light of recent studies which compare the social health of communities in which farmland is widely distributed among a large number of family farms, versus that of communities where the land is concentrated in the hands of a few giant agribusiness operations.

In short, as Neeson describes it, the commons were the difference between a community of free and independent people and a collection of dependent wage laborers:

> Living off the produce of commons encouraged frugality, economy, thrift. Productive commons had always been the insurance, the reserves, the hidden wealth of commoners—they were the oldest part of an ancient economy. They gave commoners the fuel, food and materials that kept them out of the market for labour and out of the market for consumption too. And the more productive the common the more independent the commoners.
>
> The habit of living off commons made the habit of regular employment less necessary. For commoners it was customary to make a living first out of the materials on hand; after all, the common came first, wage labour was a relatively recent arrival. This is not to deny the existence of wage labour; earning wages was necessary, but until they became the lion's share of income they were supplementary not central to a commoning economy. Looking for regular, constant employment was unnecessary where commons were rich reserves. It is no accident that the loudest complaints about the unavailability of commoners for work come from the Hampshire downs and the East Anglian fens. Time there was customarily spent on

---
[118]Ibid., pp. 180-182.

other things as well as work for wages. Grazing a cow or a donkey, getting in a store of fuel, finding repair wood and thatch, or gathering winter browse for a cow or pigs and food for the larder were other older kinds of employment. This time was never available to employers, it was never purchasable....

One consequence was that commoners who were able to live on a little were unlikely to develop expensive wants. As long as they had what they thought of as enough they had no need to spend time getting more. From this freedom came time to spend doing things other than work, as well as the ability to refuse work. This is the evidence for the accusation by critics of commons that commoners were lazy, that they spent too much time at the market or going horseracing.... Clearly sporting, indolence, laziness, taking time off, enjoying life, lack of ambition (all the words are loaded with values of one kind or another) [the fact that most working and middle class people today share those values is evidence of Methodism's success in reshaping consciousness in the late-eighteenth and early nineteenth centuries —K. C.] had their origins in other things as well as a life outside the market economy. In particular, celebration and recreation had economic functions as well as social. They established connection and obligation.... But the effect of having relatively few needs was liberating of time as well as paid labour. Having relatively few needs that the market could satisfy meant that commoners could work less.... In other words: commoners had a life as well as a living.

George Bourne, who wrote most compellingly about thrift, also argued that the life commoners got was particularly satisfying. On one level, satisfaction came from the varied nature of the work. Commoners had a variety of tasks, many calling for skill and invention, and they had a sure knowledge of their value. But there is more to it than versatility and the inter-

> est it ensures.... Bourne thought that a commoner's sense of well-being came from a sense of ownership or possession, a sense of belonging, and an overwhelming localness. This was not the ownership of a few acres (though that is surely important too) but the possession of a landscape.[119]

Anyone today who works at wage labor, who experiences clocking in as cutting off a piece of her life and flushing it down the toilet, as entering someone else's place and being a poor relation in someone else's house, of leaving her own judgment and values at the door and becoming a tool in someone else's hand, a means to someone else's ends rather than an end in her own right, knows exactly what Bourne meant. The untold millions of people who punch a time-card with a sick feeling in the pits of their stomachs at the prospect of "How much shit am I going to have to eat today to keep my job?" know what a sense of belonging and ownership are mainly from their lack.

Neeson's description reminded me of a comment about the Highland crofters, by science-fiction author Ken Macleod.

> A lot of these highlanders are Heinlein's omnicompetent man—they can turn their hand to anything. They're also rather like Marx's doodle about the post-class society where you could hunt in the morning, fish in the afternoon and be a critic after dinner without ever being hunter, fisherman or critic. That is literally what these guys are like....
>
> ...The highlanders are often people who own a croft, work for wages during the day and go poaching in the evening, and who read a lot. They are people who've never really been hammered into industrial society and therefore have a flexibility.[120]

---

[119]Ibid., pp. 177-179.
[120]Duncan Lawie, "ken macleod interview," zone-sf.com, 2001. http://www.zone-sf.com/kenmacleod.html

So when Chambers and Mingay refer to the loss of commons being "compensated...by an increase in the volume and regularity of employment after enclosure," they sort of miss the point.[121] The commons were of value to their possessors precisely because they were trying to get shut of "volume and regularity of employment." It was the propertied classes, as we saw above, who promoted Enclosures as a way of extracting as much "employment" from the labored classes as possible, regardless of whether the laborers themselves wanted it.

Against arguments by Enclosure apologists that the population of the countryside increased after Enclosure, McNally responded:

> One important recent study has shown that, during the main period of parliamentary enclosure, population rose in both enclosed and unenclosed villages, and that the rate of growth was no faster in the former. Enclosure cannot therefore be said to have had a uniquely stimulative effect on population growth. The same study also demonstrates that there was a "positive association" between enclosure and migration out of villages. Finally, a definite correlation has been established between the extent of enclosure and reliance on poor rates.... The heart of the modern liberal account has thus been refuted; indeed, the older socialist picture now seems remarkably accurate—parliamentary enclosure resulted in outmigration and a higher level of pauperization.[122]

McNally also argues that Mingay neglected the extent to which Enclosure was a tipping point for small, marginal

---

[121] Chambers and Mingay, *The Agricultural Revolution*, p. 98.

[122] David McNally, *Against the Market: Political Economy, Market Socialism and the Marxist Critique* (Verso, 1993), pp. 13-14. Citing N. F. R. Crafts, "Enclosure and Labor Supply Revisited," *Explorations in Economic History* 15, 1978, pp. 176-7,180. K. D. M. Snell, *Annals of the Labouring Poor: Social Change and Agrarian England 1660-1990*, (Cambridge: Cambridge University Press, 1985), pp. 197-206.

tenant farmers, rendering them non-viable and pushing them into wage labor:

> As Mingay has noted in another context, "the very small farmers—occupiers of perhaps 25 acres and less—could hardly survive without some additional form of income; the land itself, unless used for specialized production or amply supplemented by common, would hardly yield sufficient to pay the rent and keep the family." ...He goes on to point out that only in rare circumstances could such small occupiers engage in specialized farming for the market. Yet the other means of support—farming "amply supplemented by common"—is precisely that which was being destroyed by parliamentary enclosure, to the tune of six million acres via enclosure Act (about one-quarter of the cultivated area of England) and another 8 million acres by "agreement".... The impact of enclosure on small tenants, whose lands were inadequate to procure subsistence, can only have been dramatic, forcing them into growing reliance on wage-labour—as proponents of enclosure said it should.[123]

A lot of the trouble with twentieth century pro-Enclosure arguments like those of Chambers and Mingay is that, in many regards, they take eighteenth-century accounts by pro-Enclosure writers at face value, when in fact the latter were were—as J. M. Neeson pointed out—"making a case, not conducting an enquiry."[124]

But although modern revisionists like Chambers agree with the enclosers on the squalor and misgovernment of the commons, what's really interesting is the areas in which the pro-Enclosure writers of the eighteenth century agreed with their contemporary adversaries, rather than with their sympathizers today. According to Neeson, pro- and anti-Enclosure writers of the eighteenth century

---

[123]Ibid., p. 14.
[124]Neeson, *Commoners*, p. 7.

> [f]irst...believed commoners to be numerous and well-dispersed in space and time through the country and the century; second, they thought common right gave commoners an income and a status or independence they found valuable; third, they agreed that the extinction of common right at enclosure marked the decline of small farms and a transition for commoners from some degree of independence to complete dependence on a wage. All eighteenth-century commentators saw a relationship between the survival and decline of common right and the nature of social relations in England.[125]
>
> ....It becomes clear that beneath the argument between these writers lay a fundamental agreement. Opponents agreed on the nature of English rural society before enclosure, and they agreed on enclosure's effect: it turned commoners into labourers. Their disagreement was about the worth of each class; neither side doubted that the transformation occurred, and had profound consequences.[126]

Indeed, as we saw earlier, many of the strongest advocates for Enclosure were deliberately and avowedly motivated not so much by a desire to improve the efficiency of cultivation and animal husbandry, as by a desire to improve the efficiency of extracting labor from the rural population. Advocates for enclosure were explicitly motivated, in part, by the prediction of "complete wage dependence."

> ...many pamphleteers and most reporters to the Board of Agriculture did recommend the creation of complete wage dependence. They said that the discipline was valuable. They argued that the sanction of real or threatened unemployment would benefit farmers presently dependent on the whims of partly self-sufficient commoners. For them...the justification

---

[125]Ibid., p. 9.
[126]Ibid., p. 18.

for ending common right was the creation of an agricultural proletariat.[127]

A central theme running through all Enclosure advocacy in the eighteenth century was that "commoners were lazy." And their very obsession with this "problem" is itself an indication of the economic significance of the commons.

> They used laziness as a term of moral disapproval. But what they meant was that commoners were not always available for farmers to employ. We might ask why were they *un*available? ...In fact...every commoner was lazy, whether wages were high or not. This suggests that they refused to work because they could live without wages, or regular wages. Their laziness becomes an indicator of their independence of the wage. And the degree of frustration critics felt when they saw this laziness may be a guide to how well commoners could do without it.[128]

Those today who minimize the significance of Enclosure as the margin of difference between independence and wage-slavery do so in direct contradiction to the conscious and stated motives of Enclosure advocates—which we quoted at length in the section on English history in the main body of this paper—in the eighteenth century.

Apologists for Enclosure sometimes emphasize the alleged due process entailed in it. But in fact the formal procedure of Enclosure—behind all the rhetoric—amounted to a railroad job. The Hammonds described the formal process of Enclosure as it was justified in legal theory, but argued that in fact it was a naked power grab. The lord of the manor typically worked out the plan of Enclosure and drafted the petition to Parliament, presenting it as a *fait accompli* to the peasantry only after everything was neatly stitched up. If anyone balked

---
[127]Ibid., p. 28.
[128]Ibid., pp. 39-40.

at the terms of Enclosure, they were likely to be warned by the landlord—quite unofficially—that the Enclosure was inevitable, and "that those who obstructed it would suffer, as those who assisted it would gain, in the final award." If they persisted in obstinacy, the only recourse was to appeal to "a dim and distant Parliament of great landlords to come to his rescue."[129]

The membership of the Board of Commissioners that carried out an Enclosure was appointed by the big landowners who initially promoted the Enclosure, before the petition was ever publicly submitted for signatures. So the lord of the manor and other big owners were disproportionately represented on the Board, and the small owners poorly or not at all; and aside from the mandatory assignment of defined portions of the common to the lord of the manor and the owner of the tithes, the commissioners were otherwise given "a free hand, their powers...virtually absolute" in regard to arbitrary assignments of land to the small owners.[130]

And interestingly—interesting, anyway, to those who make a hobby of seeing just how low the depths of human nature can sink—it was common for the same names to appear on the list of commissioners in a long series of Enclosure petitions. Although in theory a commissioner represented no particular interest, in fact he did.

> ...it often says, however, what amounts to much the same thing—that if he "dies, becomes incapacitated or refuses to act" he shall be replaced by a nominee of (a) the lord of the manor, (b) the appropriator and/or other tithe owner(s), etc., or (c) the remaining proprietors. So clearly he has been chosen to represent a particular point of view. Thus in Oxfordshire, Thomas Hopcraft appears in five different commissions, always as representing manorial interests; the

---

[129] J. L. and Barbara Hammond, *Village Labourer*, p. 45.
[130] Ibid., pp. 58-60.

Rev. John Horseman is shown nine times, always acting on behalf of rector, appropriator or vicar. John Chamberl(a)in sat on sixteen commissions, 1789-1803, and on twelve of them represented "other proprietors." An enclosure commissioner combined the delicate functions of advocate and judge.[131]

Chambers and Mingay, interestingly, made mention—albeit in a much more panglossian tone—of the same substantive fact:

> The conduct of an enclosure was such a complex matter that in practice it became a professional occupation for the country gentlemen, land agents and large farmers who were experienced in it, and we find the same commissioners acting at a variety of different places.[132]

Yeah, the English gentry were good to help out that way. Part of that "unbought grace of life" Burke talked about, I guess.

The majority of small holders with rights in the common were disadvantaged in another way. Consider how, as described by the Hammonds, the procedure would have seemed to a small peasant:

> Let us imagine the cottager, unable to read or write, enjoying certain customary rights of common without any idea of their origin or history or legal basis: knowing only that as long as he can remember he has kept a cow, driven geese across the waste, pulled his fuel out of the neighbouring brushwood, and cut turf from the common, and that his father did all these things before him. The cottager learns that before a certain day he has to present to his landlord's bailiff, or to the parson, or to one of the magistrates into

---

[131] W. E. Tate, *The Enclosure Movement*, p. 109.
[132] Chambers and Mingay, *The Agricultural Revolution*, p. 86.

whose hands perhaps he has fallen before now over a little matter of a hare or a partridge, or to some solicitor from the country town, a clear and correct statement of his rights and his claim to a share in the award. Let us remember at the same time all that we know from Fielding and Smollett of the reputation of lawyers for cruelty to the poor. Is a cottager to be trusted to face the ordeal, or to be in time with his statement, or to have that statement in proper legal form? The commissioners can reject his claim on the ground of any technical irregularity.... It is significant that in the case of Sedgmoor, out of 4063 claims sent in, only 1793 were allowed.[133]

Christopher Hill, in language much like the Hammonds', mocked similar claims by Mingay that no coercion was involved in Enclosure.

There was no coercion, we are assured. True, when the big landowner or landowners to whom four-fifths of the land in a village belonged wanted to enclose, the wishes of the majority of small men who occupied the remaining twenty per cent could be disregarded. True, Parliament took no interest in the details of an enclosure bill, referring them to be worked out by its promoters, who distributed the land as they thought best. But the poorest cottager was always free to oppose a Parliamentary enclosure bill. All he had to do was to learn to read, hire an expensive lawyer, spend a few weeks in London and be prepared to face the wrath of the powerful men in his village. If he left his home after enclosure, this was entirely voluntary: though the loss of his rights to graze cattle on the common, to pick up fuel there, the cost of fencing his own little allotment if he got one, his lack of capital to buy the fertilizers necessary to profit by enclosure, the fact that rents, in the Midlands at

---

[133] J. L. and Barbara Hammond, *Village Labourer*, pp. 63-64.

least, doubled in consequence of enclosure—all these might assist him in making his free decision. But coercion—oh dear no! Nothing so un-British as that. There was a job waiting for him, either as agricultural labourer in his village or in a factory somewhere, if he could find out where to go and if he and his family could trudge there. "Only the really small owners," say Professor Chambers and Dr Mingay reassuringly, would be forced to sell out.[134]

In Parliament itself, Enclosure bills required evidence of a three-fourths majority of proprietors in favor in order to proceed. But the possible units for tallying this figure—acreage, common rights, cottages with rights of common, total rack-rental value of land with common right—varied widely, and with them the possible measures of support. The committee sometimes chose between these measures based on which would show the highest degree of support.[135]

Second, even taking at face value the claim that the commons were divided between the property owners of the manor on a pro rata basis, the preexisting distribution of property—as we've already seen from accounts of the enclosure of Church and monastic lands and of arable fields under the Tudors—doesn't bear much looking into. In effect the lord of the manor, the heir of predecessors who encroached on perhaps a majority of common lands over previous centuries, finally offers to divide up the remaining common land according to the distribution of property resulting from those centuries of theft. The process was much like that of the modern urban "improvement district," which is formed with the approval of owners of the majority of property owners in the proposed district, and subsequently levies taxes on advocates and opponents alike. The old saw about the wolf and the sheep voting on what to have for dinner comes to mind here.

---

[134] Hill, *Reformation to Industrial Revolution*, p. 223.
[135] Tate, *The Enclosure Movement*, p. 100.

And third, as we saw above, customary rights of common—probably including a majority of small claims—were seldom compensated. The division of the common land among proprietors left out the cottagers and squatters who had no formal property right in the common recognized by the royal courts, but who had rights of access under village custom—rights of access which had meant the margin for independent survival.[136] And it left out the benefit, which had previously accrued to the poor under the customary regime, of gleaning the common fields after harvest.[137]

Pro-enclosure writers, whether contemporaries or historians like Clapham, Chambers, and Mingay, frequently state in so many words that customary claims were not by legal right, and therefore should not have been compensated. Clapham argued that customary rights of common like turning geese onto pasture or onto the harvested fields were not actually rights at all, but merely on "sufferance."[138]

Customary rights of common were seldom preserved in official manorial records like rolls and field orders. And in Enclosure proceedings, the burden of proof was on peasants to provide documentation for their claims.[139]

Given the history of land ownership in the countryside, and the glaring fact that a peasantry had been reduced over a millennium to tenant status by feudalization and land engrossment, the burden of proof should have been on the other side. As Ludwig von Mises wrote:

> Nowhere and at no time has the large scale ownership of land come into being through the workings of economic forces in the market. It is the result of military and political effort. Founded by violence, it

---

[136] J. L. and Barbara Hammond, *Village Labourer*, p. 52.

[137] Ibid., p. 107.

[138] J. H. Clapham, *An Economic History of Modern Britain: The Early Railway Age 1820-1850* (Cambridge, 1926; 2nd ed., 1930; repr. 1950), pp. 115-117.

[139] Neeson, *Commoners*, pp. 78-79.

has been upheld by violence and that alone. As soon as the latifundia are drawn into the sphere of market transactions they begin to crumble, until at last they disappear completely.[140]

What customs were recognized in the eighteenth century were the remnant of claims that once had been of right. And as Neeson remarked in regard to the right of gathering wood from private woods: "It would take many years, if it happened at all, before this idea of *right*, no matter what its origin, was worn down into a privilege, and before commoners would accept that privileges could be taken away."[141]

Regarding Mingay's contention that the countryside was not depopulated by Enclosure, Hill responded: "Yes, but so what?" One reason the population did not fall in many villages after Enclosure is that "population was increasing anyway. Extension of the cultivated area and intensification of agriculture demanded more labour." But in any case, regardless of how *many* people lived in the countryside, the real question is *how* they lived. Rather than living with the security and independence that came with guaranteed customary access to land, they were permanently relegated to the precarious status of wage laborers dependent on their employer's good will and liable to be discharged without notice on his merest whim.[142]

In addition, regardless of how many people were suffered to live off the land as laborers, the question remains of how much work was required for a given unit of consumption after Enclosure compared to before. As agricultural wages fell after 1765 and rents were driven up by Enclosure, a much larger share of the agricultural laborer's total produce was sold in the towns rather than consumed by him and his family.[143]

---

[140]Ludwig von Mises, *Socialism: An Economic and Sociological Analysis* (London, 1951), p. 375.
[141]Neeson, *Commoners*, p. 163.
[142]Hill, *Reformation to Industrial Revolution*, p. 223.
[143]Ibid., pp. 223-224.

Mingay might as well have boasted that horses were better off based on their comparative numbers in wild herds versus in domestication as draft animals—or the comparatively larger numbers of chickens packed hip to hip in industrial chickenhouses than of the wild fowl from which they descended. Wild sheep may have been fewer in number than their domesticated cousins in pasture; but they no doubt kept more of their own wool and mutton. As for the increased productivity, increased output of labor doesn't matter much to the person doing the work, if the increase is appropriated by someone else.

In the Hammonds' view, the Parliamentary Enclosures of the eighteenth and nineteenth centuries were "the second and greater of two waves," exceeding the Tudor era enclosures of open fields for pasturage in scale.[144] And Dobb claimed that the total percentage of land enclosed under the Tudors "never touched 10 per cent. even in the four counties most affected."[145]

✽ The Question of Efficiency in the Enclosures

Apologists for the Enclosures in England argue that they were necessary for the introduction of efficient new agricultural techniques like improved crop rotation, the use of clover to improve wasteland, and the wintering of livestock.[146]

Chambers and Mingay enumerated a long bill of indictments against the open fields and common pastures in *The Agricultural Revolution*. The particulars included

> the dispersal and fragmentation of the holdings and the time wasted in journeying with implements from one part of the field to another; the unimproved nature of the soil, and the waste of the land in balks

---

[144] J. L. and Barbara Hammond, *Village Labourer*, p. 34.
[145] Dobb, *Studies in the Development of Capitalism*, p. 227.
[146] Hill, *Century of Revolution*, p. 150.

> (although these served as additional pieces of pasture as well as paths between lands and headlands for turning the plough); the rigid rotation of two crops and a fallow; the impossibility of improving the livestock, and the risks of wildfire spread of disease among beasts herded together on the commons and fields....
>
> Perhaps the most striking weakness of the system...was the annual fallowing of a proportion, generally from a quarter to a third, of the arable land. This was necessary in order to restore fertility after two or three years of cropping....[147]

According to subsequent critics of Chambers and Mingay, pro-Enclosure writers of the eighteenth century greatly exaggerated the extent of misgovernment and presented a deliberately one-sided picture out of self-interest; and modern writers like Mingay swallowed it because it was exactly what they wanted to hear.

For example, J. M. Neeson presents evidence that cottagers didn't "graze the commons bare": "[t]hey were unlikely to overstock their rights, they might not even stock them fully."[148]

She also presents numerous examples of effective commons management from manorial records. Far from overrunning the commons or grazing them bare, in most places commoners regulated the commoning of livestock by strictly stinting their commons—restricting the amount of stock which each commoner might graze. Neeson refers to many cases in which village juries introduced stints and carefully enforced them. Even in villages where commons were unstinted, common rights were not unlimited. The stocking, rather, was limited by "the common rights immemorially attached to land or cottage or residency: the original, unabated level of stocking."[149]

---

[147]Chambers and Mingay, *Agricultural Revolution*, pp. 48-49.
[148]Neeson, *Commoners*, p. 86.
[149]Ibid., pp. 113-117.

On the other hand, the rich land-grabbing interests—e.g., "[f]armers who could afford to buy up cottages in order to engross their rights"—were typically owners of large flocks and herds who "might overstock, certainly they would stock the full stint." "The threat to common pasture came less from the clearly defined rights of cottagers than from the larger flocks and herds of richer men."[150] Where village institutions were unable to enforce strict regulations, or stints were too generous, it frequently resulted from the political influence of a few large farmers who overran the commons with their own livestock and left no room for the majority of small owners.[151] And once Enclosure proceedings had begun, large farmers and lords of manors often deliberately overstocked the commons in order to drive down the value of the cottagers' common rights, and thereby reduce the amount of their compensation.[152] Although pro-Enclosure writers took such overstocking as evidence of mismanagement of the commons, in fact it was a side-effect of Enclosure itself.[153]

Assertions by Enclosure advocates and apologists in regard to the spread of disease were similarly slipshod. In this as in other things, Chambers and Mingay uncritically repeated interest-driven accusations by writers two centuries earlier. Besides starvation and malnourishment, pro-Enclosure writers have asserted that "common pasture led to promiscuous breeding and the spread of disease." In particular, "unregulated mixing of animals in large common pastures caused contagion and made control difficult." These writers assume with little ground that "little intelligent attempt was made to control animal diseases in common pasture."[154]

In fact, though, village juries "used by-laws and fines to prevent the spread of disease." Just as much as enclosers,

---

[150]Ibid., p. 86.
[151]Ibid., p. 155.
[152]Ibid., pp. 87-88, 156.
[153]Ibid., p. 156.
[154]Ibid., p. 124.

they believed that contagion from proximity was the source of infection. Grazing diseased livestock like mangy horses or sheep with the scab carried high fines. "Paid herdsmen and women almost constantly supervised common cattle and sheep," which made it extremely difficult to graze a diseased animal without detection. The intense economic interest of commoners in preserving the health of their livestock, and the ease of detection facilitated by "the very public assembly, movement and supervision of common flocks and herds," were powerful safeguards against infection. It was still possible to graze diseased animals for a short time in "partially supervised pastures where horses or cows could be tethered," but they were only in contact with only small numbers of other animals.[155]

What's more, contemporary and modern advocates of Enclosure indicted the livestock management practices of commoners completely out of any context. The most important comparison—to livestock management practices *after* Enclosure—was almost never made. "Perhaps the most important point to make is that the limited understanding of how many diseases spread made prevention difficult both before and after enclosure." The enclosers, as much as the commoners, mistakenly believed that all disease was caused by contagion and were unaware of other vectors—like clothing—for transmitting disease.

> Clearly most of these sources of infection were not affected by separation into herds after enclosure; and the long incubation period of the disease (30-60 days, and up to six months in some cases) made it very difficult to prevent the introduction of diseased animals into uncontaminated herds either before or after enclosure.[156]

The fences of enclosed farms, likewise, could not prevent the

---

[155]Ibid., pp. 124-125.
[156]Ibid., pp. 126-128.

transmission of diseases like leptospirosis through contaminated watercourses or rodents.[157] Diseases associated with wet commons and poor drainage were managed as well by commoners as by enclosers; "post-enclosure improvements in drainage came fifty years after most enclosures were complete."[158]

Finally, the irrelevance of Enclosure to disease is suggested by the disconnect between the chronology of Enclosure and that of "diminution of animal disease." Pandemics continued to decimate flocks well into the nineteenth century. For example, sheep rot—the most prominent item in the enclosers' indictment of the commons—killed one to two million sheep in the winter of 1830-1831.[159]

Another bit of uncritically received wisdom is "the 'impossibility' of improving animals on common pastures by selective breeding." But in fact village juries closely controlled breeding. Bulls were not allowed to run free, and rams and bulls were only allowed on the common "at stated times."[160] Lords of manors and large farmers were required by custom to put superior bulls out to stud, pasturing them periodically with commoners' herds.[161]

As for the requirement of letting a large portion of land lie fallow, Chambers and Mingay themselves concede that "open field farmers...showed enterprise" in such matters as using legumes and turnips to restore the fertility of soil—suggesting that "the ancient structure was not so backward nor so incapable of improvement as was once supposed."[162]

Where peasants were not economically crushed by rents and taxes, and where some of their members had leisure to improve their minds, open- or common-field villages were

---

[157] Ibid., p. 128.
[158] Ibid., p. 129.
[159] Ibid., p. 130.
[160] Ibid., pp. 130-131.
[161] Ibid., p. 131.
[162] Chambers and Mingay, *The Agricultural Revolution*, pp. 51-52.

frequently quite progressive in introducing new agricultural methods. According to Neeson, in the Midlands especially, common-field villages in England in the period running up to Enclosure were open to innovations—for example redividing the common fields for crop rotation and introducing clover as a fodder crop on fallow land—"impressive developments" entailing a "flexibility in agricultural practice which led to all-around increases in fertility and production long before parliamentary enclosure."[163]

According to W. E. Tate, the introduction of turnips as a field crop was entirely feasible within the bounds of the open-field system; it required only the reorganization of the arable mark to add a fourth field. Even before the act of Parliament in 1773 which made it legal for villagers to do so—apparently on the assumption that unauthorized reorganizations had been legally suspects—villages had previously voted to create fourth fields for root crops.[164]

The same later held true in the open fields of the Russian *mir*, after the emancipation of the serfs. Kropotkin, in the eighth chapter of *Mutual Aid*, cited numerous examples of villagers experimenting with new techniques on their common lands. Many of the examples referred to the efficient and progressive management of commons where they persisted in Germany, and even more so in Switzerland where they thrived in much greater vigor. But even in Russia, where most historians view the alleged backwardness of the *mir* through Stolypin's lens:

> The facts which we have before us show, on the contrary, that wherever the Russian peasants, owing to a concurrence of favourable circumstances, are less miserable than they are on the average, and wherever they find men of knowledge and initiative among their neighbours, the village community becomes the

---

[163] Neeson, *Commoners*, p. 8.
[164] Tate, *The Enclosure Movement*, p. 80.

very means for introducing various improvements in
agriculture and village life altogether.¹⁶⁵

Improved steel plows spread rapidly in southern Russia, "and
in many cases the village communities were instrumental in
spreading their use."

> A plough was bought by the community, experimented with upon on [sic] a portion of the communal land, and the necessary improvements were indicated to the makers, whom the communes often aided in starting the manufacture of cheap ploughs as a village industry.

The main impetus for the adoption of over fifteen hundred improved plows over a five-year period in the Moscow district came from "those communes which rented lands as a body for the special purpose of improved culture." In Samara, Saratov, and Kherson provinces the adoption of threshing machines came about mainly "due to the peasant associations, which can afford to buy a costly engine, while the individual peasant cannot."

And contrary to the received wisdom from agricultural historians that "the village community was doomed to disappear" when crop rotation replaced the three-field system, in fact "we see in Russia many village communities taking the initiative of introducing the rotation of crops." If experiments with crop-rotation prove successful, the peasants "find no difficulty whatever in re-dividing their fields...."¹⁶⁶

The peasant communes, on their own initiative, introduced crop rotation and dug drainage works in hundreds of villages in the provinces around Moscow, and built thousands of dams for ponds and dug many hundreds of deep wells in the dry steppe country.¹⁶⁷

---

¹⁶⁵Kropotkin, *Mutual Aid*, p. 255.
¹⁶⁶Kropotkin, *Mutual Aid*, pp. 257-258.
¹⁶⁷Ibid., pp. 258-259.

Recall, in regard to all the examples above of progressive action by peasant communes, Kropotkin's observation that they were most likely to take place in areas where peasants were least crushed by exploitation. And then consider the fact that all these heroic efforts at self-improvement come from a time when the peasantry still lived under heavy taxation to indemnify their former owners for the lands given the peasants at the time of the liberation of the serfs. Bear in mind that these people lived a generation or less after most of the peasant majority of Russia had been illiterate serfs in a state of near-slavery. Now imagine what things they might have accomplished had they lived free of that yoke in previous centuries, and held their land free from the exaction of tribute by the state and the landed aristocracy.

Seen in this light, all the arguments that "the peasants were better off" or "it was necessary for progress" seem as shameful as the old arguments for the White Man's Burden. I suspect those who dismiss traditional peasant property rights as an atavistic barrier to progress are close kin to the consequentialists who argue that technological progress would have been impossible had not the peasants been evicted from the land and driven into the factories like beasts, or that the state must promote progress and increase the tax base by seizing inefficiently used property and giving it to favored business enterprises.

W. E. Tate's description of the "benefits" envisioned for the poor by Enclosure advocates is very much on the mark:

> The deserving poor would find small plots in severalty, or small pasture closes, more useful than scattered scraps in the open fields, and vague grazing rights. Certainly they would be no worse off without the largely illusory advantages of the common, and the very real temptations to idleness which its presence entailed. The undeserving poor, especially the insubordinate squatters, living in riotous squalor in their tumbledown hovels on the common, would prosper

morally and economically if they were compelled to do regular work for an employer.[168]

To borrow a line from Cool Hand Luke, "I wish you'd stop being so good to me, cap'n."

There's also more than a little implicit collectivism in the complaint, in J. M. Neeson's words, that "[c]ommoners stood in the way of national economic growth."[169] It reminds me of a comment by some neoconservative talking head on Fox News at the outset of the Iraq War in 2003, who boasted of American cowboy capitalism's superiority to a European model that provided shorter workweeks and six-week vacations. "Maybe Americans," he said, "prefer to work longer hours and take less vacation, so we can afford all those aircraft carriers." Indeed: no true patriot will mind that BB has reduced (er, ahem, "increased") the chocoration to 20 grams a week, if it means another Floating Fortress off the Malabar Front.

Missing from all the discussion of "increased efficiency" is any consideration of qui bono. Coase's argument that it doesn't matter who owns a resource, because it will wind up in the hands of the most efficient user, has always struck me as nonsensical. It matters a great deal to the person who was robbed. Such arguments remind me a great deal of arguments for eminent domain, by which land will be put to its "most productive use." But since—as the Austrians never tire of asserting elsewhere—utility is subjective, what is "efficient" is very much in the eyes of a potential user of the land.

> Tell the fenmen, Fuller said, 'of the great benefit to the public, because where a pike or duck fed formerly, now a bullock or sheep is fatted; they will be ready to return that if they be taken in taking that bullock or sheep, the rich owner indicteth them for felons;

---
[168]Tate, *The Enclosure Movement*, p. 23.
[169]Neeson, *Commoners*, p. 32.

> whereas that pike or duck were their own goods, only for their pains of catching them'.[170]

W. E. Tate, in similar vein, describes the skepticism of commoners in the face of the propertied classes' visions of prosperity:

> They much preferred rearing poor specimens of cattle on the commons for their own benefit, to tending prize stock in enclosures for someone else's. They were not in the least attracted by the prospect set forth by one of the Reporters, seeing the commons 'to wave with luxuriant crops of grain—be covered with innumerable flocks and herds, or clothed with stately timber', since not grain, herds nor timber would be theirs.[171]

Critics of the "inefficiency" of the commons ignore the value of independence and self-sufficiency, the possession of sources of subsistence that could not be taken away at someone else's whim.

> When critics of commons weighed the value of common right they did so in their own terms, the terms of the market. They talked about wage labour and the efficient use of resources. But commoners lived off the shared use of land. To some extent they lived outside the market. They lived in part on the invisible earnings of grazing and gathering. Much of this was inconceivable to critics, either because they did not look or because they did not want to see. In their eyes commoners were lazy, insubordinate and poor. But when historians come to assess these assessments we have to understand that none of these conditions, except poverty, is a measure of the inadequacy of a

---

[170]Hill, *Reformation to Industrial Revolution*, p. 121.
[171]Tate, *The Enclosure Movement*, p. 165.

standard of living. Even poverty, in the case of commoners, may have been in the eye of the beholder: commoners did not think themselves poor.[172]

---

[172]Neeson, *Commoners*, pp. 41-42.

CHAPTER SEVEN

GOVERNANCE, AGENCY, AND AUTONOMY: ANARCHIST THEMES IN THE WORK OF ELINOR OSTROM

KEVIN CARSON

✻ *INTRODUCTION*

This paper is intended as one in a series, to be read along with my previous one on James C. Scott,[1] on anarchist and decentralist thinkers whose affection for the particularity of local, human-scale institutions overrides any doctrinaire ideological labels.

✻ *The Governance of Common Pool Resources*

Ostrom begins by noting the problem of natural resource depletion—what she calls "common pool resources"—and then goes on to survey three largely complementary ("closely related concepts") major theories that attempt to explain

---

Center for a Stateless Society Paper No. 16 (Second Half 2013): c4ss.org/content/23644

[1] Kevin Carson, "Legibility & Control: Themes in the Work of James C. Scott." *Center for a Stateless Society Paper* No. 12 (Winter/Spring 2011). http://c4ss.org/wp-content/uploads/2011/05/James-Scott.pdf

"the many problems that individuals face when attempting to achieve collective benefits": Hardin's "tragedy of the commons," the prisoner's dilemma, and Olson's "logic of collective action."[2]

Unfortunately, these models (or this model) ossified into a dogma, serving more often as a substitute for thought than a starting point. Even more than twenty years after Ostrom's seminal work, it's still common to state as a truism—backed only by a passing allusion to Hardin or the prisoner's dilemma—that the actual users of resources will inevitably deplete them in the absence of governance by some higher authority or other. Ostrom cites one blithe assertion, in an article on fisheries in *The Economist*: "left to their own devices, fishermen will overexploit stocks.... [T]o avoid disaster, managers must have effective hegemony over them."[3]

This last quote exemplifies perfectly the common approach to the governance of common pool resources taken by advocates both of state regulation and corporate privatization. Garrett Hardin himself, later revisiting his article on the tragedy of the commons, argued that the problem of resource depletion would have to be addressed either by "a private enterprise system" (i.e., ownership by for-profit business firms) or "socialism" (i.e., ownership and regulation by the state).[4] (The assumption that "private enterprise" and "socialism" both require managerial hierarchies of one sort or another, and are incompatible with horizontal, self-organized institutions, speaks volumes about the internalized values of the intellectual stratum.)

Ostrom goes on to consider the unsatisfactory performance of both the state and the market[5] in addressing the problem.

---

[2]Elinor Ostrom, *Governing the Commons: The Evolution of Institutions for Collective Action* (Cambridge University Press, 1990), pp. 1-7.
[3]Ibid., p. 8.
[4]Ibid., p. 9.
[5]Ostrom consistently uses the term "market" in the sense of "cash

It should be noted right off that the juxtaposition between "common property" and "private property" put forward by mainstream capitalist libertarians is just plain silly. In cases where parceling out a common resource to individuals is by the nature of the case impossible, Ostrom says, one is hard-pressed to understand just what is meant by "private." Open fields or common pasture can be divided up into separate plots and distributed to individuals; but fisheries?[6] Common pool resources, by the nature of things, must be owned and governed by some sort of collective institution, whether it be the state, a corporation—or a self-organized, horizontal association of the users themselves.

Ownership by a for-profit corporation is no more "private" than (or if you prefer, just as "collectivist" as) the administration of a commons by its users. In corporate law, a firm's property is owned, and its management employed, by a unitary person created under the terms of the corporate charter. No individual shareholder or group of shareholders has any right of ownership over the firm's assets or authority over its management.

Both the conventional "privatization" and "state regulation" approaches amount, when all the legal fictions are stripped away, to substituting the judgment of managers working for some absentee central authority (perhaps only in theory, working in fact for their own interests) for that of users. So we might expect it to result in the same knowledge and incentive problems that always result from externalizing costs and benefits, when ownership and control are divorced from direct knowledge of the situation.

On the other hand, we might expect that placing control directly in the hands of those with Hayekian local knowledge of a situation results in outcomes far preferable to either of

---

nexus" or "for-profit business sector," rather than a general legal regime of voluntary contract and enforceable property rights. Unless specified otherwise, I will be using the term in her sense.

[6]Ibid., p. 19.

the other two approaches based on verticality and absentee control.

And Ostrom's findings bear out that expectation.

Rather than starting from the assumption that the users of common resources are helpless without an outside authority intervening to protect them from themselves, she assumes that "the capacity of individuals to extricate themselves from various types of dilemma situations *varies* from situation to situation," and then adopts the empirical approach of surveying "both successful and unsuccessful efforts to escape tragic outcomes."[7]

To the two orthodox models of state and corporate ownership, Ostrom juxtaposes the administration of a commons by a binding contract among the commoners themselves, "to commit themselves to a cooperative strategy that they themselves will work out."

Of course there are ways they could go wrong; livestock owners "can overestimate or underestimate the carrying capacity of the meadow," or their monitoring system can break down. But even so, these potential points of failure arguably exist in stronger form in the case of absentee governance by a central institution. The monitoring system is based on the users themselves, who are neighbors and who as users have a strong incentive to prevent defection by the others, observing each other directly—considerably more effective, one would think, than the typical inspection regime of a state regulatory authority (my mother, who worked in a poultry processing plant and came into daily contact with USDA inspectors, could have told you that). And their calculations of carrying capacity and sustainable yield, while fallible, at least "are not dependent on the accuracy of the information obtained by a distant government official [or corporate home office, I might add] regarding their strategies."[8]

Ostrom's empirical survey casts light not so much on

---

[7] Ibid., p. 14.
[8] Ibid., pp. 15-18.

whether such horizontal governance of a commons by the commoners themselves works—obviously sometimes it does—but on what particular governance rules produce optimal results.

Really, it stands to reason that cooperative governance of common pool resources, all other things being equal, will be more effective in formulating and enforcing rules than governance by either a government agency or a corporation. "Because the individuals involved gain a major part of their economic return from the CPRs, they are strongly motivated to try to solve common problems to enhance their own productivity over time."[9]

So what remains, in the course of Ostrom's investigation, is "to identify the underlying design principles of the institutions used by those who have successfully managed their own CPRs over extended periods of time...."[10] What measures, in particular, did they take to address the real problems presented by "temptations to free-ride, shirk, or otherwise act opportunistically"?[11] The middle part of her book is accordingly devoted to a survey of

> field settings in which (1) appropriators have devised, applied, and monitored their own rules to control the use of their CPRs and (2) the resource systems, as well as the institutions, have survived for long periods of time. The youngest set of institutions to be analyzed...is already more than 100 years old. The history of the oldest system to be examined exceeds 1,000 years.[12]

The rules for governing common pool resources, in the instances Ostrom examined, worked in situations where game theory would have predicted incentives to defect were strong

---

[9]Ibid., p. 26.
[10]Ibid., p. 27.
[11]Ibid., p. 29.
[12]Ibid., p. 58.

and negative consequences of defection were weak (as in common governance systems for irrigation water in the Spanish Philippines, where monitoring was relatively weak and fines were low compared to the benefits of defection, and stealing water in a drought might save an entire season's crop).[13]

And far from reflecting "an anachronistic holdover from the past," governance systems for common pool resources have typically reflected close empirical reasoning from historical experience. In the case of communal for pastoral mountain land,

> for at least five centuries these Swiss villagers have been intimately familiar with the advantages and disadvantages of both private and communal tenure systems and have carefully matched particular types of land tenure to particular types of land use.[14]

Based on her survey, Ostrom distilled this list of common design principles from the experience of successful governance institutions:

1. *Clearly defined boundaries.* Individuals or households who have rights to withdraw resource units from the CPR must be clearly defined, as must the boundaries of the CPR itself.

2. *Congruence between appropriation and provision rules and local conditions.* Appropriation rules restricting time, place, technology, and/or quantity of resource units are related to local conditions and to provision rules requiring labour, material, and/or money.

3. *Collective-choice arrangements.* Most individuals affected by the operational rules can participate in modifying the operational rules.

---

[13]Ibid., p. 59.
[14]Ibid., p. 63.

4. *Monitoring.* Monitors, who actively audit CPR conditions and appropriator behaviour, are accountable to the appropriators or are the appropriators.

5. *Graduated sanctions.* Appropriators who violate operational rules are likely to be assessed graduated sanctions (depending on the seriousness and context of the offence) by other appropriators, by officials accountable to these appropriators, or by both.

6. *Conflict-resolution mechanisms.* Appropriators and their officials have rapid access to low-cost local arenas to resolve conflicts among appropriators or between appropriators and officials.

7. *Minimal recognition of rights to organize.* The rights of appropriators to devise their own institutions are not challenged by external governmental authorities.

For CPRs that are parts of larger systems:

8. *Nested enterprises.* Appropriation, provision, monitoring, enforcement, conflict resolution, and governance activities are organized in multiple layers of nested enterprises.[15]

Here are some thoughts that occurred to me as I read through Ostrom's common principles. Historically, many commons governance regimes have failed as a result of outside interference, by states and landed elites, with the spirit of No. 7. That was true of both Stolypin's "reform" and Stalin's forced collectivization, which both ran roughshod over the *mir*'s internal rights of self-governance. In addition, Stolypin's land policy in its substance violated No. 1, by allowing individual households to withdraw aliquot shares of land from the village's common fields as a close (in English terms) without the

---
[15]Ibid., p. 90.

consent of the *mir* as a whole. In so doing, it violated the basic social understanding of the nature of property ownership built into the system from its founding.

To put it in terms understandable by the kind of right-wing libertarian who instinctively cheers for the word "private" and boos "common," imagine if a legislature overrode the terms of a corporate charter and let individual shareholders barge into factories with front-end loaders and carry off some aliquot share of machinery—under the terms of the charter owned solely by the corporation as a single person—from assembly lines. Imagine how that would disrupt production planning within a factory. That's what Stolypin's policies did to land-use planning by the *mir* for those lands remaining within the open-fields.

No. 3, the right of those affected by the rules to have a say in devising them, is—normative theories of participatory democracy aside—a prerequisite for an efficiently functioning institution. As Ostrom says:

> CPR institutions that use this principle are better able to tailor their rules to local circumstances, because the individuals who directly interact with one another and with the physical world can modify the rules over time so as to better fit them to the specific characteristics of their setting.[16]

The separation of decision-making power from both distributed situational knowledge and experience of the consequences is key to all the knowledge and incentive problems of hierarchical, authoritarian institutions, whether they be governments or corporations. Top-down authority is a mechanism for expropriating the benefits of others' work for oneself, and externalizing cost and inconvenience downward.

Given the obvious knowledge and incentive problems resulting from separation of authority from competence, why

---

[16] Ibid., p. 93.

is hierarchy ever adopted in the first place? The answer lies in clearing our minds of unconscious assumptions that institutional design is something that "we" or "society" do in order to maximize some vague idea of the "common good." Hierarchy exists because those who run the dominant institutions of state and corporation have a fundamental conflict of interest with those who possess the situational knowledge, such that the former cannot trust the latter to use their own best judgment. The manager of a hierarchical institution, like the owner of a slave plantation, cannot trust her subordinates to use their own best judgment lest she find her throat cut in the middle of the night. And subordinates know full well that if they use their situational knowledge to maximize efficiency, any productivity gains will be expropriated by management in the form of downsizings, speedups, and management bonuses.

Most production jobs involve a fair amount of hidden or distributed knowledge, and depend on the initiative of workers to improvise, to apply skills in new ways, in the face of events which are either totally unpredictable or cannot be fully anticipated. Rigid hierarchies and rigid work rules only work in a predictable environment. When the environment is unpredictable, the key to success lies with empowerment and autonomy for those in direct contact with the situation.

The problem with authority relations in a hierarchy is that, given the conflict of interest created by the presence of power, those in authority cannot *afford* to allow discretion to those in direct contact with the situation. Systematic stupidity results, of necessity, from a situation in which a bureaucratic hierarchy must develop some metric for assessing the skills or work quality of a labor force whose actual work they know nothing about, and whose material interests militate against remedying management's ignorance. When management doesn't know (in Paul Goodman's words) "what a good job of work is," they are forced to rely on arbitrary metrics.

Weberian work rules are necessary because those at the

top of the pyramid cannot afford to allow those at the bottom the discretion to use their own common sense. Because the subordinate has a fundamental conflict of interest with the superior, and does not internalize the benefits of applying her intelligence, she cannot be trusted to use her intelligence for the benefit of the organization. In such a zero-sum relationship, any discretion can be abused.

On the other hand, subordinates cannot afford to contribute the knowledge necessary to design an efficient work process. R. A. Wilson's analogy of the person in authority confronting the subordinate as a "highwayman" is a good one. The party with residual claimancy in any economic institution—like a business firm—will use the powers associated with ownership to obtain a disproportionate share of the surplus. Those who lack ownership stakes will have a corresponding incentive to under-invest their knowledge and skills in the performance of the enterprise. Hence, the most rational approach to maximizing productivity is to assign residual claimancy or ownership rights to stakeholders in accordance with their contribution to productivity.[17]

This almost never happens, because it's in management's perceived self-interest to engage in self-dealing even at the expense of the overall productivity of the firm. So workers instead hoard knowledge and minimize their legibility (in James Scott's terms) to management and minimize the chance that the increased productivity resulting from their hidden knowledge will be used against them or expropriated. Hence, hierarchies are a very inefficient way of organizing activity, from the standpoint of harnessing the full capabilities and knowledge of the workforce.

But when given a choice between efficiency and control—between a larger pie and a larger slice of a smaller pie—management usually prefers to maximize the size of their

---

[17]Sanford J. Grossman and Oliver D. Hart, "The Costs and Benefits of Ownership: A Theory of Vertical and Lateral Integration," *Journal of Political Economy* 94:4 (1986), pp. 716-717.

slice rather than the size of the pie. Hierarchy is a way of organizing human activity so as to facilitate the extraction of rents from it, even at the expense of a severe degradation in efficiency.

Monitoring systems, No. 4, are best designed when "actors most concerned with cheating [are placed] in direct contact with one another." For example, in an irrigation rotation system the actor whose turn it currently is is prevented from extending their turn past its scheduled end by the presence of the actors whose turn is next, eagerly waiting to take over.[18] Grandma's practice of letting one child cut the cake in half and the other take first pick is the classic example of this principle. In many cases monitoring others' use of a commons is "a natural by-product of using the commons." And successful monitoring is further encouraged by informal sanctions and rewards, sometimes as simple as the social approval or disapproval of one's neighbors.[19]

The cost of front-line supervision is generally about a quarter as much in the plywood cooperatives of the Pacific Northwest as in conventional capitalist operations, because of employee self-monitoring.[20]

Under graduated sanctions, the modest penalties actually serve as a mutual confidence-building regime. Users who enter into a governance system suspicious their neighbors will violate the rules and thus having an incentive to defect themselves, will, on being detected and paying a modest penalty, be reassured that enforcement is credible, compliance is widespread, and they can expect to benefit rather than being taken advantage of by participating in the system.

There will always be a small minority, of course, who are immune to such moral sanctions. But the majority on whom

---

[18] Ostrom, *Governing the Commons*, p. 95.
[19] Ibid., p. 96.
[20] Edward S. Greenberg, "Producer Cooperatives and Democratic Theory" in Jackall and Levin, eds., *Worker Cooperatives in America* (University of California Press, 1986), p. 193.

such sanctions do work will reduce the cost of monitoring those who need closer surveillance.

Ostrom also considers the optimal conditions for overcoming the transaction costs of incrementally improving on a CPR governance system. She starts with the assumption that appropriators are "in a remote location under a political regime that is basically indifferent to what happens with regard to CPRs of this type," and therefore unlikely to interfere either to promote or impede local governance decisions. Under such conditions,

> the likelihood of CPR appropriators adopting a series of incremental changes in operational rules to improve joint welfare will be positively related to the following internal characteristics:
>
> 1. Most appropriators share a common judgment that they will be harmed if they do not adopt an alternative rule.
> 2. Most appropriators will be affected in similar ways by the proposed rule changes.
> 3. Most appropriators highly value the continuation activities from this CPR....
> 4. Appropriators face relatively low information, transformation, and enforcement costs.
> 5. Most appropriators share generalized norms of reciprocity and trust that can be used as initial social capital.
> 6. The group appropriating from the CPR is relatively small and stable.[21]

In other words, the same conditions under which Ostrom's earlier list of eight prerequisites for successful CPR governance are likely to be met in the first place.

---

[21]Ostrom, *Governing the Commons*, p. 211.

As we shall see in the next section, states have exacerbated problems by artificially inflating the extent of background conditions—e.g., large, anonymous market areas with one-off dealings, social atomization, etc.—in which Ostrom's prerequisites for successful self-governance do not exist.

The existence of an interventionist state can hamper formation of local CPR governance regimes in another way, even when intentions are good. When locals in an area without CPR governance regimes already in place are aware of a central government with an interest in regulating CPRs, the temptation will be greatly increased to "wait and see" in hopes of free-riding off a central government regulatory policy.[22]

And of course the difficulty faced by officials from a central government in obtaining sufficient knowledge of local conditions to formulate governance rules as effective as those designed by local appropriators in direct contact with local conditions, and the constant temptation to devise uniform policies for all jurisdictions, will impede good governance.[23]

✻ Centralization, Atomization, and Sustainability

Ostrom, surveying the value of self-organized governance institutions, writes:

> ...we will all be the poorer if local, self-organized institutions are not a substantial portion of the institutional portfolio of the twenty-first century. Many indigenous institutions developed to govern and manage local common pool resources have proven themselves capable of enabling individuals to make intensive use of these resources over the long run—centuries or even millennia—without destroying the delicate resource base on which individuals and their future offspring depend for their livelihood....

---
[22]Ibid., p. 213.
[23]Ibid., pp. 213-214.

> Under banners associated with conserving the environment for future generations, international donors, national governments, international nongovernmental organizations, national charities, and others have, in many cases, unwittingly destroyed the very social capital—the shared relationships, norms, knowledge, and understanding—that has been used by resource users to sustain the productivity of natural capital over the ages.
>
> These institutions are most in jeopardy when central government officials presume they do not exist (or are not effective).[24]

Unfortunately, the conventional ideological framework for understanding governance institutions presumes that the natural state of affairs absent rules introduced from above is a Hobbesian war of all against all; the proper question, it follows from this starting point, is what policies governments should formulate to impose order on the chaos of voluntary interaction.

This mindset represents centuries' worth of ingrained habits of thought, resulting from a shift from social organizations primarily (to James Scott's terminology in *Seeing Like a State*) "legible" or transparent to the people of local communities organized horizontally and opaque to the state, to social organizations that are primarily "legible" to the state from above.[25]

The former kind of architecture, as described by Pyotr Kropotkin, was what prevailed in the networked free towns of late medieval Europe. The primary pattern of social organization was horizontal (guilds, etc.), with quality certification

---

[24]Ostrom, "Neither Market Nor State: Governance of Common Pool Resources in the Twenty-first Century," lecture presented June 2, 1994 at the International Food Policy Research Institute, Washington, D. C., p. 2.

[25]James Scott, *Seeing Like a State* (New Haven and London: Yale University Press, 1998).

and reputational functions aimed mainly at making individuals' reliability transparent to one another. To the state, such local formations were opaque.

With the rise of the absolute state, the primary focus became making society transparent (or "legible") from above. Things like the systematic adoption of family surnames that persisted from one generation to the next (and the twentieth-century follow-up of Social Security Numbers and other citizen ID numbers), the systematic mapping of urban addresses for postal or 911 service, etc., were all for the purpose of making society legible to the state. Like us, the state wants to keep track of where its stuff is—and guess what we are?

Before this transformation, for example, surnames existed mainly for the convenience of people in local communities, so they could tell each other apart. Surnames were adopted on an ad hoc basis for clarification, when there was some danger of confusion, and rarely continued from one generation to the next. If there were multiple Johns in a village, they might be distinguished at any particular time by trade ("John the Miller"), location ("John on the Hill"), patronymic ("John Richard's Son"), etc. By contrast, everywhere there have been family surnames with cross-generational continuity, they have been imposed by centralized states as a way of cataloguing and tracking the population—making it legible to the state, in Scott's terminology.[26]

During the ascendancy of the modern state, the horizontal institutions of the free towns were at best barely tolerated— and usually not even that. Kropotkin wrote:

> For the next three centuries the States, both on the Continent and in these islands, systematically weeded out all institutions in which the mutual-aid tendency had formerly found its expression. The village communities were bereft of their folkmotes, their courts and independent administration; their lands were

---

[26]Ibid., pp. 64-73.

> confiscated. The guilds were spoliated of their possessions and liberties, and placed under the control, the fancy, and the bribery of the State's official.... It was taught in the Universities and from the pulpit that the institutions in which men formerly used to embody their needs of mutual support could not be tolerated in a properly organized State; that the State alone could represent the bonds of union between its subjects; that federalism and "particularism" were the enemies of progress, and the State was the only proper initiator of further development. By the end of the last century, the kings on the Continent, the Parliament in these isles, and the revolutionary Convention in France, although they were at war with each other, agreed in asserting that no separate unions between citizens must exist within the State.... "No state within the State!" The State alone...must take care of matters of general interest, while the subjects must represent loose aggregations of individuals, connected by no particular bonds, bound to appeal to the Government each time that they feel a common need....
>
> The absorption of all social functions by the State necessarily favoured the development of an unbridled, narrow-minded individualism. In proportion as the obligations towards the state grew in numbers the citizens were evidently relieved from their obligations towards each other.[27]

Likewise, the preemption and absorption—or suppression—of all regulatory functions by the state favored the development of a mindset by which providers of goods and services were relieved of their obligations to provide reliable certifications of the quality of their wares to consumers, and consumers were relieved of their obligations to scrutinize their quality and the reputations of the vendors. It was'the state's job to

---

[27] Pyotr Kropotkin, *Mutual Aid: A Factor of Evolution* (New York: Doubleday, Page & Company, 1909), pp. 226-227.

take care of that business for us, and we needn't bother our heads about it.

To accomplish a shift back to horizontal transparency, it will be necessary to overcome a powerful residual cultural habit, among the general public, of thinking of such things through the mind's eye of the state: i.e., if "we" didn't have some way of verifying compliance with this regulation or that, some business somewhere might be able to get away with something or other. We must overcome six hundred years or so of almost inbred habits of thought, in which the state is the all-seeing guardian of society protecting us from the possibility that someone, somewhere might do something wrong if "the authorities" don't prevent it.

In place of this habit of thought, we must think instead of *ourselves* creating mechanisms on a networked basis, to make us as transparent as possible to *each other* as providers of goods and services, to prevent businesses from getting away with poor behavior by informing *each other*, to prevent *each other* from selling defective merchandise, to protect *ourselves* from fraud, etc. The state has attempted to co-opt the rhetoric of horizontality (e.g., "We are the government."). But in fact, the creation of such mechanisms—far from making us *transparent* to the regulatory state—may well require active measures to render us *opaque* to the state (e.g., encryption, darknets, etc.) for protection *against* attempts to suppress such local economic self-organization against the interests of corporate actors.

We need to lose the centuries-long habit of thinking of "society" as a hub-and-spoke mechanism and viewing the world vicariously from the imagined perspective of the hub, and instead think of it as a horizontal network and visualize things from the perspective of the individual nodes which we occupy. We need to lose the habit of thought by which transparency from above even became perceived as an issue in the first place. Because the people who are seeing things "from above," in reality, do not represent us or have anything in common with us.

Such a shift in perspective will require, in particular, overcoming the hostility of conventional liberals who are in the habit of reacting viscerally and negatively, and on principle, to anything not being done by "qualified professionals" or "the proper authorities."

Arguably conventional liberals, with their thought system originating as it did as the ideology of the managers and engineers who ran the corporations, government agencies, and other giant organizations of the late-nineteenth and early twentieth centuries, have played the same role for the corporate-state nexus that the *politiques* did for the absolute states of the early modern period.

On his old MSNBC program, Keith Olbermann routinely mocked exhortations to charity and self-help, reaching for shitkicking imagery of the nineteenth-century barn-raiser for want of any other comparison sufficient to get across just how backward and ridiculous that kind of thing really was. In Olbermann's world, of course, such ideas come only from conservatives. The only ideological choice is between plain, vanilla-flavored managerialist liberalism and the Right. In Olbermann's world, the decentralist Left of Ivan Illich, Paul Goodman, and Colin Ward—"the 'recessive Left' of anarchists, utopians and visionaries, which tends only to manifest itself when dominant genes like Lenin or Harold Wilson are off doing something else," as one of the editors of *Radical Technology* put it—doesn't even exist.

Helping your neighbor out directly, or participating in a local self-organized friendly society or mutual, is all right in its own way, of course—if nothing else is available. But it carries the inescapable taint, not only of the quaint, but of the provincial and the picayune—very much like the stigmatization of homemade bread and home-grown veggies in corporate advertising in the early twentieth century, come to think of it. People who help each other out, or organize voluntarily to pool risks and costs, are to be praised—with just the slightest hint of condescension—for heroically doing the best they can in an era of relentlessly downscaled social services. But that people are forced to resort to such expedients, rather than meeting all their social safety net needs through one-stop shopping at the Ministry of Central Services office in a giant monumental building with a statue of winged victory in the lobby, à la *Brazil*, is a damning indictment of any civilized society. The progressive society is one of comfortable and well-fed citizens, competently managed by properly credentialed authorities, contentedly milling about like ants in the shadows of miles-high buildings that look like they were designed by Albert Speer. And that kind of H. G. Wells utopia simply has no room for atavisms like the barn-raiser or the sick benefit society.

Not only does Ostrom challenge the authoritarian assumptions of the received view, but the focus of her work is almost entirely on the factors that foster horizontal legibility in forming trust networks.

> ...refocus the analysis from an assumption that individuals are hopelessly trapped in a situation from which they cannot extract themselves without an external authority deciding what should be done and imposing that decision on participants. Asking what "the" government should do assumes that external actors will always come up with wise decisions and implement them effectively and fairly. The perspective of this chapter leads the analyst to inquire how individuals facing commons problems can gain trust that others are trustworthy and that a cooperator will not be a sucker who contributes while others continue to free ride.[28]

> We should be asking how different institutions support or undermine norms of reciprocity instead of simply presuming that central authority is necessary

---

[28] Ostrom, "Building Trust to Solve Commons Dilemmas," pp. 12-13.

to enforce rules related to cooperation on participants....[29]

She lists a number of factors that facilitate the creation of an assurance commons:

> When the structure of a situation includes repeated interactions, the level of cooperation achieved is likely to increase in those contexts in which the following attributes occur:
>
> 4. Information about past actions is made available;
> 5. Repeated interactions occur with the same set of participants;
> 6. Participants can signal one another by sending pre-structured information;
> 7. Prescriptions are adopted and enforced that when followed do lead to higher outcomes;
> 8. Participants are able to engage in full communication (via writing or "chat room" without knowing the identity of the others involved);
> 9. Participants are able to engage in full communication with known others (via face-to-face discussions or other mechanisms). In addition to communication, participants can sanction (or reward) each other for the past actions they have taken; and
> 10. Participants can design their own rules related to levels of cooperation and sanctions that are to be assigned to those who do not follow agreed-upon rules.[30]

Communication is central to Ostrom's model for formulating viable governance systems. The "pure theory" behind the Prisoner's Dilemma game, she writes,

---

[29] Ibid., p. 25.
[30] Ibid., p. 22.

is about individuals who do not know one another, do not share a common history, and cannot communicate with one another. In this model, game theory predicts that individuals jointly using a commons will overharvest, leading to Hardin's (1968) "Tragedy of the Commons."

...When a set of anonymous subjects makes decisions without communication about appropriation from a one-shot or finitely repeated, common pool resource in a laboratory setting based on Gordon's (1954) bioeconomic theory, they behave broadly as game theory predicts.... They overharvest....

This is, however, not the end of the story. Making one simple change in the design of a laboratory experiment, allowing participants to engage in face-to-face communication (cheap talk), enables them to reduce overharvesting substantially.... When given a chance to communicate, most subjects first try to figure out what is the best joint strategy. Subjects, who are most successful, use communication to help build a group identity and commitment to follow their agreed-upon strategy.... Behavior changes dramatically and subjects greatly increase their joint payoffs....

...Further, when given an opportunity to devise their own sanctioning rules, those who adopt their own rules tend to follow these rules closely, achieve higher joint returns, and the use of punishment drops to almost zero (Ostrom et al. 1992). Parallel to laboratory findings, field researchers have recorded a large number of empirical settings where those directly involved in a commons have themselves devised, adopted, and monitored rules over time that have led to robust common pool resource institutions....[31]

---

[31] Elinor Ostrom, "Building Trust to Solve Commons Dilemmas: Taking Small Steps to Test an Evolving Theory of Collective Action," Workshop in Political Theory and Policy Analysis, Indiana University. Center for the Study of Institutional Diversity (Arizona State University,

It's interesting that not only do pathological outcomes in the Prisoner's Dilemma game depend on preventing horizontal communication, but the Milgram Experiment's results depended on totally isolating each subject in the face of authority—essentially the strategy of "individualization" that Foucault described in *Discipline and Punish*. Pro-social, cooperative behavior depends on people being in ongoing situations with horizontal communication channels, in which they know they're going to be dealing with each other in the future, and have an incentive not to shit where they eat.

Elsewhere, shared norms figure prominently in Ostrom's list of the attributes of community that are relevant for sustainable local systems of rules for governing common resources:

> the values of behavior generally accepted in the community; the level of common understanding that potential participants share...about the structure of particular types of action arenas; the extent of homogeneity in the preferences of those living in a community; the size and composition of the relevant community; and the extent of inequality of basic assets among those affected.[32]

Shared local cultural norms and cognitive templates for interpreting others' behavior are important for a sustainable system of rules.[33] When participants share cultural norms against defection, they are likely to behave more cooperatively than game theory based on purely utility-maximizing considerations would predict.[34]

Of course, individuals start out with more innate inclination toward cooperation than game theory would predict.

2008), pp. 2-3.

[32]Ostrom, *Understanding Institutional Diversity* (Princeton and Oxford: Princeton University Press, 2005), pp. 26-27.

[33]Ibid., pp. 106-108.

[34]Ibid., p. 122.

Ostrom echoes Kropotkin's cooperative take on evolutionary psychology in this regard:

> Human evolution occurred mostly during the long Pleistocene era that lasted for about 3 million years to about 10,000 years ago. During this era, humans roamed the earth in small bands of hunter-gatherers who were dependent on each other for mutual protection, sharing food, and providing for the young. Survival was dependent not only on aggressively seeking individual returns but also on solving many day-to-day collective action problems. Those of our ancestors who solved these problems most effectively and learned how to recognize who was deceitful and who was a trustworthy reciprocator had a selective advantage over those who did not.... Humans have acquired well-honed skills at facial recognition and strong abilities to detect cheating. Research provides evidence that humans keep rough internal accounts—both in regard to goodwill...and threats....[35]

On top of this, behavior also evolves on a Lamarckian pattern, with successful strategies quickly catching on and being propagated culturally.[36]

Individuals are also more likely to behave cooperatively, and to formulate a sustainable set of governance rules, if they are engaged in an ongoing relationship in which present defection has future consequences and confidence increases from continued interaction, rather than in a one-off exchange with people they'll never see again. The outcomes of Prisoner's Dilemma games vary a great deal, depending on "whether the participants are engaged in a one-time encounter or over an indefinitely long sequence of plays."[37]

---

[35]Ibid., p. 125.
[36]Ibid., pp. 126-127.
[37]Ibid, p. 53.

The issue isn't simply whether states are *necessary* for creating cooperative governance systems. The model of corporate capitalism promoted by modern states, arguably, fosters levels of centralization, atomization, and anonymity that directly undermine the conditions required for stable local governance rule systems, and are instead conducive to individual adoption of rational egoist strategies at the expense of more cooperative ones.

As William Gillis put it, "States create game theoretic environments around their peripheries that suppress cooperation and reward antisocial strategies."[38]

The social capital embodied in self-organized governance systems takes generations of lived experience to build up, and can be quickly dissipated when state policies are destructive to it.

> The shared cognitive aspects of social capital help to account for two of its unusual characteristics that differ from those of physical capital. First, social capital does not wear out the more it is used. It may, in fact, improve with use so long as participants continue to keep prior commitments. Using social capital for an initial purpose creates mutual understanding and ways of relating that can frequently be used to accomplish entirely different joint activities at much lower start-up costs. It is not that learning curves for new activities disappear entirely. Rather, one of the steepest sections of a learning curve—learning to make commitments and to trust one another in a joint undertaking—has already been surmounted. A group that has learned to work effectively together in one task can take on other similar tasks at a cost in time and effort that is far less than bringing an entirely new group together who must learn everything from scratch. The fungibility of social capital is, of course,

---

[38] William Gillis, "The Retreat of the Immediate," *Center for a Stateless Society*, November 17, 2013. http://c4ss.org/content/22627

limited to broadly similar activities. No tool is useful for all tasks. Social capital that is well adapted to one broad set of joint activities may not be easily molded to activities that require vastly different patterns of expectation, authority, and distribution of rewards and costs than those used in the initial activities.

Second, if unused, social capital deteriorates at a relatively rapid rate. Individuals who do not exercise their own skills can lose human capital relatively rapidly. When several individuals must all remember the same routine in the same manner, however, the probability that at least one of them forgets some aspect increases rapidly over time. Further, as time goes on, some individuals leave and others enter any social group. If newcomers are not introduced to an established pattern of interaction as they enter (through job training, initiation, or any of the myriad of other ways that social capital is passed from one generation to the next), social capital can dissipate through nonuse. Then no one is quite sure how a particular joint activity used to be done. Either the group has to pay some of the start-up costs all over again or forgo the joint advantages that they had achieved at an earlier time.[39]

✽ Authority, Legibility, and Authoritarian High Modernism: Paging James Scott

According to Ostrom, most of the literature is "silent" on questions involving the factors that influence the adoption of common pool resource governance rules by appropriators, "since the presumption is made in this literature that making policies is what government officials, rather than those who are directly affected by problems, do."[40]

Unfortunately—from the perspective of government of-

---

[39] Ostrom, "Neither Market Nor State," p. 21.
[40] Ostrom, *Understanding Institutional Diversity*, p. 220.

ficials, anyway—the kinds of policies made by government officials rather than those directly affected by problems almost always result in stupidity, irrationality, and suboptimality. In fact this is true of all situations—including decisions by corporate management—in which authority-based rules override the judgment of those in direct contact with a situation.

Ostrom cites a wide range of studies showing that "national government agencies have been notably unsuccessful in their efforts to design effective and uniform sets of rules to regulate important common pool resources across a broad domain," including government policies of nationalizing forests, fisheries, etc., previously governed by local user-groups.[41] Many newly independent developing countries nationalized land and water resources in the period from the 1950s through the 1970s, with disappointing results.

> The institutional arrangements that local resource users had devised to limit entry and use lost their legal standing. The national governments that assumed these new and difficult tasks lacked adequate funds and personnel to monitor resource use effectively. They frequently turned to private forestry firms to gain revenue from these resources. Governments in these countries wanted to convert common pool resources to a de jure government-property regime, but their actions frequently resulted in de facto open-access regimes.... The incentives of an open-access commons were accentuated since local users had specifically been told that they would not receive the long-term benefits of their own costly stewardship efforts.[42]

> As concern for the protection of natural resources mounted during the 1960s, any developing countries nationalized all land and water resources that had

---

[41] Ibid., p. 221.
[42] Ibid., pp. 221-222.

> not yet been recorded as private property. The institutional arrangements that local users had devised to limit entry and use lost their legal standing, but the national governments lacked monetary resources and personnel to monitor the use of these resources effectively. Thus, resources that had been under a de facto common-property regime enforced by local users were converted to a de jure government-property regime, but reverted to a de facto open-access regime. When resources that were previously controlled by local participants have been nationalized, state control has usually proved to be less effective and efficient than control by those directly affected, if not disastrous in its consequences.... The harmful effects of nationalizing forests that had earlier been governed by local user groups have been well documented for Thailand..., Nepal..., and India.... Similar results have occurred in regard to inshore fisheries taken over by state or national agencies from local control by the inshore fishermen themselves....[43]

Two things are worth noting here. First, authority relations create both knowledge and incentive problems that result from faulty internalization. The main effect of authority is to decouple decision-making power both from situational knowledge and from experiencing the consequences of the decision. This stands to reason, since power is by definition the ability to override the judgment of others, shift costs onto others, and appropriate benefits for oneself. Depriving commoners of the benefits of wise stewardship of a common pool resource destroys their incentive to effectively monitor and enforce use.

This leads us to the second note-worthy point: policies adopted by those in authority frequently reflect a zero-sum

---

[43] Elinor Ostrom and Charlotte Hess, "Private and Common Property Rights," Workshop in Political Theory and Policy Analysis, Indiana University W07-25 11/29/07, pp. 7-8.

relationship between their interests and those over whom they exercise authority, in which the practical effect of a policy—despite its framing and ideological legitimization in terms of "efficiency," "conservation," or some other sort of "general welfare" consideration—is to directly promote the interests of authorities and their allies at the expense of the governed. The reference to collusive relationships between regulatory authorities and private forestry firms in the block quote above is a classic example of this.

Ostrom goes on to cite findings that "large-scale government irrigation systems do not tend to perform at the same level as smaller-scale, farmer-managed systems," and "in terms of cropping intensity and agricultural yield, crudely constructed irrigation systems using mud, rock, timber, and sticks significantly outperform systems built with modern concrete and iron headworks operated by national agencies."[44]

The situational knowledge of participants is key to governing complex adaptive systems. And because the total number of possible components of a policy is too great for a decision-maker to consider all possible combinations of them, the most successful approach to decision-making is often to select from a number of possible combinations based on intuition and past performance—combined with the ability of those in contact with the situation to quickly tweak and adjust in the face of immediate feedback. Ostrom uses the example of aircraft design.

> For far too long, social scientists have viewed the physics of static, simple systems as the model of science we should try to emulate. Those who want to emulate the science of static, simple systems are grossly out-of-date when it comes to understanding contemporary science and particularly contemporary engineering. The engineers responsible for the design of airplanes and bridges—and now computers—have

---

[44]Ostrom, *Understanding Institutional Diversity*, p. 222.

long coped with complex dynamic systems. The Boeing 777, for example, has 150,000 distinct subsystems that are composed, in some instances, of highly complex components.

Design engineers of complex systems long ago gave up hope of even doing complete analyses of all combinations of subsystems under all combinations of external environmental conditions. Obviously, they invest heavily in trying out diverse design elements under a variety of conditions. Testing designs by building models, using wind tunnels and computer simulations, increases the likelihood that engineers can produce a viable combination of design elements that are robust under many conditions. They also invest in complex backup systems that enable these designed systems to achieve a high degree of robustness—meaning the capacity to maintain some desired system characteristics under changing circumstances. All such robust systems are, however, fragile to a variety of small perturbations.... Small, rare disturbances can cause a disastrous cascade of failure in any highly complex designed system.

Instead of assuming that designing rules that approach optimality, or even improve performance, is a relatively simple analytical task that can be undertaken by distant, objective analysts, we need to understand the policy design process as involving an effort to tinker with a large number of component parts.... Those who tinker with any tools—including rules—are trying to find combinations that work together more effectively than other combinations. Policy changes are experiments based on more or less informed expectations about potential outcomes.... Whenever individuals decide to add a rule, change a rule, or adopt someone else's proposed rule set, they are conducting a policy experiment. Further, the complexity of the ever-changing biophysical and socioeconomic world combined with the complexity of rule systems means that any proposed rule change faces a nontrivial probability of error.[45]

Ostrom then describes a viable approach to formulating governance rules for common pool resources, based on the engineering analogy:

> Officials and/or the appropriators themselves may try to improve performance by changing one or more rules in an adaptive process. Participants adapt the rules, norms, and strategies of their parents and elders as well as those who are viewed as highly successful in a particular culture. They learn about neighboring systems that work better than theirs and try to discern which rules are helping their neighbors to do better. Human agents try to use reason and persuasion in their efforts to devise better rules, but the process of choice from the vast array of rules they might use always involves experimentation. Self-organized resource governance systems use many types of decision rules to make collective choices ranging from deferring to the judgment of one person or elders to using majority voting to relying on unanimity.[46]

And she lists variables that increase the likelihood of appropriators successfully improving governance rules in the face of experience:

Attributes of the Resource:

R1. Feasible improvement: Resource conditions are not at a point of deterioration such that it is useless to organize or so underutilized that little advantage results from organizing.

R2. Indicators: Reliable and valid indicators of the condition of the resource system are frequently available at a relatively low cost.

---

[45]Ibid., pp. 242-243.
[46]Ibid, p. 244.

R3. Predictability: The flow of resource units is relatively predictable.

R4. Spatial extent: The resource system is sufficiently small, given the transportation and communication technology in use, that appropriators can develop accurate knowledge of external boundaries and internal micro-environments.

Attributes of the Appropriators:

A1. Salience: Appropriators depend on the resource system for a major portion of their livelihood or the achievement of important social or religious values.

A2. Common understanding: Appropriators have a shared image of how the resource system operates (attributes R1, 2, 3, and 4 above) and how their actions affect each other and the resource system.

A3. Low discount rate: Appropriators use a sufficiently low discount rate in relation to future benefits to be achieved from the resource.

A4. Trust and reciprocity: Appropriators trust one another to keep promises and relate to one another with reciprocity.

A5. Autonomy: Appropriators are able to determine access and harvesting rules without external authorities countermanding them.

A6. Prior organizational experience and leadership: Appropriators have learned at least minimal skills of organization and leadership through participation in other local associations or learning about ways that neighboring groups have organized.[47]

---

[47]Ibid., pp. 244-245.

Of course these are all attributes that are facilitated by Ostrom's third design principle for common pool resource governance from *Governing the Commons*: "collective-choice arrangements."

> The third design principle is that most of the individuals affected by a resource regime are authorized to participate in making and modifying their rules. Resource regimes that use this principle are both better able to tailor rules to local circumstances and to devise rules that are considered fair by participants. As environments change over time, being able to craft local rules is particularly important as officials located far away do not know of the change. When a local elite is empowered at the collective-choice level, policies that primarily benefit them can be expected...
>
> In a study of forty-eight irrigation systems in India, Bardhan (2000) finds that the quality of maintenance of irrigation canals is significantly lower on those systems where farmers perceive the rules to have been made by a local elite. On the other hand, those farmers (of the 480 interviewed) who responded that the rules for their system have been crafted by most of the farmers, as contrasted to the elite or the government, have a more positive attitude about the water allocation rules and the rule compliance of other farmers. Further, in all of the villages where a government agency decides how water is to be allocated and distributed, frequent rule violations are reported, and farmers tend to contribute less to the local village fund. Consistent with this is the finding by Ray and Williams (1999) that the dead weight loss from upstream farmers stealing water on government-owned irrigation systems in Maharashtra, India, approaches one-fourth of the revenues that could be earned in an efficient water allocation and pricing regime.
>
> Knox and Meinzen-Dick (2001, 22) note that property rights "are significantly more likely to address

the interests and needs of local people when they are not imposed from the outside but rather are based on existing rights and reflect local values and norms." As they point out, these rules take time and effort to develop, try out, modify, and then experiment with again. Users who have been engaged in this process for some time understand the rules that they have crafted, agree on why they are using one rule rather than another, and tend to follow their own rules to a greater extent than those that are imposed on them. Sekher (2000) conducted a study of villages in Orissa, India, that varied in regard to the extent of participation of local villagers in making rules related to nearby forests that they used. He found that the "wider the representation of the community in the organization, the better are its chances of securing local cooperation and rule confirmation for managing and preserving the resource"....

In a comparative study of farmer-designed and -governed irrigation systems (FMIS), as contrasted to those designed and operated by engineers without involvement of the farmers in making rules to govern these systems, Shukla (2002, 83), a water engineer himself, is relatively critical of the "unrealistic planning and design, incomplete development, non-systematic and inadequate maintenance program, deficit operation, and lack of participation of the users that characterized many of these systems in Nepal. Drawing on the earlier research of Pant and Lohani (1983), Yoder (1994), Lam (1998), and Pradhan (1989), Shukla identifies the following as the strengths of the farmer-designed systems: "(1) Their technical deficiencies are compensated by management inputs; (2) they are low cost and based on local resources; (3) effective irrigation organizations exist in most FMIS; (4) most FMIS have well-defined rules and roles for water allocation, distribution, resource mobilization, and conflict resolution; and (5) the leaders of these systems are accountable to the users....[48]

Conversely, they are undermined by state policies that promote (as we considered in the previous section) centralization, social atomization, and anonymity.

Ostrom argues that central government policy regimes are relevant mainly to the extent to which they facilitate or hinder the primary local efforts to formulate governance rules. The best central government approach is simply to provide information and a supportive atmosphere without active interference. She puts forth, as an ideal case, the U. S. Geological Survey:

> Let me use the example of the important role that the U. S. Geological Survey has played in the development of more effective local groundwater institutions in some parts of the United States. What is important to stress is that the Geological Survey does not construct engineering works or do anything other than obtain and disseminate accurate information about hydrologic and geologic structures within the United States. When a local set of water users wants to obtain better information about a local groundwater basin, they can contract with the Geological Survey to conduct an intensive study in their area. Water producers would pay a portion of the cost of such a survey. The Geological Survey would pay the other portion. The information contained in such a survey is then public information available to all interested parties. The Geological Survey employs a highly professional staff who rely on the most recent scientific techniques for determining the structure and condition of groundwater basins. Local water producers obtain the very best available information from an agency that is not trying to push any particular future project that the agency is interested in

---

[48]Ibid., pp. 263-265.

conducting.[49]

The interesting thing is that this function—providing an information commons—is about as close as any government function can come to the non-coercive "administration of things." In considering how the same function might be provided by institutions altogether outside the state framework, networked/crowdsourced models like amateur astronomy may be relevant.

In any case, the concrete knowledge advantages Ostrom lists for local governance by common pool resource users are things both Friedrich Hayek and James Scott would recognize:

> Local knowledge. Appropriators who have lived and appropriated from a resource system over a long period of time have developed relatively accurate mental models of how the biophysical system itself operates, since the very success of their appropriation efforts depends on such knowledge. They also know others living in the area well and what norms of behavior are considered appropriate.
> Inclusion of trustworthy participants. Appropriators can devise rules that increase the probability that others are trustworthy and will use reciprocity. This lowers the cost of relying entirely on formal sanctions and paying for extensive guarding.
> Reliance on disaggregated knowledge. Feedback about how the resource system responds to changes in actions of appropriators is provided in a disaggregated way. Fishers are quite aware, for example, if the size and species distribution of their catch is changing over time. Irrigators learn whether a particular rotation system allows most farmers to grow the crops they most prefer by examining the resulting productivity of specific fields.
> Better adapted rules. Given the above, appropriators are more likely to craft rules over time that

---
[49]Ibid., pp. 278-279.

are better adapted to each of the local common pool resources than any general system of rules.

Lower enforcement costs. Since local appropriators have to bear the cost of monitoring, they are apt to craft rules that make infractions highly obvious so that monitoring costs are lower. Further, by creating rules that are seen as legitimate, rule conformance will tend to be higher.

Parallel autonomous systems. The probability of failure throughout a large region is greatly reduced by the establishment of parallel systems of rule making, interpretation, and enforcement.[50]

Aside from cognitive issues, one reason systems imposed from outside by central authorities are so failure-prone is they're perceived as illegitimate. As Ostrom notes:

If individuals voluntarily participate in a situation, they must share some general sense that most of the rules governing the situation are appropriate. Otherwise, the cost of enforcement within voluntary activities becomes high enough that it is difficult, if not impossible, to maintain predictability in an ongoing voluntary activity.[51]

People are instinctively alienated by rules-systems in which they feel powerless, and question the legitimacy of rules imposed by an authority over whom they have no control.

Psychological research provides evidence that positive intrinsic motivation is increased when individuals feel that their own self-determination or self-esteem is enhanced.... This leads to the possibility that intrinsic motivation can be "crowded out" in situations where individuals do not perceive themselves to have sufficient self-control over the actions they take.[52]

---

[50]Ibid., pp. 281-282.
[51]Ibid., p. 21.
[52]Ibid., p. 112.

Ostrom goes on to cite a number of experiments providing "strong evidence for the crowding out of reciprocity by the imposition of external sanctions," quoting the findings of one that:

> 1. External interventions *crowd out* intrinsic motivation if the individuals affected perceive them to be *controlling*. In that case, both self-determination and self-esteem suffer, and the individuals react by reducing their intrinsic motivation in the activity controlled.
>
> 2. External interventions *crowd in* intrinsic motivation if the individuals concerned perceive it as *supportive*. In that case, self-esteem is fostered, and the individuals feel that they are given more freedom to act, which enlarges self-determination.[53]

This is closely associated with the tendency of external imposed rules to "'crowd out' endogenous cooperative behavior." In one experiment, players of a prisoner's game on whom external incentives for cooperation were imposed were less cooperative after the incentives were withdrawn than were the players in a control group who played the regular game without incentives for cooperation and spontaneously evolved their own strategies.[54]

> A social norm, especially in a setting where there is communication between parties, can work as well or nearly as well at generating cooperative behavior as an externally imposed set of rules and system of monitoring and sanctioning. Moreover, norms seem to have a certain staying power in encouraging a growth of the desire for cooperative behavior over time, while cooperation that is primarily there due to

---
[53]Ibid., pp. 112-113.
[54]Ibid., p. 130.

> externally imposed and enforced rules can disappear very quickly.[55]

❋ *Third World Development, Infrastructure Policy, and the Missing Class Dimension*

It's hard to know how much of the argument of *Institutional Incentives and Sustainable Development*[56] to assign to Ostrom, given it's coauthored with two other people. But considering her name appears first on the byline, and it's a direct development of her approach in *Governing the Commons*, I think it's safe to treat it as speaking largely with her voice.

Ostrom is great, in her analysis of Third World development policy (and more specifically of infrastructure projects), at treating the way multilateral development agencies and national governments tend to adopt James Scott's "authoritarian high modernist" approach, and ignore local, distributed knowledge. Western development experts, for the most part, saw local social infrastructures in Third World countries as atavistic, and conflated them with tribalism, corruption, nepotism, inequality, and authoritarianism.

> When massive amounts of physical capital were introduced by donor countries into the countries of Africa, Asia, and Latin America, that had been through long periods of colonization, little attention was paid to the massive destruction of social capital that had occurred under colonization. Tribal communities in India, for example, had organized themselves for centuries to derive their food, fodder, tools, and building materials in a sustainable manner from forest lands that they governed and managed as common property.

[55] Ibid., p. 130.

[56] Elinor Ostrom, Larry Schroeder, and Susan Wynne. *Institutional Incentives and Sustainable Development: Infrastructure Policies in Perspective* (Boulder, San Francisco, Oxford: Westview Press, 1993).

The British government did not recognize community ownership and, in fact, passed legislation during the 1860s to create a forestry department and to exert monopoly power over ever greater territories.... By the time of independence, the government of India exerted full control over more than 40 percent of the total forested area of India. Similar stripping away of the legitimacy of local institutions occurred throughout Africa, Asia, and Latin America.

To the extent that attention was paid to the earlier social capital of the people living in these areas, it was assumed that the former patterns of relationships were "primitive" and not worth saving. Many colonial and postcolonial officials felt that prior institutions had to be destroyed before development could really occur. The diversity of different ways of life was seen as an obstacle to be replaced by modern, centralized institutions that could energize economic activity from the capital.[57]

Instead, ...donors from the Eastern and Western blocs proceeded, or as was the case with the former imperial powers, continued to support the destruction of indigenous institutional infrastructure in LDCs and the replacement of this social infrastructure with institutional arrangements that were familiar to the donors. They found willing accomplices in the new national leaders of LDCs who hoped to suppress any organizational activity outside their control in order to prevent the emergence of viable political competitors....

The one institutional feature of LDCs that all donors found potentially useful as a foundation for development was the highly centralized national governments, which were primarily the legacy of the colonial period. National governments were viewed as the instruments through which change and economic

---

[57] Ostrom, "Neither Market nor State," pp. 21-22.

development would be accomplished. They were considered so crucial, in fact, that development efforts were specially fashioned, for most of the past half century, to enhance the capacity and authority of these national governments at the expense of subnational public agencies and private sector institutions. In the most recent "structural adjustment" phase, this tendency to reinforce national institutions has been accelerated. Major policy reforms have been devised by small teams composed almost exclusively of representatives from ministries of finance and central banks working with consultants engaged by the World Bank and IMF.[58]

Ostrom produces considerable evidence from case studies to show that infrastructure projects undertaken in such an atmosphere of disregard for local knowledge tend to have less than optimal results—a finding that should come as no surprise to readers of her larger body of work.

Ostrom is quite right in assuming that "[i]ndividuals, who are expected to invest resources...in sustaining rural infrastructure, must perceive that the benefits they obtain...exceed the costs of the resources they devote to this effort."[59] And she addresses problems of rent-seeking, in which projects are promoted by interests that get more out of them than they put in.

But she considers rent-seeking mainly at the micro-level, rather than treating rent-seeking as built into the macro-structure of the system and central to its goals. Even the one time she specifically mentions rent-seeking in the case of infrastructure projects that generate "disproportionate benefits" for "certain groups of potential users, such as large landowners,"[60] she treats it as just a deviation to be fixed by

---

[58]Ostrom, et al., *Institutional Incentives and Sustainable Development*, pp. 6-7.
[59]Ibid., p. 9.
[60]Ibid., p. 96.

technical jiggering with the incentive structure.

The glaring omission in all this, the elephant in the living room she fails to mention, is class conflict and the role of states in promoting the interests of the economic classes that control them.

Modern societies do indeed, as Ivan Illich pointed out in *Tools for Conviviality*, adopt particular forms of technology and organization beyond the point of counterproductivity or diminishing returns. But they only do so because the coercive state, by creating externalities, shifts the costs and burdens of adoption to a different class of people from those who receive the benefits. Since the full cost of adoption of a technology does not appear on the ledger of its adopters, their decision of how far to adopt it is not based on a full social accounting of the costs and benefits. The market price of adopting the technology, which informs the adopter of the full costs and benefits and enables her to make a rational decision, is disrupted.

Ostrom adopts the World Bank's metric for "sustainability" of infrastructure projects: "whether or not the rate of return was equal to, or greater than, the current opportunity cost of the capital invested in each project." The project, in other words, pays in what its output adds to the GDP.[61] This ignores the central question—as Lenin phrased it—of "Kto-kogo?" Who pays for the inputs, and who benefits from the outputs?

The issue is not simply that centralized development agencies, because of knowledge problems resulting from their centralism, make mistakes in pursuing some disinterested goal of "development." The issue is also that the kind of development they're pursuing reflects a particular coalition of interests and their perception of the world. These interests, and their perceptions, are those commonly associated with the terms "export-oriented development" and "neoliberalism."

---

[61]Ibid., pp. 14-16.

The larger functional role of the World Bank, IMF and Western national foreign aid projects since WWII was well summed up by Kwame Nkrumah in *Neo-Colonialism*: foreign aid, under neo-colonialism, is what under colonialism used to be called simply "foreign capital investment."

In the specific case of Third World rural infrastructure, the dominant model of rural development centers on large-scale, export-oriented cash crop production on large tracts of land—often situated on land stolen from evicted peasants with the help of colonial or post-colonial governments—held by native landed oligarchs.

So in a sense the attention Ostrom devotes to free-riders in the design of local infrastructure systems is misleading; free-riding, or rent-seeking, is the primary purpose of most big large-scale rural infrastructure projects like irrigation systems. Their purpose is to provide subsidized inputs to a model of agricultural production heavily dependent on such subsidized inputs, on stolen land held by local landed elites.

She discusses "equity" in financing infrastructure in the context of two rival approaches: 1) beneficiaries pay in proportion to the marginal cost of supplying the portion of output they consume; and 2) beneficiaries pay in proportion to their ability to pay.[62] But from the perspective of the powerful economic interests served by big infrastructure projects, either approach would violate the whole purpose: to externalize their operating costs on someone else.

Stepping back still further, capitalism by definition depends on the inequitable shifting of benefits and costs to different parties. Capitalism has been defined by more than one radical critic as the socialization of cost and risk and the privatization of profit.

Sadly, Ostrom (and/or one or both of her coauthors) dismiss such considerations as "conspiracy theories." "At times, the criticism presumes conspiratorial motivation, with

---

[62]Ibid., pp. 113-115.

donor agencies characterized as fronts for a new form of conscious imperialism."[63]

> But anyone who has observed infrastructure projects in operation is struck by the number of extremely hard-working, highly motivated individuals in both the host governments and the donor agencies whose principal goal is clearly to improve the well-being of those living in countries receiving foreign aid. Yet, realistic assessments of the many projects designed by donor and host government staff repeatedly reveal unintended negative outcomes. Evaluations show that the projects have increased or reinforced the overcentralization of recipient countries' governments, were poorly designed (given local circumstances), and generated inappropriately large debt burdens for the recipient countries. How is it possible for highly motivated, hard-working people who sincerely want to improve conditions in these recipient countries to be repeatedly involved in the design and implementation of projects that do not accomplish this goal?[64]

Ostrom points to several quite plausible structural factors, some of which would cause readers of James Scott's work to smile and nod. The U. S. Congressional mandate to spend a certain portion of foreign aid on purchases of American-made equipment create, to some extent, a structural bias in favor of projects involving heavy equipment.[65] The fiscal incentives all government agencies face, of spending this year's entire budget by the end of the year in order to secure the same levels of funding next year, creates a bias toward a smaller number of expensive projects that can be processed quickly by a limited staff.[66] And the need for what Scott would call "legibility" results, given political pressure to reduce

---

[63] Ibid., p. 156.
[64] Ibid., pp. 156-157.
[65] Ibid., p. 157.
[66] Ibid., p. 157.

embarrassing levels of skimming off the top by local officials in recipient countries, in a focus on large-scale projects for the sake of reduced monitoring costs.[67]

The problem is that Ostrom posits all these entirely valid and plausible factors as an alternative to "conspiracy theories." One doesn't have to visualize World Bank policy wonks literally twirling their mustaches like Snidely Whiplash, or saying with Milton's Lucifer "Evil be thou my good," in order to see them as actively and enthusiastically serving the interests of global corporate capital. Sincerely promoting some vision of the "general welfare," as they see it, is perfectly compatible with having internalized an ideology in which the present system is natural and inevitable, and the only feasible alternative for organizing human society.

And the neoliberal institutions that coordinate foreign aid are guided by an ideology in which the most efficient model of development—indeed, the only one conceivable by right-thinking people—is large-scale capital-intensive industry and large-scale, mechanized, chemical-intensive, export-oriented agriculture.

※ *We're All Humans Here*

In all her work, Ostrom never lost sight of one central truth: collective institutions, whether they're called governments, corporations, or commons, are all framed from the same crooked human timber. Advocates of government activity and critics/skeptics of anarchism, all too often, simply assume a level of omniscience on the part of the state that's denied to the state, or handwave away the actual problem of detecting and punishing infractions. For example, those who are skeptical about anarchism ask the supposedly telling question of how a stateless society would prevent something like the Deepwater Horizons oil spill—without stopping to

---

[67]Ibid., p. 159.

consider whether the EPA and its regulations in our actual statist society managed to prevent it.

Giving an official name to the collectivity does nothing to alter the fact that it's just a bunch of human beings doing stuff together. And they don't cease to be fallible, limited in perspective, and influenced by self-interest just because they have official titles or claim to be working in the name of the public or the shareholders.

> Obviously, I do not know if these appropriators reached optimal solutions to their problems. I strongly doubt it. They solved their problems the same way that most individuals solve difficult and complex problems: as well as they were able, given the problems involved, the information they had, the tools they had to work with, the costs of various known options, and the resources at hand.[68]

> Resource users are explicitly thought of [in mainstream conservation policy literature] as rational agents who plunder local resources so as to maximize their own short-term benefits. Government officials are implicitly depicted, on the other hand, as seeking the more general public interest, having the relevant information at hand, and the capability of designing optimal policies....
>
> One should not, however, presume that all government officials are "saints" while assuming that all resource users are "sinners." Nor should we presume that officials have all the relevant knowledge to manage complex dynamic systems while local appropriators are ignorant. The knowledge base of government officials may not, in reality, be better than that of local appropriators who have used a particular resource for years and know its characteristics in considerable detail. Even when the knowledge base is similar, no guarantee exists that government officials

---

[68] Ostrom, *Governing the Commons*, p. 56.

(or the researchers who advise them) will use available information to make efficient and/or sustainable decisions.[69]

BIBLIOGRAPHY

Kevin Carson. "Legibility & Control: Themes in the Work of James C. Scott." *Center for a Stateless Society Paper* No. 12 (Winter/Spring 2011). http://c4ss.org/wp-content/uploads/2011/05/James-Scott.pdf

William Gillis. "The Retreat of the Immediate." *Center for a Stateless Society*, November 17, 2013. http://c4ss.org/content/22627

Sanford J. Grossman and Oliver D. Hart. "The Costs and Benefits of Ownership: A Theory of Vertical and Lateral Integration." *Journal of Political Economy* 94:4 (1986).

Edward S. Greenberg. "Producer Cooperatives and Democratic Theory." In Jackall and Levin, eds., *Worker Cooperatives in America* (University of California Press, 1986).

Bonnie J. McCay and James M. Acheson, eds. *The Question of the Commons: The Culture and Ecology of Communal Resources* (GF49 .Q47 1987).

Elinor Ostrom. "Building Trust to Solve Commons Dilemmas: Taking Small Steps to Test an Evolving Theory of Collective Action." Workshop in Political Theory and Policy Analysis, Indiana University. Center for the Study of Institutional Diversity (Arizona State University, 2008).

Ostrom. *Governing the Commons: The Evolution of Institutions for Collective Action* (Cambridge University Press, 1990).

---

[69]Ostrom, *Understanding Institutional Diversity*, p. 238.

Ostrom. "Neither Market Nor State: Governance of Common Pool Resources in the Twenty-first Century." Lecture presented June 2, 1994 at the International Food Policy Research Institute, Washington, D. C.

Ostrom. *Understanding Institutional Diversity* (Princeton and Oxford: Princeton University Press, 2005).

Ostrom and Charlotte Hess. "Private and Common Property Rights." Workshop in Political Theory and Policy Analysis, Indiana University (W07-25 11/29/07).

Ostrom, Larry Schroeder, and Susan Wynne. *Institutional Incentives and Sustainable Development: Infrastructure Policies in Perspective* (Boulder, San Francisco, Oxford: Westview Press, 1993).

CHAPTER
EIGHT

DAVID GRAEBER'S ANARCHIST THOUGHT: A SURVEY

KEVIN CARSON

❋ *Introduction: The Primacy of Everyday Life*

David Graeber chose, as the epigraph to his book *Fragments of an Anarchist Anthropology*, a quote from Pyotr Kropotkin's article on anarchism for the *Encyclopedia Britannica*. In it, Kropotkin stated that, in an anarchist society, harmony would be

> obtained, not by submission to law, or by obedience to any authority, but by free arrangements concluded between the various groups, territorial and professional, freely constituted for the sake of production and consumption, as also for the satisfaction of the infinite variety of needs and aspirations of a civilized being.[1]

The interesting thing about this is that it could serve as an accurate description of virtually any anarchist society, including

---

c4ss.org/content/27752

[1] David Graeber, *Fragments of an Anarchist Anthropology* (Chicago: Prickly Paradigm Press, 2004), p. 1.

the libertarian communist sort favored by Kropotkin, Goldman, or Malatesta, the kind of anarcho-syndicalism favored by most of the Wobblies and CNT, the anarcho-collectivism of Bakunin, the mutualism of Proudhon, or the market anarchism of Thomas Hodgskin and Benjamin Tucker. And it's appropriate that Graeber chose it as his epigraph, because his affection for "freely constituted groups" and the "free arrangements" concluded between them is bigger than any doctrinaire attempt to pigeonhole such groups and arrangements as business firms operating in the cash nexus or moneyless collectives.

Graeber, as we already saw to be the case with Elinor Ostrom, is characterized above all by a faith in human creativity and agency, and an unwillingness to let *a priori* theoretical formulations preempt either his perceptions of the particularity and "is-ness" of history, or to interfere with the ability of ordinary, face-to-face groupings of people on the spot to develop workable arrangements—whatever they may be—among themselves. Graeber is one of those anarchist (or anarchist-ish) thinkers who, despite possibly identifying with a particular hyphenated variant of anarchism, have an affection for the variety and particularity of self-organized, human-scale institutions that goes beyond ideological label. These people, likewise, see the relationships between individual human beings in ways that can't be reduced to simple abstractions like the cash nexus or doctrinaire socialism.[2]

> If we really want to understand the moral grounds of economic life and, by extension, human life, it seems to me that we must start...with the very small things: the everyday details of social existence, the way we treat our friends, enemies, and children—often

---

[2]I selected James Scott and Elinor Ostrom for earlier C4SS research papers based on this quality. I expect to continue with papers on Voltairine DeCleyre, Pyotr Kropotkin, and Colin Ward who, despite identifying as libertarian communists, cannot be reduced to any ideological pigeonhole based on that label.

> with gestures so tiny (passing the salt, bumming a cigarette) that we ordinarily never stop to think about them at all. Anthropology has shown us just how different and numerous are the ways in which humans have been known to organize themselves. But it also reveals some remarkable commonalities....[3]

Graeber's anarchism is, above all else, human-centered. It entails a high regard for human agency and reasonableness. Rather than fitting actual human beings into some idealized anarchist paradigm, he displays an openness to—and celebration of—whatever humans may actually do in exercising that agency and reasonableness. Anarchy isn't what people will do "after the Revolution," when some sort of "New Anarchist Man" has emerged who can be trusted with autonomy; it's what they do right now. "Anarchists are simply people who believe human beings are capable of behaving in a reasonable fashion without having to be forced to."[4]

At their very simplest, anarchist beliefs turn on two elementary assumptions. The first is that human beings are, under ordinary circumstances, about as reasonable and decent as they are allowed to be, and can organize themselves and their communities without needing to be told how. The second is that power corrupts. Most of all, anarchism is just a matter of having the courage to take the simple principles of common decency that we all live by and follow them through to their logical conclusions. Odd though this may seem, in most important ways you are probably already an anarchist—you just don't realize it.

Let's start by taking a few examples from everyday life.

- If there's a line to get on a crowded bus, do you wait

---

[3]Graeber, *Debt: The First 5,000 Years* (Brooklyn and London: Melville House, 2011), p. 89.

[4]Graeber, "Are You an Anarchist? The Answer May Surprise You" (Anarchist Library, 2000). http://theanarchistlibrary.org/library/david-gr aeber-are-you-an-anarchist-the-answer-may-surprise-you

your turn and refrain from elbowing your way past others even in the absence of police?

If you answered "yes," then you are used to acting like an anarchist! The most basic anarchist principle is self-organization: the assumption that human beings do not need to be threatened with prosecution in order to be able to come to reasonable understandings with each other, or to treat each other with dignity and respect....

To cut a long story short: anarchists believe that for the most part it is power itself, and the effects of power, that make people stupid and irresponsible.

- Are you a member of a club or sports team or any other voluntary organization where decisions are not imposed by one leader but made on the basis of general consent?

If you answered "yes," then you belong to an organization which works on anarchist principles! Another basic anarchist principle is voluntary association. This is simply a matter of applying democratic principles to ordinary life. The only difference is that anarchists believe it should be possible to have a society in which everything could be organized along these lines, all groups based on the free consent of their members, and therefore, that all top-down, military styles of organization like armies or bureaucracies or large corporations, based on chains of command, would no longer be necessary. Perhaps you don't believe that would be possible. Perhaps you do. But every time you reach an agreement by consensus, rather than threats, every time you make a voluntary arrangement with another person, come to an understanding, or reach a compromise by taking due consideration of the other person's particular situation or needs, you are being an anarchist—even if you don't realize it.

Anarchism is just the way people act when they are free to do as they choose, and when they deal with others who are equally free—and therefore aware of the responsibility to others that entails.[5]

Graeber's approach to the form of a hypothetical anarchist society is simple: take away all forms of domination, or of unilateral, unaccountable authority by some people over others, put people together, and see what they come up with.

As we shall see below, Graeber critiques totalizing and idealized visions of the state. Similarly, anarchy itself, rather than a totalizing system, is just a way people interact with one another, and that (as Colin Ward notes in *Anarchy in Action*) it's all around us right now.

> We could start with a kind of sociology of micro-utopias, the counterpart of a parallel typology of forms of alienation, alienated and nonalienated forms of action.... The moment we stop insisting on viewing all forms of action only by their function in reproducing larger, total, forms of inequality of power, we will also be able to see that anarchist social relations and non-alienated forms of action are all around us. And this is critical because it shows that anarchism is, already, and has always been, one of the main bases for human interaction. We self-organize and engage in mutual aid all the time. We always have.[6]

Graeber's definition of "Anarchy," accordingly, is quite simple. It's whatever people decide to do, whatever arrangements out of the countless ones possible they make among themselves, when they're not threatened with violence:

> ...a political movement that aims to bring about a genuinely free society—and that defines a "free society" as one where humans only enter those kinds of relations with one another that would not have to be enforced by the constant threat of violence.

---
[5]Ibid.
[6]Ibid., p. 76.

> History has shown that vast inequalities of wealth, institutions like slavery, debt peonage, or wage labor, can only exist if backed up by armies, prisons, and police. Even deeper structural inequalities like racism and sexism are ultimately based on the (more subtle and insidious) threat of force. Anarchists thus envision a world based on equality and solidarity, in which human beings would be free to associate with one another to pursue any endless variety of visions, projects, and conceptions of what they find valuable in life. When people ask me what sorts of organization could exist in an anarchist society, I always answer: any form of organization one can imagine, and probably many we presently can't, with only one proviso—they would be limited to ones that could exist without anyone having the ability, at any point, to call on armed men to show up and say "I don't care what you have to say about this; shut up and do what you're told."[7]

Graeber considers himself "a small-a anarchist," on the side of whatever particular social forms free, mutually consenting people work out for themselves when out from under the thumb of authority.

> I'm less interested in figuring out what sort of anarchist I am than in working in broad coalitions that operate in accord with anarchist principles: movements that are not trying to work through or become governments; movements uninterested in assuming the role of de facto government institutions like trade organizations or capitalist firms; groups that focus on making our relations with each other a model of the world we wish to create. In other words, people working toward truly free societies. After all, it's hard to figure out exactly what kind of anarchism makes

---

[7]Graeber, *The Democracy Project: A History, a Crisis, a Movement* (Spiegel & Grau, 2013), pp. 187-188.

> the most sense when so many questions can only be answered further down the road. Would there be a role for markets in a truly free society? How could we know? I myself am confident, based on history, that even if we did try to maintain a market economy in such a free society— that is, one in which there would be no state to enforce contracts, so that agreements came to be based only on trust—economic relations would rapidly morph into something libertarians would find completely unrecognizable, and would soon not resemble anything we are used to thinking of as a "market" at all. I certainly can't imagine anyone agreeing to work for wages if they have any other options. But who knows, maybe I'm wrong. I am less interested in working out what the detailed architecture of what a free society would be like than in creating the conditions that would enable us to find out.[8]
>
> Myself, I am less interested in deciding what sort of economic system we should have in a free society than in creating the means by which people can make such decisions for themselves.[9]

It's highly unlikely this would turn out to resemble any particular monolithic hyphenated model of anarchism, like anarcho-syndicalism, anarcho-communism, or any other schematized vision of society. It would be much more likely to include a blend of all sorts of things, most of which already probably exist in nascent form today all around us. In addition to gift and sharing economies, peer-production, etc., it might very well include significant elements of market exchange—although Graeber is highly skeptical that anything remotely resembling "anarcho-capitalism" could come about or be sustained entirely through voluntary agreement.

---

[8] Ibid., pp. 192-193.
[9] Graeber, "A Practical Utopians's Guide to the Coming Collapse," *The Baffler* 23 (2013). http://www.thebaffler.com/past/practical_utopian s_guide

Even what now seem like major screaming ideological divides are likely to sort themselves easily enough in practice. I used to frequent Internet newsgroups in the 1990s, which at the time were full of creatures that called themselves "anarcho-capitalists." ...Most spent a good deal of their time condemning left anarchists as proponents of violence. "How can you be for a free society and be against wage labor? If I want to hire someone to pick my tomatoes, how are you going to stop me except through force?" Logically then any attempt to abolish the wage system can only be enforced by some new version of the KGB. One hears such arguments frequently. What one never hears, significantly, is anyone saying "If I want to hire myself out to pick someone else's tomatoes, how are you going to stop me except through force?" Everyone seems to imagine that in a future stateless society, they will somehow end up members of the employing class. Nobody seems to think they'll be the tomato pickers. But where, exactly, do they imagine these tomato pickers are going to come from? Here one might employ a little thought experiment: let's call it the parable of the divided island. Two groups of idealists each claim half of an island. They agree to draw the border in such a way that there are roughly equal resources on each side. One group proceeds to create an economic system where certain members have property, others have none, and those who have none have no social guarantees: they will be left to starve to death unless they seek employment on any terms the wealthy are willing to offer. The other group creates a system where everyone is guaranteed at least the basic means of existence and welcomes all comers. What possible reason would those slated to be the night watchmen, nurses, and bauxite miners on the anarcho-capitalist side of the island have to stay there? The capitalists would be bereft of their labor force in a matter of weeks. As a result, they'd be forced to patrol their own grounds, empty their own bedpans, and operate their own heavy machinery—that is, unless they quickly began offering their workers such an extravagantly good deal that they might as well be living in a socialist utopia after all.

For this and any number of other reasons, I'm sure that in practice any attempt to create a market economy without armies, police, and prisons to back it up will end up looking nothing like capitalism very quickly. In fact I strongly suspect it will soon look very little like what we are used to thinking of as a market. Obviously I could be wrong. It's possible someone will attempt this, and the results will be very different than I imagined. In which case, fine, I'll be wrong. Mainly I'm interested in creating the conditions where we can find out.[10]

(It's worth bearing in mind that the "voluntary arrangement" between Robinson Crusoe and "Friday" was possible only because Crusoe was able to claim "ownership" of the entire island with the help of a gun.)

Graeber is fairly confident in the ability of average people to work out ways of getting along in the absence of authority. The cases in which the collapse of a state results in a Hobbesian "war of all against all," like Somalia, are actually a minority. The violence in Somalia resulted mainly from the fact that the state collapsed in the middle of a preexisting war between major warlords, who continued to fight after the state collapsed.[11]

> But in most cases, as I myself observed in parts of rural Madagascar, very little happens. Obviously, statistics are unavailable, since the absence of states generally also means the absence of anyone gathering

---

[10]Graeber, *The Democracy Project*, pp. 296-297.
[11]Ibid., p. 206.

statistics. However, I've talked to many anthropologists and others who've been in such places and their accounts are surprisingly similar. The police disappear, people stop paying taxes, otherwise they pretty much carry on as they had before. Certainly they do not break into a Hobbesian "war of all against all."

As a result, we almost never hear about such places at all....

So the real question we have to ask becomes: what is it about the experience of living under a state, that is, in a society where rules are enforced by the threat of prisons and police, and all the forms of inequality and alienation that makes possible, that makes it seem obvious to us that people, under such conditions, would behave in a way that it turns out they don't actually behave?

The anarchist answer is simple. If you treat people like children, they will tend to act like children. The only successful method anyone has ever devised to encourage others to act like adults is to treat them as if they already are. It's not infallible. Nothing is. But no other approach has any real chance of success. And the historical experience of what actually does happen in crisis situations demonstrates that even those who have not grown up in a culture of participatory democracy, if you take away their guns or ability to call their lawyers, can suddenly become extremely reasonable. This is all that anarchists are really proposing to do.[12]

So anarchism isn't just a grand theory that was invented by some big-league thinker, like Marx in the London Museum. It's what people actually do.

> The basic principles of anarchism—self-organization, voluntary association, mutual aid—referred to forms

---

[12]Ibid., pp. 206-207.

> of human behavior they [the so-called "founding figures" of nineteenth-century anarchist thought] assumed to have been around about as long as humanity.[13]

❋ I. Everyday Democracy

Graeber's respect for the capacity of ordinary people to achieve their goals through voluntary cooperation is reflected in his view of democracy, not as something the human race suffered in ignorance for millennia waiting for some smart guys in the Athenian *agora*, French Enlightenment, or Philadelphia State House to come up with, but something that people have instinctively done throughout history when they meet each other as equals.

He points to the "wave of indignant responses in conservative web pages" when Western academic intellectuals' claims that the Greeks, British, colonial Americans, or some other branch of "Western Civilization," are met by Amartya Sen making "the obvious point that democracy can just as easily be found in village councils in southern Africa, or India."[14]

> In this sense democracy is as old as history, as human intelligence itself. No one could possibly own it. I suppose...one could argue it emerged the moment hominids ceased merely trying to bully one another and developed the communication skills to work out a common problem collectively. But such speculation is idle; the point is that democratic assemblies can be attested in all times and places, from Balinese seka to Bolivian ayllu, employing an endless variety of formal procedures, and will always crop up wherever a large group of people sat down together to make a collective decision on the principle that all taking part should have an equal say.[15]

---

[13] Graeber, *Fragments of an Anarchist Anthropology*, p. 3.
[14] Graeber, *The Democracy Project*, p. 183.
[15] Ibid., p. 184.

In other words, he sees institutions for self-governance and decision-making in general much as Elinor Ostrom saw institutions for governing common pool resources: not as something created by "great men" or duly constituted authorities and institutions, but by ordinary people who sat down together and started talking.

So for Graeber, democracy is something that emerges "when one has a diverse collection of participants, drawn from very different traditions, with an urgent need to improvise some means to regulate their common affairs, free of a preexisting overarching authority."

And from such conditions it has frequently so emerged throughout human history, improvised by human beings in stations of life far more varied than the well-to-do Athenians who had endless time to kill in the *agora*, or the propertied elites who assembled in Philadelphia to represent the interests of Continental war bond speculators and land barons. Historical examples of actual democracy included, for example, the democracy of pirate ships:

> Pirates were generally mutineers, sailors often originally pressed into service against their will in port towns across the Atlantic, who had mutinied against tyrannical captains and "declared war against the whole world." They often became classic social bandits, wreaking vengeance against captains who abused their crews, and releasing or even rewarding those against whom they found no complaints. The makeup of crews was often extraordinarily heterogeneous. According to Marcus Rediker's book *Villains of All Nations*, "Black Sam Bellamy's crew of 1717 was a Mix'd Multitude of all Country's, including British, French, Dutch, Spanish, Swedish, Native American, African American, and two dozen Africans who had been liberated from a slave ship." In other words, we are dealing with a collection of people in which there was likely to be at least some firsthand knowledge of

a very wide range of directly democratic institutions, ranging from Swedish *things* (councils) to African village assemblies to Native American federal structures, suddenly finding themselves forced to improvise some mode of self-government in the complete absence of any state. It was the perfect intercultural space of experiment. There was likely to be no more conducive ground for the development of New Democratic institutions anywhere in the Atlantic world at the time.[16]

The frontier settlements of North America, whose inhabitants also had little in common with the classically educated delegates to the Philadelphia Convention, improvised democratic forms of self-governance much like the pirates.

...those early colonies were far more similar to pirate ships than we are given to imagine. Frontier communities might not have been as densely populated as pirate ships, or in as immediate need of constant cooperation, but they were spaces of intercultural improvisation, and, like the pirate ships, largely outside the purview of any states. It's only recently that historians have begun to document just how thoroughly entangled the societies of settlers and natives were in those early days, with settlers adopting Indian crops, clothes, medicines, customs, and styles of warfare. They engaged in trading, often living side by side, sometimes intermarrying, while others lived for years as captives in Indian communities before returning to their homes having learned native languages, habits, and mores. Most of all, historians have noted the endless fears among the leaders of colonial communities and military units that their subordinates were—in the same way that they had taken up the use of tomahawks, wampum, and canoes—beginning to absorb Indian attitudes of equality and individual liberty.

---

[16]Ibid., pp. 178-179.

In the 1690s, at the same time as the famous Boston Calvinist minister Cotton Mather was inveighing against pirates as a blaspheming scourge of mankind, he was also complaining that his fellow settlers, led astray by the ease of the climate in the New World and relaxed attitudes of its native inhabitants, had begun to undergo what he called "Indianization"—refusing to apply corporal punishment to their children, and thus undermining the principles of discipline, hierarchy, and formality that should govern relations between masters and servants, men and women, or young and old...

What was true in towns like Boston was all the more true on the frontiers, especially in those communities often made up of escaped slaves and servants who "became Indians" outside the control of colonial governments entirely, or island enclaves of what historians Peter Linebaugh and Marcus Rediker have called "the Atlantic proletariat," the motley collection of freedmen, sailors, ship's whores, renegades, Antinomians, and rebels who developed in the port cities of the North Atlantic world before the emergence of modern racism, and from whom much of the democratic impulse of the American—and other—revolutions seems to have first emerged. Men like Mather would have agreed with that as well: he often wrote that Indian attacks on frontier settlements were God's punishment on such folk for abandoning their rightful masters and living like Indians themselves.

If the history were truly written, it seems to me that the real origin of the democratic spirit—and most likely, many democratic institutions—lies precisely in those spaces of improvisation just outside the control of governments and organized churches.[17]

New World colonial elites' hatred and fear of the "wildness" of frontier communities, when we read between the lines,

---

[17]Ibid., pp. 179-182.

centered very much on their illegibility. "We don't know what they're up to."

There is a strong parallel between the spontaneous origins of democracy on pirate ships and in frontier communities, and Kropotkin's account in *The State* of the rise of the towns of Europe in the late Middle Ages. The towns started out as marginal, ungovernable areas on the frontiers of feudal control, settled from refugees from the feudal system of power. The typical late-medieval town began as a large village on an important crossroads or ford, or a fair, which became swollen with populations of runaway peasants and eventually erected walls and declared their independence from the nominal feudal overlord of the area. The solidaritarian institutions of these newly risen towns showed close continuity with the institutions of the villages they grew from, or of the peasants who fled to them; their charters of self-government, in defiance of local feudal authorities, amounted to desperate pledges of "life, fortunes and sacred honor." And the governance institutions of federated guilds displayed a communal and egalitarian ethos much like those of the village, with its open field system and non-state governance.

But the conventional Western tradition sees "democracy" as a privileged concept properly applicable only to Periclean Athens, England in 1688, and Philadelphia in 1787.

> Of course it's the peculiar bias of Western historiography that this is the only sort of democracy that is seen to count as "democracy" at all. We are usually told that democracy originated in ancient Athens—like science, or philosophy, it was a Greek invention. It's never entirely clear what this is supposed to mean. Are we supposed to believe that before the Athenians, it never really occurred to anyone, anywhere, to gather all the members of their community in order to make joint decisions in a way that gave everyone equal say? That would be ridiculous. Clearly there have been plenty of egalitarian societies in history—

many far more egalitarian than Athens, many that must have existed before 500 BCE—and obviously, they must have had some kind of procedure for coming to decisions for matters of collective importance. Yet somehow, it is always assumed that these procedures, whatever they might have been, could not have been, properly speaking, "democratic."[18]

The real reason for the unwillingness of most scholars to see a Sulawezi or Tallensi village council as "democratic"—well, aside from simple racism, the reluctance to admit anyone Westerners slaughtered with such relative impunity were quite on the level as Pericles—is that they do not vote. Now, admittedly, this is an interesting fact. Why not? If we accept the idea that a show of hands, or having everyone who supports a proposition stand on one side of the plaza and everyone against stand on the other, are not really such incredibly sophisticated ideas that they never would have occurred to anyone until some ancient genius "invented" them, then why are they so rarely employed? Again, we seem to have an example of explicit rejection. Over and over, across the world, from Australia to Siberia, egalitarian communities have preferred some variation on consensus process. Why?

The explanation I would propose is this: it is much easier, in a face-to-face community, to figure out what most members of that community want to do, than to figure out how to convince those who do not to go along with it. Consensus decision-making is typical of societies where there would be no way to compel a minority to agree with a majority decision—either because there is no state with a monopoly of coercive force, or because the state has nothing to do with local decision-making. If there is no way to compel those who find a majority decision distasteful

---

[18]Graeber, *Fragments of an Anarchist Anthropology*, p. 87.

to go along with it, then the last thing one would want to do is to hold a vote: a public contest which someone will be seen to lose. Voting would be the most likely means to guarantee humiliations, resentments, hatreds, in the end, the destruction of communities. What is seen as an elaborate and difficult process of finding consensus is, in fact, a long process of making sure no one walks away feeling that their views have been totally ignored.

Majority democracy, we might say, can only emerge when two factors coincide:

1. a feeling that people should have equal say in making group decisions, and
2. a coercive apparatus capable of enforcing those decisions.

For most of human history, it has been extremely unusual to have both at the same time. Where egalitarian societies exist, it is also usually considered wrong to impose systematic coercion. Where a machinery of coercion did exist, it did not even occur to those wielding it that they were enforcing any sort of popular will.[19]

In the cases where formally majoritarian institutions did emerge within preexisting coercive states (as with the Western liberal democracies of the past two centuries), it has generally been a case in which dissenting elements in a ruling elite defended their own rights against the ruler in terms that sounded more generally applicable than they were actually intended to be (Magna Carta), or used democratic rhetoric to enlist a popular majority as allies in its struggle for dominance—as Emmanuel Goldstein put it in *1984*, the middle enlisting the low as allies against the high. And when formally majoritarian institutions have been put in place, in practice the systems continued to be governed by the Iron

---

[19]Ibid., pp. 88-89.

Law of Oligarchy and the use of all the techniques Edward Bernays elaborated for "manufacturing consent."

> ...It's for this reason the new global movement has begun by reinventing the very meaning of democracy. To do so ultimately means, once again, coming to terms with the fact that "we"—whether as "the West" (whatever that means), as the "modern world," or anything else—are not really as special as we like to think we are; that we're not the only people ever to have practiced democracy; that in fact, rather than disseminating democracy around the world, "Western" governments have been spending at least as much time inserting themselves into the lives of people who have been practicing democracy for thousands of years, and in one way or another, telling them to cut it out.[20]

Graeber contrasts ruling class notions of "rationality" (which they naturally possess much more of than the ruled) with "reasonableness," which is "the ability to compare and co-ordinate contrasting perspectives"—something people used to being in a position of command, like the ruling classes with their pose of superior rationality, rarely have to do.[21] The consensus-based decision-making preferred by anarchists comes from feminist praxis ("the intellectual tradition of those who have, historically, tended not to be vested with the power of command"). "Consensus is an attempt to create a politics founded on the principle of reasonableness...." It requires the ability to listen to those with different perspectives, engage in give-and-take, and find pragmatic common ground with one's equals.[22] In other words, it's the kind of thing done by ordinary people who have to work out a solution to a common problem by sitting down and talking to

---
[20]Ibid., p. 93.
[21]Graeber, *The Democracy Project*, pp. 200-201.
[22]Graeber, *Fragments of an Anarchist Anthropology*, pp. 202-203.

each other as equals—far different from the "rationality" of "crackpot realists" who are so utterly unself-critical about the real biases of their supposedly neutral and self-evident ways of doing things.

Part of the explanation for Western elites' hostility to historical manifestations of direct democracy and self-governance by ordinary people is that it both disempowers them and puts them out of a job. As Larry Gambone argues:

> Representative democracy, such as exists in Parliament and Congress, effectively isolates people. Once every four or five years you get to have your five minutes of democracy, casting your vote for one group or another, groups over which you have zero control. Meanwhile, you have been subject to a 24-7 propaganda bombardment from the media. This onslaught works upon and bolsters your fears, anxieties and prejudices. In isolation, both at home in front of the TV and later the ballot box, you are more likely to vote against your own interests with knee-jerk fears and prejudices.
>
> Direct democracy links individuals, involves them in discussion in an assembly. Issues are debated, and without the censorship and demonization indulged in by the media, people can hear other viewpoints and make their own decisions. Fence-sitters can be swayed by the assembly in a positive direction, whereas in isolation and subject to propaganda bombardment, they might support policies that work against their real interests.
>
> Direct democracy can only function in a relatively small group—no more than a few thousand people. This means a community or neighborhood assembly, and thus questions get discussed in relation to the needs and desires of that community and are not abstract debates at the provincial or national level. Positive NIMBY can take place. A possible example—no one wants a nuclear waste dump in their community,

> but in a national referendum they might allow one if they thought it might be put somewhere other than their region. If the vote was *by community only*, there would be no nuclear waste dumps allowed anywhere.
>
> It isn't hard to see why the dominators hate direct democracy. Their power to dominate would quickly fade. The claim that right-wingers sometimes make that direct democracy is a form of tyranny is easy to understand. It seems like tyranny to them, because they are no longer in control and telling us what to do. Our freedom is despotism to them. Their freedom can only rest upon our servitude.[23]

Graeber, incidentally, sees anarchy—like democracy—as a spontaneous and common sense phenomenon that emerges as a matter of course when ordinary people confront each other as equals outside the state's jurisdiction. Historically democratic practices of self-governance were most likely to grow from the same soil as anarchistic movements—especially what James Scott would call Zomian or nonstate spaces, areas outside the reach of powerful states where runaway serfs, slaves and debtors, draft evaders, and other fugitives from authority would tend to gravitate.

> In China around 400 B.C...., there was a philosophical movement that came to be known as the "School of the Tillers," which held that both merchants and government officials were both useless parasites, and attempted to create communities of equals where the only leadership would be by example, and the economy would be democratically regulated in unclaimed territories between the major states. Apparently, the movement was created by an alliance between renegade intellectuals who fled to such free

---

[23]Larry Gambone, "Why the Dominators Hate Direct Democracy," *Porcupine Blog*, May 25, 2014. http://porkupineblog.blogspot.com/2014/05/why-dominators-hate-direct-democracy.html

villages and the peasant intellectuals they encountered there. Their ultimate aim appears to have been to gradually draw off defectors from surrounding kingdoms and thus, eventually, cause their collapse. This kind of encouragement of mass defection is a classic anarchist strategy. Needless to say they were not ultimately successful, but their ideas had enormous influence on court philosophers of later generations.

Indirectly, they ultimately influenced the anarchistic aspects of Lao Tzu's thought.[24] Graeber himself points out that this was just a better-documented-than-average version of what people have done all over the world when they managed to set up new communities on the margin of state authority—people like Scott's Zomians, the Cossacks, Romani and Irish Travelers, Hakim Bey's "pirate utopias," "tri-racial isolates" in the North American back country, etc.[25]

✳ *II. Everyday Communism*

Although the conventional economic narrative treats money exchange as a spontaneous and natural outgrowth of barter, and a society dominated by commodity production as the logical outgrowth of this, in fact this separate sphere of atomized cash nexus exchange has never existed in any human society except where it was artificially created by the state. The common pattern throughout human history, including communities where significant elements of exchange existed, was for production, exchange, and consumption to be embedded in a context of social relationships, religion, love, and family life. If anything, the common denominator throughout human history—even in our society, despite the capitalist state's attempt either to destroy it or harness it as an auxiliary of the cash nexus—has been what Graeber calls "the

---

[24] Graeber, *The Democracy Project*, pp. 188-189.
[25] Ibid., p. 189.

communism of everyday life." Every society in human history has been a foundation built out of this everyday communism of family, household, self-provisioning, gifting, and sharing among friends and neighbors, etc., with a scaffolding of market exchange and hierarchies erected on top of it.

For Graeber, this kind of communism is the basis of everyday life in most societies, in the same sense that many anarchists like to point out that most of our lives are characterized by anarchy. He means by it the same thing as the classic definition conveyed: "from each according to their abilities, to each according to their needs." Without this universal kind of communism, based on voluntary association and self-organization, both what we refer to as "capitalist" and what we refer to as "state socialist" societies simply could not sustain themselves. To a large extent, the cash nexus and hierarchical institutions are parasitic on this basic stratum of communism in which human life and culture are reproduced.

> In fact, "communism" is not some magical utopia, and neither does it have anything to do with ownership of the means of production. It is something that exists right now—that exists, to some degree, in any human society, although there has never been one in which *everything* has been organized in that way, and it would be difficult to imagine how there could be. All of us act like communists a good deal of the time.... "Communist society"...could never exist. But all social systems, even social systems like capitalism, have been built on top of a bedrock of actually-existing communism.[26]

> ...[C]ommunism really just means any situation where people act according to this principle: from each according to his abilities, to each according to his needs. This is, in fact, the way pretty much everyone acts if they are working together. If, for example, two people

---
[26] Graeber, *Debt*, p. 95.

> are fixing a pipe and one says "hand me the wrench," the other doesn't say "and what do I get for it?" This is true even if they happen to be employed by Bechtel or Citigroup. They apply the principles of communism because they're the only ones that really work. This is also the reason entire cities and countries revert to some form of rough-and-ready communism in the wake of natural disasters or economic collapse—markets and hierarchical chains of command become luxuries they can't afford. The more creativity is required and the more people have to improvise at a given task, the more egalitarian the resulting form of communism is likely to be. That's why even Republican computer engineers trying to develop new software ideas tend to form small democratic collectives. It's only when work becomes standardized and boring (think production lines) that it becomes possible to impose more authoritarian, even fascistic forms of communism. But the fact is that even private companies are internally organized according to communist principles.[27]

Whenever we look at the nuts and bolts of "who has access to what sorts of things and under what sorts of conditions"—even among two or a few people—and see sharing, "we can say we are in the presence of a sort of communism."[28]

The domain of communism extends further in "less impersonal" communities, like medieval villages, where it is commonly accepted that anyone with enough of the basic necessities of life to spare will share some with a neighbor in distress.[29] I would add that most pre-state societies in human history, and most agrarian villages even under the state until it was actively suppressed by either Enclosure or forced collectivization, were organized around the principle of

---

[27]Graeber, "The Machinery of Hopelessness."
[28]Graeber, *Debt*, p. 95.
[29]Ibid., p. 98.

access to common pasture, wood and waste, and periodically redivided shares in the open fields; even formally landless peasants with no strips in the open fields would maintain a passable level of subsistence by erecting cottages in the common waste and foraging for berries, game and firewood in fen and wood, and keeping a few pigs or geese on the common pasture.

And society—the communities actually on the spot—reverts to this baseline communism after a major disaster, with people stepping in to contribute their labor or risk their lives in the same extraordinary—yet ordinary—ways that Kropotkin described in *Mutual Aid*.[30]

But even within formally capitalist or state socialist hierarchies—corporations, state-owned factories, etc.—hierarchies often unofficially rely on the informal communism of those at the bottom rung working together to solve problems that are opaque to the idiots at the top (when not actually caused by them). Capitalism is just "a poor system for managing communism."[31]

The actual efficiency of large hierarchical institutions comes from the communism of those actually engaged in the work, and contributing their efforts to the common endeavor in the manner typically ascribed to commons-based peer production. Of course this communism takes place in a larger institutional framework characterized by military chains of command. But "...top-down chains of command are not particularly efficient: they tend to promote stupidity among those on top, resentful foot-dragging among those on the bottom."[32]

---

[30] Ibid., p. 96.
[31] Graeber, "The Machinery of Hopelessness."
[32] Graeber, *Debt*, p. 92.

* III. The Irrelevance of Standard Ideological Models

Graeber's view of the particularity and historical situatedness of human experience precludes abstracting human social relations into artificially separated spheres like, for example, the "economic man" functioning purely in the cash nexus. Much like Ostrom, Graeber sees states as simply one example of people doing stuff, one kind of patterned relationships. And the market, likewise, is just a way people relate to one another sometimes.

One of his criticisms of modern economics, as a discipline, is that

> for there even to be a discipline called "economics," a discipline that concerns itself first and foremost with how individuals see the most advantageous arrangement for the exchange of shoes for potatoes, or cloth for spears, it must assume that the exchange of such goods need have nothing to do with war, passion, adventure, mystery, sex, or death. Economics assumes a division between different spheres of human behavior that, among people like the Gunwinngu and the Nambikwara, simply does not exist.... This in turn allows us to assume that life is neatly divided between the marketplace, where we do our shopping, and the "sphere of consumption," where we concern ourselves with music, feasts, and seduction.[33]

As we saw above, the conventional account of the origin of money, stated in Smith's *The Wealth of Nations* and repeated in a thousand introductions to economics since then, is that the "cash nexus" emerges spontaneously from the human propensity to "truck and barter." People in "primitive" societies start out by bartering necessities with one another; confronted with the problem of "double coincidence

---
[33]Ibid., pp. 32-33.

of wants," these societies first address the problem by stockpiling especially widely desired commodities to use as media of exchange, proceed to adopting rare precious metals as the primary medium of exchange, and finally issue specific quantities of previous metals denominated in monetary values.

The problem, Graeber points out, is that this account is totally ahistorical. In all historical human societies, money exchange has been embedded in a larger social context, as one means among many others by which people meet their needs.

The story of the origin of money out of barter, from Smith onward, has been presented as a sort of parable set in a completely imaginary society ("To see that society benefits from a medium of exchange, imagine a barter economy." "Imagine you have roosters, but you want roses.").

> The problem is where to locate this fantasy in time and space: Are we talking about cave men, Pacific Islanders, the American frontier? One textbook, by economists Joseph Stiglitz and John Driffil, takes us to what appears to be an imaginary New England or Midwestern town...
>
> Again, this is just a make-believe land much like the present, except with money somehow plucked away. As a result it makes no sense. Who in their right mind would set up a grocery in such a place? And how would they get supplies?[34]

In short, it's as much a "bourgeois nursery fable" as the "original accumulation of capital" and the "Social Contract." That's not to say barter doesn't take place, Graeber says; just that it takes place, not between villagers, but "between strangers, even enemies."[35] Barter is used mainly for one-off transactions between people who have no common social

---
[34]Ibid., pp. 23-24.
[35]Ibid., p. 29.

context.³⁶ And, as he argues throughout *Debt*, the very kinds of currency-based cash nexus societies that Smith theorized had evolved from barter have only existed where states have stripped human beings of all social context and reduced them to atomized individuals.

In virtually all spontaneously emerging, self-organized human communities, the typical pattern has been, as we saw at the beginning, the "communism of everyday life" with some amount of more formalized market exchange on top of it—but still embedded in the larger social context, not as an abstract "economic" sphere. At the most basic level, this might take the form of one person in a village hinting to the shoemaker that her shoes are getting worn out, shortly thereafter getting the spontaneous "gift" of a pair of shoes, and later taking the opportunity to reciprocate the gift when the shoemaker needs something she can provide—or, just as likely, filling a need for someone else to whom the shoemaker owes a favor.³⁷ At a more refined level, this kind of system might evolve into virtual money, with everybody running ongoing tabs with the butcher, baker, and candle-stick maker, and keeping account of whatever nature of goods and services they provide for their neighbors. Periodically members of the community settle up whatever differences are left after all the debits and credits have cancelled each other out. This sounds, as a matter of fact, a lot like the mutual credit-clearing systems of Thomas Greco and E.C. Riegel. No "double coincidence of needs" ever arises.

❋ *IV. Prefigurative Politics*

Considering Graeber's high regard for the results of spontaneous, self-directed human interaction, it's not surprising he played a major role in the process that led to the Occupy movement taking a horizontalist path—against the wishes of

---

³⁶Ibid., p. 32.
³⁷Ibid., pp. 35-36.

many of its would-be founders.

> When Graeber and his friends showed up on Aug. 2..., they found out that the event wasn't, in fact, a general assembly, but a traditional rally, to be followed by a short meeting and a march to Wall Street to deliver a set of predetermined demands ("A massive public-private jobs program" was one, "An end to oppression and war!" was another). In anarchist argot, the event was being run by "verticals"—top-down organizations—rather than "horizontals" such as Graeber and his friends. Sagri and Graeber felt they'd been had, and they were angry.[38]

As Graeber recalled, the movement as it had evolved to that point gave every indication of being a conventional protest that would fizzle out with little notice.

> ...[A] local anti-budget cut coalition top-heavy with NGOs, unions, and socialist groups had tried to take possession of the process and called for a "General Assembly" at Bowling Green. The title proved extremely misleading. When I arrived, I found the event had been effectively taken over by a veteran protest group called the Worker's World Party, most famous for having patched together ANSWER, one of the two great anti-war coalitions, back in 2003. They had already set up their banners, megaphones, and were making speeches—after which, someone explained, they were planning on leading the 80-odd assembled people in a march past the Stock Exchange itself.[39]

---

[38] Drake Bennet, "David Graeber, the Anti-Leader of Occupy Wall Street," *BusinessWeek*, October 26, 2011. http://www.businessweek.com/printer/magazine/david-graeber-the-antileader-of-occupy-wall-street-10262011.html

[39] David Graeber, "On Playing By The Rules—The Strange Success of OccupyWallStreet," *Countercurrents.org*, October 23, 2011. http://www.countercurrents.org/graeber241011l.htm

But Graeber, noticing that most of the people who showed up weren't all that happy with the professional activists' self-appointed leadership ("the sort of people who actually like marching around with pre-issued signs and listening to spokesmen from somebody's central committee"[40]), wound up playing a role comparable to triggering the crystallization of a supersaturated solution around a random particle. The demonstration that was set up to be just another cookie-cutter effort of the institutional Left—"the old fashioned vertical politics of top-down coalitions, charismatic leaders, and marching around with signs"—instead emerged as a leaderless, horizontal movement.

> But as I paced about the Green, I noticed something. To adopt activist parlance: this wasn't really a crowd of verticals—that is, the sort of people whose idea of political action is to march around with signs under the control of one or another top-down protest movement. They were mostly pretty obviously horizontals: people more sympathetic with anarchist principles of organization, non-hierarchical forms of direct democracy, and direct action. I quickly spotted at least one Wobbly, a young Korean activist I remembered from some Food Not Bomb event, some college students wearing Zapatista paraphernalia, a Spanish couple who'd been involved with the indignados in Madrid... I found my Greek friends, an American I knew from street battles in Quebec during the Summit of the Americas in 2001, now turned labor organizer in Manhattan, a Japanese activist intellectual I'd known for years... My Greek friend looked at me and I looked at her and we both instantly realized the other was thinking the same thing: "Why are we so complacent? Why is it that every time we see something like this happening, we just mutter things and go home?"— though I think the way we put it was more like, "You

---

[40]Graeber, *The Democracy Project*, p. 27.

know something? Fuck this shit. They advertised a general assembly. Let's hold one."

So we gathered up a few obvious horizontals and formed a circle, and tried to get everyone else to join us.... We created a decision-making process (we would operate by modified consensus) broke out into working groups (outreach, action, facilitation) and then reassembled to allow each group to report its collective decisions, and set up times for new meetings of both the smaller and larger groups....

Two days later, at the Outreach meeting we were brainstorming what to put on our first flyer. *Adbusters*' idea had been that we focus on "one key demand." This was a brilliant idea from a marketing perspective, but from an organizing perspective, it made no sense at all. We put that one aside almost immediately. There were much more fundamental questions to be hashed out. Like: who were we? Who did want to appeal to? Who did we represent? Someone—this time I remember quite clearly it was me, but I wouldn't be surprised if a half dozen others had equally strong memories of being the first to come up with it—suggested, "well, why not call ourselves 'the 99%'? If 1% of the population have ended up with all the benefits of the last 10 years of economic growth, control the wealth, own the politicians...why not just say we're everybody else?" The Spanish couple quickly began to lay out a "We Are the 99%" pamphlet, and we started brainstorming ways to print and distribute it for free.

Over the next few weeks a plan began to take shape.... We quickly decided that what we really wanted to do was something like had already been accomplished in Athens, Barcelona, or Madrid: occupy a public space to create a New York General Assembly, a body that could act as a model of genuine, direct democracy to contrapose to the corrupt charade presented to us as "democracy" by the US government.

The Wall Street action would be a stepping-stone.[41]

It's also not surprising that Graeber sees the horizontalism of the EZLN, the Seattle movement, the Arab Spring, M15, Syntagma, and Occupy not only as models for the future human society that emerges from the decline of the existing corporate-state system of power, but also sees their prefigurative politics as the way to get there.

The antiglobalization movement "has in a mere two or three years managed to transform completely the sense of historical possibilities for millions across the planet."[42]

> The very notion of direct action, with its rejection of a politics which appeals to governments to modify their behaviour, in favour of physical intervention against state power in a form that itself prefigures an alternative—all of this emerges directly from the libertarian tradition. Anarchism is the heart of the movement, its soul; the source of most of what's new and hopeful about it.[43]

We remarked earlier on Graeber's openness to people's choices and concrete decisions. He regards anarchist society, accordingly, as an open-ended process:

> Where the democratic-centralist "party" puts its emphasis on achieving a complete and correct theoretical analysis, demands ideological uniformity and tends to juxtapose the vision of an egalitarian future with extremely authoritarian forms of organization in the present, these openly seek diversity. Debate always focuses on particular courses of action; it's taken for granted that no one will ever convert anyone else

---

[41] Graeber, "On Playing By the Rules."
[42] Graeber, "The New Anarchists," *New Left Review* 13 (January-February 2002). http://newleftreview.org/II/13/david-graeber-the-new-anarchists
[43] Ibid.

entirely to their point of view. The motto might be, "If you are willing to act like an anarchist now, your long-term vision is pretty much your own business." Which seems only sensible: none of us know how far these principles can actually take us, or what a complex society based on them would end up looking like. Their ideology, then, is immanent in the anti-authoritarian principles that underlie their practice, and one of their more explicit principles is that things should stay this way.[44]

And the horizontalist movements that have arisen since the Zapatista uprisings in Chiapas are Graeber's primary illustration of how these lessons actually have been put into practice. They

> rejected the very idea that one could find a solution by replacing one set of politicians with another. The slogan of the Argentine movement was, from the start, *que se vayan todas*—get rid of the lot of them. Instead, the first cycle of the new global uprising—what the press still insists on referring to, increasingly ridiculously, as "the anti-globalization movement"—began with the autonomous municipalities of Chiapas and came to a head with the *asambleas barreales* of Buenos Aires, and cities throughout Argentina. There is hardly room here to tell the whole story: beginning with the Zapatistas' rejection of the idea of seizing power and their attempt instead to create a model of democratic self-organization to inspire the rest of Mexico; their initiation of an international network (People's Global Action, or PGA) which then put out the calls for days of action against the WTO (in Seattle), IMF (in Washington, Prague…) and so on; and finally, the collapse of the Argentine economy, and the overwhelming popular uprising which, again, of a

---

[44]Ibid.

> new government they created a vast network of alternative institutions, starting with popular assemblies to govern each urban neighborhood (the only limitation on participation is that one cannot be employed by a political party), hundreds of occupied, worker-managed factories, a complex system of "barter" and newfangled alternative currency system to keep them in operation—in short, an endless variation on the theme of direct democracy.
>
> All of this has happened completely below the radar screen of the corporate media, which also missed the point of the great mobilizations. The organization of these actions was meant to be a living illustration of what a truly democratic world might be like, from the festive puppets to the careful organization of affinity groups and spokescouncils, all operating without a leadership structure, always based on principles of consensus-based direct democracy. It was the kind of organization which most people would have, had they simply heard it proposed, written off as a pipe-dream; but it worked, and so effectively that the police departments of city after city were completely flummoxed with how to deal with them....
>
> When protesters in Seattle chanted "this is what democracy looks like," they meant to be taken literally.[45]

The "core principles" are the same in all the movements, from Chiapas through the post-Seattle anti-globalization movement, the Arab Spring, Wisconsin, M15, Syntagma, Occupy, and the amazing things that have been going on more recently in places from Turkey to Brazil:

> decentralization, voluntary association, mutual aid, the network model, and above all, the rejection of any idea that the end justifies the means, let alone that the business of a revolutionary is to seize state

---

[45]Graeber, *Fragments of an Anarchist Anthropology*, pp. 82-84.

> power and then begin imposing one's vision at the point of a gun. Above all, anarchism, as an ethics of practice—the idea of building a new society "within the shell of the old"—has become the basic inspiration of the "movement of movements"..., which has from the start been less about seizing state power than about exposing, de-legitimizing, and dismantling mechanisms of rule while winning ever-larger spaces of autonomy and participatory management within it.[46]

Graeber considers the very word "protest" to be problematic, because "it sounds like you already lost." It recognizes the existing system of power, perhaps even its necessity, and simply tries to influence its functioning. Direct action, on the other hand, treats the system of power as both illegitimate and unnecessary, and involves people organizing their lives the way they want as though the system of power weren't even there at all.

> Well the reason anarchists like direct action is because it means refusing to recognise the legitimacy of structures of power. Or even the necessity of them. Nothing annoys forces of authority more than trying to bow out of the disciplinary game entirely and saying that we could just do things on our own. Direct action is a matter of acting as if you were already free.

Graeber points to the example of Madagascar, where the state has ceased to function—in the sense of collecting taxes or enforcing the law—in many rural areas. "[E]ssentially the government had ceased to exist and the people had come

---

[46] Andrej Grubacic and David Graeber, "Anarchism, Or The Revolutionary Movement Of The Twenty-first Century" (2004). In *David Graeber: Collection of Essays* (The Anarchist Library. Anti-Copyright February 5, 2012), p. 10.

up with ingenious expedients of how to deal with the fact that there was still technically a government, it was just really far away." In most cases this meant direct action—people simply solving problems on their own—coupled with the avoidance of direct confrontation with state functionaries. The people were very polite to officials, but made enforcement as difficult as possible through passive aggression, so that state functionaries learned that the path of least resistance was to play along with the charade.

✻ V. Human Scale Alternatives: Building the Successor Society

When we look at particular human ventures in local self-organization in their particularity, and not through the prism of ideological abstractions, it strikes me that local, face-to-face arrangements—whatever mixture of market exchange, gifting and sharing, or moneyless self-sufficiency they partake of—are largely irrelevant to critiques like Mises's socialist calculation argument or the anti-market socialist claim that any form of market exchange will, through the process of winners and losers, lead to a capitalist system based on concentrated absentee capital ownership and exploited wage labor. Human experience, quite simply, is too big for such theories to adequately describe.

It's hard for me to imagine a society without at least some market pricing to enable economic calculation on a macro-scale of trade involving numerous local communities, like the long-distance distribution of minerals, microprocessors, etc. Even Bakunin saw his agro-industrial communes exchanging their surpluses with each other on some kind of market. On the other hand, even calculation hawks like Mises admitted that moneyless valuation of inputs was feasible on small scales like the Robinson Crusoe scenario or a subsistence farm; and it seems to me that a village or neighborhood economic unit of several dozen people that produced most of its consumption needs on-site with intensive horticulture, micro-manufacturing, and the like, would largely fall into the same category, insofar as internal allocation of production inputs and the sharing of output could be governed by the same communist ethos as a family (although obviously some members would have to earn "foreign exchange" by selling goods or services outside, so the community could purchase locally unavailable raw materials and specialized industrial goods on the outside).

But if small-scale production technology makes localized moneyless communism feasible for a major share of consumption needs without invoking the specter of calculational chaos, it seems equally likely that a significant amount of economic activity could be governed by free markets without degenerating—as anti-market anarchists warn—into capitalism. In an anarchy without adjectives (with no central authority capable of enforcing large-scale absentee ownership of vacant land, shutting down squats or criminalizing comfortable subsistence on squatted land, or enforcing "intellectual property," with the technological feasibility of individuals and small communities engaging in sophisticated machine production for themselves with minimal capital outlays, and with an infinite proliferation of communistic institutions for solidarity and the pooling of risks and costs outside the money economy) it seems unlikely that the central prerequisite for economic exploitation would exist. Without, that is, the concentration of expensive means of production into a few hands, or the blocking of independent access to means of production and subsistence through social power, it would be unable to close off viable alternatives to accepting wage labor on the terms offered.

It is the very face-to-face element itself—the fact that human beings at a local level are interacting directly and working out ways to deal with one another—that conditions the nature of social relations:

> just as markets, when allowed to drift entirely free

> from their violent origins, invariably begin to grow into something different, into networks of honor, trust, and mutual connectedness, so too does the maintenance of systems of coercion constantly do the opposite: turn the products of human cooperation, creativity, devotion, love, and trust back into numbers once again.[47]

It is the "honor, trust, and mutual connectedness" of local, face-to-face, horizontal human relations, rather than their formally "market" or "non-market" nature, that determines their real character.

Graeber expresses frustration at arguing for the viability of anarchism with liberals who hypothesize it as a monolithic "system" adopted through some sort of large-scale agreement to remodel an entire society at once on the same pattern, or as a society organized exactly the way it is now in terms of economic and social institutions but with the government suddenly taken away.[48]

> There is a way out, which is to accept that anarchist forms of organization would not look anything like a state. That they would involve an endless variety of communities, associations, networks, projects, on every conceivable scale, overlapping and intersecting in any way we could imagine and possibly many that we can't. Some would be quite local, others global. Perhaps all they would have in common is that none would involve anyone showing up with weapons and telling everyone else to shut up and do what they were told. And that, since anarchists are not actually trying to seize power within any national territory, the process of one system replacing the other will not take the form of some sudden revolutionary cataclysm— the storming of a Bastille, the seizing of a Winter

---

[47] Graeber, *Debt*, pp. 386-387.
[48] Graeber, *Fragments of an Anarchist Anthropology*, p. 39.

> Palace—but will necessarily be gradual, the creation of alternative forms of organization on a world scale, new forms of communication, less alienated ways of organizing life, which will, eventually, make currently existing forms of power seem stupid and beside the point. That in turn would mean that there are endless examples of viable anarchism...[49]

The attempt to achieve solutions through the state is utterly misguided. Rather, we must start from the building blocks of everyday communism around us.

> ...the last decade has seen the development of thousands of forms of mutual aid associations. They range from tiny cooperatives to vast anti-capitalist experiments, from occupied factories in Paraguay and Argentina to self-organized tea plantations and fisheries in India, from autonomous institutes in Korea to insurgent communities in Chiapas and Bolivia. These associations of landless peasants, urban squatters, and neighborhood alliances spring up pretty much anywhere where state power and global capital seem to be temporarily looking the other way. They might have almost no ideological unity, many are not even aware of the others' existence, but they are all marked by a common desire to break with the logic of capital. "Economies of solidarity" exist on every continent, in at least 80 different countries. We are at the point where we can begin to conceive of these cooperatives knitting together on a global level and creating a genuine insurgent civilization.
> ...Becoming aware of alternatives allows us to see everything we are already doing in a new light. We realize we're already communists when working on common projects, already anarchists when we solve problems without recourse to lawyers or police,

---
[49] Ibid., p. 40.

already revolutionaries when we make something genuinely new.[50]

Graeber, in treating anarchism as something that already exists with a state superimposed on it, sounds a lot like Colin Ward.

> We are already practicing communism much of the time. We are already anarchists, or at least we act like anarchists, every time we come to understandings with one another that would not require physical threats as a means of enforcement. It's not a question of building an entirely new society whole cloth. It's a question of building on what we are already doing, expanding the zones of freedom, until freedom becomes the ultimate organizing principle. I actually don't think the technical aspects of coming up with how to produce and distribute manufactured objects is likely to be the great problem, though we are constantly told to believe it's the only problem. There are many things in short supply in the world. One thing of which we have a well-nigh unlimited supply is intelligent, creative people able to come up with solutions to problems like that. The problem is not a lack of imagination. The problem is the stifling systems of debt and violence, created to ensure that those powers of imagination are not used—or not used to create anything beyond financial derivatives, new weapons systems, or new Internet platforms for the filling out of forms. This is, of course, exactly what brought so many to places like Zuccotti Park.[51]

He proposes, as a revolutionary model for anarchists, "an eggshell theory of revolution," in which "[y]ou just hollow it out until there's nothing left and eventually it will collapse."

---

[50]Graeber, "The Machinery of Hopelessness."
[51]Graeber, *The Democracy Project*, pp. 295-296.

That means an extended period of dual power, finally culminating at the point where "the forces of order refuse to shoot."[52]

✻ VI. The Other Side: The Stupidity of Power

Graeber is in agreement with James Scott, R. A. Wilson, and a wide range of other libertarian and anarchist thinkers that power makes those who wield it stupid.

> ...[W]hile people can be reasonable and considerate when they are dealing with equals, human nature is such that they cannot be trusted to do so when given power over others. Give someone such power, they will almost invariably abuse it in some way or another.[53]

More fundamentally, it is differentials of power, which enable one side to disregard communications from the other and to substitute violence for reason, that create stupidity. Power and violence eliminate the need to understand. Instead, those in power are able to force reality into an easy-to-understand schema. And because those in power can repress anyone who disobeys or fails to follow the script, they can externalize the negative consequences of irrationality on their subordinates. Power means having neither to perceive or suffer from the negative effects of one's own actions.

One benefit of power—rendering society legible, in James Scott's terminology—is that it creates a situation in which the powerful can *afford* to be stupid. You've probably heard the old joke about the drunk who looks for his car keys under the street lamp, despite having lost them somewhere else, because the light is better. The enforcement of legibility by

---

[52] Ellen Evans and Jon Moses, "Interview with David Graeber" *White Review*, December 7, 2011. http://www.thewhitereview.org/interviews/interview-with-david-graeber/

[53] Graeber, "Are You an Anarchist?"

those in power is a way of moving all the car keys under street lamps, or at least getting everybody to pretend that's where they are. (We'll have more to say in the next section about deliberately building our new society outside the street lamp's circle of illumination.)

> What I would like to argue is that situations created by violence—particularly structural violence, by which I mean forms of pervasive social inequality that are ultimately backed up by the threat of physical harm—invariably tend to create the kinds of willful blindness we normally associate with bureaucratic procedures. To put it crudely: it is not so much that bureaucratic procedures are inherently stupid, or even that they tend to produce behavior that they themselves define as stupid, but rather, that are invariably ways of managing social situations that are already stupid because they are founded on structural violence. I think this approach allows potential insights into matters that are, in fact, both interesting and important: for instance, the actual relationship between those forms of simplification typical of social theory, and those typical of administrative procedures.[54]

> Comparative analysis suggests there is a direct relation, however, between the level of violence employed in a bureaucratic system, and the level of absurdity it is seen to produce.[55]

> Violence's capacity to allow arbitrary decisions, and thus to avoid the kind of debate, clarification, and renegotiation typical of more egalitarian social relations, is obviously what allows its victims to see procedures created on the basis of violence as stupid

---

[54]Graeber, *Beyond Power/Knowledge: An Exploration of the Relation of Power, Ignorance, and Stupidity* (Malinowski Memorial Lecture: Thursday 25 May 2006), pp. 4-5.

[55]Ibid., p. 6

or unreasonable. One might say, those relying on the fear of force are not obliged to engage in a lot of interpretative labor, and thus, generally speaking, do not.[56]

Subordinates *have* to understand the situation, because they're the ones dealing with reality.

It's important to bear in mind that most human relations—particularly ongoing ones, whether between longstanding friends or longstanding enemies—are extremely complicated, dense with experience and meaning. Maintaining them requires a constant and often subtle work of interpretation, of endlessly imagining others' points of view. Threatening others with physical harm allows the possibility of cutting through all this. It makes possible relations of a far more schematic kind (i.e., "cross this line and I will shoot you"). This is of course why violence is so often the preferred weapon of the stupid: indeed, one might say it is one of the tragedies of human existence that this is the one form of stupidity to which it is most difficult to come up with an intelligent response.

I do need to introduce one crucial qualification here. If two parties engage in a contest of violence—say, generals commanding opposing armies—they have good reason to try to get inside each other's heads. It is really only when one side has an overwhelming advantage in their capacity to cause physical harm that they no longer need to do so. But this has very profound effects, because it means that the most characteristic effect of violence—its ability to obviate the need for interpretive labor—becomes most salient when the violence itself is least visible, in fact, where acts of spectacular physical violence are least likely to occur. These are situations of what

---

[56]Ibid., p. 7.

> I've referred to as structural violence, on the assumption that systematic inequalities backed up by the threat of force can be treated as forms of violence in themselves. For this reason, situations of structural violence invariably produce extreme lopsided structures of imaginative identification.[57]

There's a great scene in *Patton* where the general, after defeating Rommel, says "Rommel, you magnificent bastard, I read your book." The greater the equality of power, the greater the need to take each other into account. He refers to

> the process of imaginative identification as a form of knowledge, the fact that within relations of domination, it is generally the subordinates who are effectively relegated the work of understanding how the social relations in question really work. Anyone who has ever worked in a restaurant kitchen, for example, knows that if something goes terribly wrong and an angry boss appears to size things up, he is unlikely to carry out a detailed investigation, or even, to pay serious attention to the workers all scrambling to explain their version of what happened. He is much more likely to tell them all to shut up and arbitrarily impose a story that allows instant judgment: i.e., "you're the new guy, you messed up—if you do it again, you're fired." It's those who do not have the power to hire and fire who are left with the work of figuring out what actually did go wrong so as to make sure it doesn't happen again. The same thing usually happens with ongoing relations: everyone knows that servants tend to know a great deal about their employers' families, but the opposite almost never occurs.... [So] while those on the bottom of a social ladder spend a great deal of time imagining the perspectives of, and actually caring about, those on the top, it almost never happens the other way around.

---

[57]Ibid., pp. 7-8.

> Whether one is dealing with masters and servants, men and women, employers and employees, rich and poor, structural inequality—what I've been calling structural violence—invariably creates highly lopsided structures of the imagination. Since I think Smith was right to observe that imagination tends to bring with it sympathy: the result is that victims of structural violence tend to care about its beneficiaries far more than those beneficiaries care about them. This might well be, after the violence itself, the single most powerful force preserving such relations.[58]

As James Scott argued, those in power try to render society legible. But more than that, they also *pretend* that it *is* legible when it is not, and act on that assumption.

> Bureaucratic knowledge is all about schematization. In practice, bureaucratic procedure invariably means ignoring all the subtleties of real social existence and reducing everything to preconceived mechanical or statistical formulae. Whether it's a matter of forms, rules, statistics, or questionnaires, it is always a matter of simplification. Usually it's not so different than the boss who walks into the kitchen to make arbitrary snap decisions as to what went wrong: in either case it is a matter of applying very simple pre-existing templates to complex and often ambiguous situations.[59]

> A former LAPD officer turned sociologist (Cooper 1991) observed that the overwhelming majority of those beaten by police turn out not to be guilty of any crime. "Cops don't beat up burglars," he observed. The reason, he explained, is simple: the one thing most guaranteed to evoke a violent reaction from police is to challenge their right to "define the situation." If what I've been saying is true this is just

---

[58] Ibid., pp. 8-9.
[59] Ibid., p. 9.

what we'd expect. The police truncheon is precisely the point where the state's bureaucratic imperative for imposing simple administrative schema, and its monopoly of coercive force, come together. It only makes sense then that bureaucratic violence should consist first and foremost of attacks on those who insist on alternative schemas or interpretations. At the same time, if one accepts Piaget's famous definition of mature intelligence as the ability to coordinate between multiple perspectives (or possible perspectives) one can see, here, precisely how bureaucratic power, at the moment it turns to violence, becomes literally a form of infantile stupidity.[60]

✻ VII. Undermining Enforcement: Autonomy, Opacity, and Zomianism

As we saw above, Graeber treats the experience of so-called "primitive" societies, not as material of quaint antiquarian interest to be studied as a naturalist studies ants under a microscope, but as a common treasury of human knowledge that's relevant to the issues facing "developed" societies. Accordingly, he draws close parallels between the forms of self-governance used by Third World peoples in anthropological field studies, and the forms of organization adopted by protest movements like Occupy.

Graeber points out that the consensus decision-making process in the Occupy movement and other horizontalist movements—which actually had its modern origins in the feminist and other social justice movements and was practiced by the Zapatistas, post-Seattle movement, Arab Spring, M15, and Syntagma—is much like that used in face-to-face groups of human beings throughout history.

He argues—in terms that sound a great deal like Scott's description of Zomian law—that the lack of a political state in

---

[60]Ibid., p. 11.

so-called "primitive" societies reflects, not a lack of awareness that such "advanced" levels of organization are possible, but a deliberate choice to structure social organization so as to prevent them from arising. In the predominant linear framing, the state is "a more sophisticated form of organization than what had come before," and "stateless peoples, such as the Amazonian societies..., were tacitly assumed not to have attained the levels of say, the Aztecs or the Inca."

> But what if...Amazonians were not entirely unaware of what the elementary forms of state power might be like—what it would mean to allow some men to give everyone else orders which could not be questioned, since they were backed up by the threat of force—and were for that very reason determined to ensure such things never came about? What if they considered the fundamental premises of our political science morally objectionable?

Graeber compares it to the rules built into a gift economy to prevent the concentration of wealth and power.

> In gift economies there are, often, venues for enterprising individuals. But everything is arranged in such a way they could never be used as a platform for creating permanent inequalities of wealth, since self-aggrandizing types all end up competing to see who can give the most away. In Amazonian (or North American) societies, the institution of the chief played the same role on a political level: the position was so demanding, and so little rewarding, so hedged about by safeguards, that there was no way for power-hungry individuals to do much with it....
>
> By these lights these were all, in a very real sense, anarchist societies. They were founded on an explicit rejection of the logic of the state and of the market.[61]

---
[61]Graeber, *Fragments of an Anarchist Anthropology*, pp. 22-23.

> Anarchistic societies are no more unaware of human capacities for greed or vainglory than modern Americans are unaware of human capacities for envy, gluttony, or sloth; they would just find them equally unappealing as the basis for their civilization. In fact, they see these as moral dangers so dire they end up organizing much of their social life around containing them.[62]

Here Graeber turns the tables. To the anarchist, it's the advocate of the state who's a naïve utopian lacking in a commonsense understanding of human nature. "That would be all right on paper, if we were all angels."

So it follows that counterpower can not only emerge in opposition to a system of power already in existence, but can also be aimed at preventing the rise of a system of power which does not yet exist.

> In typical revolutionary discourse a "counterpower" is a collection of social institutions set in opposition to the state and capital: from self-governing communities to radical labor unions to popular militias. Sometimes it is also referred to as an "anti-power." When such institutions maintain themselves in the face of the state, this is usually referred to as a "dual power" situation. By this definition most of human history is actually characterized by dual power situations, since few historical states had the means to root such institutions out, even assuming that they would have wanted to. But [this line of argument] suggests something even more radical. It suggests that counterpower, at least in the most elementary sense, actually exists where the states and markets are not even present; that in such cases, rather than being embodied in popular institutions which pose themselves against the power of lords, or kings, or plutocrats, they are embodied in institutions which

---

[62]Ibid., p. 24.

> ensure such types of person never come about. What it is "counter" to, then, is a potential, a latent aspect, or dialectical possibility if you prefer, within the society itself.[63]

> In egalitarian societies, counterpower might be said to be the predominant form of social power. It stands guard over what are seen as certain frightening possibilities within the society itself: notably against the emergence of systematic forms of political or economic dominance.[64]

Graeber's treatment of marginal cultures on the frontiers of authoritarian states, and his thoughts on autonomy and exodus, share many parallels with James Scott's work on Zomian society, non-state spaces, and other attempts by populations to make themselves illegible to their rulers.

Scott's theme in *Seeing Like a State* was "a state's attempt to make society legible, to arrange the population in ways that simplified the classic state functions of taxation, conscription, and prevention of rebellion."

> The premodern state was, in many crucial respects, partially blind; it knew precious little about its subjects, their wealth, their landholdings and yields, their location, their very identity. It lacked anything like a detailed "map" of its terrain and its people. It lacked, for the most part, a measure, a metric, that would allow it to "translate" what it knew into a common standard necessary for a synoptic view. As a result, its interventions were often crude and self-defeating.
> ...How did the state gradually get a handle on its subjects and their environment? Suddenly, processes as disparate as the creation of permanent last names, the standardization of weights and measures,

---

[63]Ibid., pp. 24-25.
[64]Ibid., p. 35.

> the establishment of cadastral surveys and population registers, the invention of freehold tenure, the standardization of language and legal discourse, the design of cities, and the organization of transportation seemed comprehensible as attempts at legibility and simplification. In each case, officials took exceptionally complex, illegible, and local social practices, such as land tenure customs or naming customs, and created a standard grid whereby it could be centrally recorded and monitored....[65]

Historically, state attempts to render the population legible entailed the suppression of local forms of Hayekian distributed knowledge, like customary modes of governance, that were illegible to the state.

> How were the agents of the state to begin measuring and codifying, throughout each region of an entire kingdom, its population, their landholdings, their harvests, their wealth, the volume of commerce, and so on?
> ...Each undertaking...exemplified a pattern of relations between local knowledge and practices on one hand and state administrative routines on the other.... In each case, local practices of measurement and landholding were "illegible" to the state in their raw form. They exhibited a diversity and intricacy that reflected a great variety of purely local, not state, interests. That is to say, they could not be assimilated into an administrative grid without being either transformed or reduced to a convenient, if partly fictional, shorthand. The logic behind the required shorthand was provided...by the pressing material requirements of rulers: fiscal receipts, military manpower, and state security. In turn, this shorthand functioned...as not just a description, however inadequate. Backed by

---

[65]James Scott, *Seeing Like a State* (New Haven and London: Yale University Press, 1998), p. 2.

state power through records, courts, and ultimately coercion, these state fictions transformed the reality they presumed to observe, although never so thoroughly as to precisely fit the grid.[66]

With the distinction between legibility and illegibility came another distinction, that between areas where the state was able to impose conditions of legibility with relative success (state spaces), and the nonstate spaces in which its powers of monitoring and control were relatively weak. State spaces, Scott wrote in *Seeing Like a State*, are geographical regions with high-density population and high-density grain agriculture, "producing a surplus of grain...and labor which was relatively easily appropriated by the state." The conditions of nonstate spaces were just the reverse, "thereby severely limiting the possibilities for reliable state appropriation."[67]

These nonstate spaces were the subject of his next book, *The Art of Not Being Governed*. In it he illustrated the concept primarily with reference to the populations of "Zomia," the highland areas spanning the countries of Southeast Asia, which are largely outside the reach of the governments there. He suggests areas of commonality between the Zomians and people in nonstate areas around the world, upland and frontier people like the Cossacks, Highlanders and "hillbillies," nomadic peoples like the Romani and Tinkers, and runaway slave communities in inaccessible marsh regions of the American South.

States attempt to maximize the appropriability of crops and labor, designing state space so as "to guarantee the ruler a substantial and reliable surplus of manpower and grain at least cost..." This is achieved by geographical concentration of the population and the use of concentrated, high-value forms of cultivation, in order to minimize the cost of governing the area as well as the transaction costs of appropriating

---

[66]Ibid., p. 24.
[67]Ibid., p. 186.

labor and produce.[68] State spaces tend to encompass large "core areas" of highly concentrated grain production "within a few days' march from the court center," not necessarily contiguous with the center but at least "relatively accessible to officials and soldiers from the center via trade routes or navigable waterways."[69] Governable areas are mainly areas of high-density agricultural production linked either by flat terrain or watercourses.[70]

The nonstate space is a direct inversion of the state space: it is "state repelling"; i.e., "it represents an agro-ecological setting singularly unfavorable to manpower- and grain-amassing strategies of states." States "will hesitate to incorporate such areas, inasmuch as the return, in manpower and grain, is likely to be less than the administrative and military costs of appropriating it."

Nonstate spaces benefit from various forms of "friction" that increase the transaction costs of appropriating labor and output, and of extending the reach of the state's enforcement arm into such regions. These forms of friction include the friction of distance[71] (which amounts to a distance tax on centralized control), the friction of terrain or altitude, and the friction of seasonal weather.[72] In regard to the latter, for example, the local population might "wait for the rains, when supply lines broke down (or were easier to cut) and the garrison was faced with starvation or retreat."[73]

In Zomia, as Scott describes it:

> Virtually everything about these people's livelihoods, social organization, ideologies, ...can be read as strate-

---

[68] James Scott, *The Art of Not Being Governed: An Anarchist History of Upland Southeast Asia* (New Haven and London: Yale University Press, 2009), pp. 40-41.
[69] Ibid., p. 53.
[70] Ibid., p. 58.
[71] Ibid., p. 51.
[72] Ibid., p. 61.
[73] Ibid., p. 63.

gic positionings designed to keep the state at arm's length. Their physical dispersion in rugged terrain, their mobility, their cropping practices, their kinship structure, their pliable ethnic identities, and their devotion to prophetic, millenarian leaders effectively serve to avoid incorporation into states and to prevent states from springing up among them.[74]

One of Graeber's primary examples of what Scott would call a nonstate space comes from Madagascar, where the western coast from the sixteenth through the nineteenth centuries was divided into several related kingdoms under a common dynasty, collectively known as the Sakalava. In the difficult, hilly terrain of northwest Madagascar there lived a people called the Tsimihety, whose name is derived from their refusal—as required by the custom of the surrounding kingdoms—to cut their hair in honor of a deceased monarch. Like Zomians, they organize their societies is mostly egalitarian ways, outside the administrative reach of surrounding states. And like Zomians, they rely on mobility and distance to avoid governance by any would-be authorities.[75]

> ...under the French administrators would complain that they could send delegations to arrange for labor to build a road near a Tsimihety village, negotiate the terms with apparently cooperative elders, and return with the equipment a week later only to discover the village entirely abandoned—every single inhabitant had moved in with some relative in another part of the country.[76]

They are regarded as an ethnic group in Madagascar. But their origins lie entirely in their political project of refusing governance by the institutions to which surrounding peoples,

---

[74]Ibid., x.
[75]Graeber, *Fragments*, pp. 54-55.
[76]Ibid., p. 55.

who speak essentially the same language and share most of the same traditions, have submitted.

> The desire to live free of Sakalava domination was translated into a desire—one which came to suffuse all social institutions from village assemblies to mortuary ritual—to live in a society free of markers of hierarchy. This then became institutionalized as a way of life of a community living together, which then in turn came to be thought of as a particular "kind" of people, an ethnic group—people who also, since they tend to intermarry, come to be seen as united by common ancestry.[77]

This model of ethnogenesis—through deliberate fission and withdrawal—is, Graeber says, a relatively new concept to anthropologists. But as we saw in my previous paper on James Scott, it's central to his analysis of Zomian populations.

A central feature of Graeber's thought, as we have already seen, is his general view of the continuity between "primitive" and "modern" (i.e., Western) societies, and his view of the body of knowledge of anthropology concerning the experiences of people in so-called "primitive" societies as a common heritage of humanity that's directly relevant to our own concerns in the West.

Scott does not explicitly develop the analogy between Zomian/nonstate spaces, and autonomist technology and liberatory technology in the West. But Graeber very much does so, relating his Zomian model of counterpower and ethnogenesis to the concept of "exodus" in Western autonomist theory. Is his analysis of the Tsimihety and similar people "relevant to contemporary concerns?" he asks.

> Very much so, it seems to me. Autonomist thinkers in Italy have, over the last couple decades, developed a theory of what they call revolutionary "exodus." It

---

[77]Ibid., p. 55.

> is inspired in part by particularly Italian conditions—the broad refusal of factory work among young people, the flourishing of squats and occupied "social centers" in so many Italian cities.... But in all this Italy seems to have acted as a kind of laboratory for future social movements, anticipating trends that are now beginning to happen on a global scale.
>
> The theory of exodus proposes that the most effective way of opposing capitalism and the liberal state is not through direct confrontation but by means of what Paolo Virno has called "engaged withdrawal," mass defection by those wishing to create new forms of community. One need only glance at the historical record to confirm that most successful forms of popular resistance have taken precisely this form. They have not involved challenging power head on (this usually leads to being slaughtered, or if not, turning into some—often even uglier—variant of the very thing one first challenged) but from one or another strategy of slipping away from its grasp, from flight, desertion, the founding of new communities.[78]

This is a parallel I tried to draw in my analysis of Scott, as a model for anarchists in advanced technological societies: withdrawal into "nonstate spaces" based, not on actual spatial separation or withdrawal, but on reducing legibility and governability, and creating counterpower, while remaining where we are.

The concepts of "state space" and "nonstate space," if removed from Scott's immediate spatial context and applied by way of analogy to spheres of social and economic life that are more or less amenable to state control, can be useful for us in the kinds of developed Western societies where to all appearances there are no geographical spaces beyond the control of the state.

State spaces in our economy are sectors which are closely

---

[78] Ibid., pp. 60-61.

allied to and legible to the state. Nonstate spaces are those which are hard to monitor and where regulations are hard to enforce. State spaces, especially, are associated with legible forms of production. In the Western economies, the economic sectors most legible to and closely allied to the state are those dominated by large corporations in oligopoly markets.

The same effects achieved through spatial distance and isolation and the high costs of physical transportation in Scott's Zomia can be achieved in our economy, without all the inconvenience, through expedients such as encryption and the use of darknets, and the dispersal of physical production into small cooperative spaces through cheap micromanufacturing technologies. Recent technological developments have drastically expanded the potential for non-spatially, non-territorially based versions of the nonstate spaces that Scott describes. People can remove themselves from state space by adopting technologies and methods of organization that make them illegible to the state, without any actual movement in space.

Anything that reduces the "EROEI" of the system, the size of the net surplus which the state is able to extract, will cause the state to shrink to a smaller equilibrium scale of activity. The more costly enforcement is and the smaller the revenues the state (and its corporate allies, as in the case of enforcing digital copyright law or suppressing shanzhai knockoffs) can obtain per unit of enforcement effort, the hollower the state capitalist or corporatist system becomes and the more areas of life it retreats from as not worth the cost of governing.

This attempt to draw a parallel between ungovernable Third World areas and ungovernable spaces in Western societies is another example of Graeber's project for "tearing down of conceptual walls" between anthropological analysis of "primitive" cultures and the analysis of political, economic, and social alternatives within the "advanced" societies. The lessons of anthropology are not of purely antiquarian interest, concerning what people lived like before they became advanced enough to invent states. They're a common conceptual treasury of humankind, with lessons for *us* about what our alternatives are *here and now*—"an infinitely richer conception of how alternative forms of revolutionary action might work."[79]

Graeber goes on to cite Peter Lamborn's (aka Hakim Bey's) work on "pirate utopias" as an example of how historical case-studies of autonomous spaces provide models for secession and exodus from the system for us.[80]

He discusses, in particular, what examples from anthropology have to say about exodus and counter-institution building as alternatives to directly confronting the state.

> Most of these little utopias were even more marginal than the Vezo or Tsimihety were in Madagascar; all of them were eventually gobbled up. Which leads to the question of how to neutralize the state apparatus itself, in the absence of a politics of direct confrontation. No doubt some states and corporate elites will collapse of their own dead weight; a few already have; but it's hard to imagine a scenario in which they all will. Here, the Sakalava and BaKongo might be able to provide us some useful suggestions. What cannot be destroyed can, nonetheless, be diverted, frozen, transformed, and gradually deprived of its substance—which in the case of states, is ultimately their capacity to inspire terror. What would this mean under contemporary conditions? It's not entirely clear. Perhaps existing state apparati will gradually be reduced to window-dressing as the substance is pulled out of them from above and below: i.e., both from the growth of international institutions, and from devolution to local and regional forms of self-governance. Perhaps government by media spectacle

---

[79]Ibid., p. 61.
[80]Ibid., p. 62.

will devolve into spectacle pure and simple (somewhat along the lines of what Paul Lafargue, Marx's West Indian son-in-law and author of *The Right to Be Lazy*, implied when he suggested that after the revolution, politicians would still be able to fulfill a useful social function in the entertainment industry). More likely it will happen in ways we cannot even anticipate. But no doubt there are ways in which it is happening already. As Neoliberal states move towards new forms of feudalism, concentrating their guns increasingly around gated communities, insurrectionary spaces open up that we don't even know about. The Merina rice farmers described in the last section understand what many would-be revolutionaries do not: that there are times when the stupidest thing one could possibly do is raise a red or black flag and issue defiant declarations. Sometimes the sensible thing is just to pretend nothing has changed, allow official state representatives to keep their dignity, even show up at their offices and fill out a form now and then, but otherwise, ignore them.[81]

In other words, the most cost-effective way of supplanting the state is evasion—attacking it indirectly, through its power of enforcement. Fighting within the system to change the law, as much of the establishment Left does, is a loser's game. Participating in the process requires enormous resources of funding and effort—giving the advantage to the participants with the most money and the most lobbyists and lawyers on retainer. For a tiny fraction of the cost of getting "a seat at the table" and getting a few minor changes in punctuation in regulations drafted by the regulated industries, we can instead develop technologies of evasion that make those regulations unenforceable. As Charles Johnson argues:

> If you put all your hope for social change in legal reform...then...you will find yourself outmaneuvered

---
[81]Ibid., pp. 62-64.

at every turn by those who have the deepest pockets
and the best media access and the tightest connections. There is no hope for turning this system against
them; because, after all, the system was made for
them and the system was made by them. Reformist
political campaigns inevitably turn out to suck a lot
of time and money into the politics—with just about
none of the reform coming out on the other end.

Far more cost-effective is "bypassing those laws and making them irrelevant to your life." [82] A law that can't be enforced is as good as no law at all. And a society where no laws can be enforced, despite the continued existence of a state claiming authority to make such laws on behalf of a given territory, is as good as an anarchist society—indeed, it *is* an anarchist society.

John Robb, a specialist on asymmetric warfare and networked organization, argues that to disrupt centralized, hierarchical systems, it's not necessary to take over or destroy even a significant portion of their infrastructures. It's only necessary to destroy the most vulnerable of their key nodes and render the overall system non-functional.

These vulnerable, high-value nodes are what Robb calls the *Systempunkt*. It's a concept borrowed from German blitzkrieg doctrine. The *Schwerpunkt* was the most vulnerable point in an enemy's defenses, on which an offensive should concentrate most of its force in order to achieve a breakthrough. Once this small portion of the enemy's forces was destroyed, the rest could be bypassed and encircled without direct engagement. Likewise, according to Robb's *Systempunkt* concept, a few thousand dollars spent incapacitating several nodes in a gas or oil pipeline system can result in disruption that costs billions in economic damage from fuel shortages and spikes in prices.[83]

---

[82]Charles Johnson, "Counter-Economic Optimism," *Rad Geek People's Daily*, February 7, 2009.

[83]John Robb, "THE SYSTEMPUNKT," *Global Guerrillas*, December

Actually capturing the bulk of the system's infrastructure would be enormously costly—quite possibly costing the attacker more than it cost the enemy in economic damage.

We can apply these lessons to our own movement to supplant the state. Conventional politics aims at taking over the state's policy apparatus and using it to implement one's own goals. But taking over the state through conventional politics is enormously costly.

To a certain extent, from the perspective of the plutocrats and crony capitalists who run the system, the state itself is a *Systempunkt*—if, that is, you start out with enough money to make seizing the key node a realistic possibility. A large corporation may donate a few hundred thousands to campaign funds or spend a similar amount hiring lobbyists, and in return secure billions in corporate welfare or regulatory benefits from the state.

But from our standpoint, that's out of the question. Victory in conventional politics means we have to out-compete billionaires in a bidding war to control the state, and outdo them in navigating the rules of a policy-making process that their money already controls. The odds of carrying that off are about the same as the odds of beating the house in Vegas. You have to out-compete the RIAA in influencing "intellectual property" law, ADM and Cargill in setting USDA policy, the insurance industry in setting healthcare policy—and so on, ad nauseam.

So how do anarchists deal with the state? How do we respond to state interventions, which protect its privileged corporate clients from competition by suppressing low-overhead, self-organized alternatives? How do we get the freedom to organize our lives the way we want, in the face of a government dedicated to keeping us on the corporate reservation in order to meet all our needs?

We must find some weak point besides gaining control of

19, 2004. http://globalguerrillas.typepad.com/globalguerrillas/2004/12/the_systempunkt.html; Robb, *Brave New War*, pp. 99-100.

the state. For us, the state's *Systempunkt* is its enforcement capability. By attacking the state at its weak point, its ability to enforce its laws, we can neutralize its ability to interfere with our building the kind of society we want here and now—and we can do so at a tiny fraction of the cost of gaining power through conventional politics.

For example, conducting torrent downloads under cover of darknets, with the help of encryption and proxies, is a lot cheaper than trying to out-compete the money and lobbyists of the RIAA in influencing "intellectual property" law. The same is true of local zoning and licensing laws, which protect incumbent businesses from competition by low-overhead household microenterprises, and of attempts to enforce industrial patents against neighborhood micromanufacturers. To a large extent, similar measures—encrypted local currencies and barter systems, secure trust networks, etc.—can neutralize government's power to tax and regulate the counter-economy out of existence.

Trying to capture the state is a loser's game. But we don't have to sieze control of the state or change the laws in order to end the special privileges of big business and the rentier classes. We just have to make the law unenforceable, so we can ignore it.

Like Elinor Ostrom, Graeber analyzes states and other authoritarian institutions in terms of their practical power as one institution in a cluster of many, and not their idealized, totalizing projection of themselves.

> States have a peculiar dual character. They are at the same time forms of institutionalized raiding or extortion, and utopian projects. The first certainly reflects the way states are actually experienced, by any communities that retain some degree of autonomy; the second however is how they tend to appear in the written record.

In one sense states are the "imaginary totality" par excellence, and much of the confusion entailed in theories of the state historically lies in an inability or unwillingness to recognize this. For the most part, states were ideas, ways of imagining social order as something one could get a grip on, models of control. This is why the first known works of social theory, whether from Persia, or China, or ancient Greece, were always framed as theories of statecraft. This has had two disastrous effects. One is to give utopianism a bad name. (The word "utopia" first calls to mind the image of an ideal city, usually, with perfect geometry— the image seems to hearken back originally to the royal military camp: a geometrical space which is entirely the emanation of a single, individual will, a fantasy of total control.) All this has had dire political consequences, to say the least. The second is that we tend to assume that states, and social order, even societies, largely correspond. In other words, we have a tendency to take the most grandiose, even paranoid, claims of world-rulers seriously, assuming that whatever cosmological projects they claimed to be pursuing actually did correspond, at least roughly, to something on the ground. Whereas it is likely that in many such cases, these claims ordinarily only applied fully within a few dozen yards of the monarch in any direction, and most subjects were much more likely to see ruling elites, on a day-to-day basis, as something much along the lines of predatory raiders.

An adequate theory of states would then have to begin by distinguishing in each case between the relevant ideal of rulership (which can be almost anything, a need to enforce military style discipline, the ability to provide perfect theatrical representation of gracious living which will inspire others, the need to provide the gods with endless human hearts to fend off the apocalypse...), and the mechanics of rule, without assuming that there is necessarily all that much correspondence between them.[84]

His proposed theory of the state is a project "to reanalyze the state as a relation between a utopian imaginary and a messy reality involving strategies of flight and evasion, predatory elites, and a mechanics of regulation and control.[85]

Graeber's agenda of counter-institution building must be coupled with attacks on the central structural supports of the present system.

> For at least 5,000 years, before capitalism even existed, popular movements have tended to center on struggles over debt. There is a reason for this. Debt is the most efficient means ever created to make relations fundamentally based on violence and inequality seem morally upright. When this trick no longer works everything explodes, as it is now. Debt has revealed itself as the greatest weakness of the system, the point where it spirals out of control. But debt also allows endless opportunities for organizing. Some speak of a debtors' strike or debtors' cartel. Perhaps so, but at the very least we can start with a pledge against evictions. Neighborhood by neighborhood we can pledge to support each other if we are driven from our homes. This power does not solely challenge regimes of debt, it challenges the moral foundation of capitalism.[86]

The best way of attacking these structural supports, as we already considered in the case of nonstate spaces, is by undermining or evading the state's enforcement machinery, and building counter-institutions in the interstices of the present system that will eventually supplant it, rather than direct confrontation. As my friend Katherine Gallagher put it:[87]

---

[84]Graeber, *Fragments of an Anarchist Anthropology*, pp. 65-66.
[85]Ibid., p. 68.
[86]Graeber, "The Machinery of Hopelessness."
[87]Redacted into paragraph form from a series of tweets by Katherine Gallagher (@zhinxy) in July 2012.

For me it's about stretching out our networks of what's possible across borders, about decentralizing.... "We" will be transnational, and distributed. We won't be encircled by "them," but woven through their antiquated structures, impossible to quarantine off and finish. I'm not a pacifist. I'm not at all against defensive violence. That's a separate question to me of overthrow. But to oversimplify, when it comes to violence, I want it to be the last stand of a disintegrating order against an emerging order that has already done much of the hard work of building its ideals/structures. Not violent revolutionaries sure that their society will be viable, ready to build it, but a society defending itself against masters that no longer rule it. Build the society and defend it, don't go forth with the guns and attempt to bring anarchy about in the rubble.

I think technology is increasingly putting the possibility of meaningful resistance and worker independence within the realm of a meaningful future. So much of the means of our oppression is now more susceptible to being duplicated on a human scale (and so much of patent warfare seems to be aimed at preventing this).

And I think we should be working on how we plan to create a parallel industry that is not held only by those few. More and more the means to keep that industry held only by the few are held in the realm of patent law. It is no longer true that the few own the "lathe" so to speak, nearly as much as they own the patent to it. So we truly could achieve more by creating real alternative manufacture than seizing that built. Yes, there will be protective violence, but it's not as true as it was in the past that there is real necessary means of production in the hands of the few. What they control more now is access to the methods of production and try to prevent those methods being used outside of their watch. Again,

I'm not saying that the "last days" of the state won't be marked by violence. But I am saying we now have real tactical options beyond confronting them directly *until* they come to us.

BIBLIOGRAPHY

Bennet, Drake. "David Graeber, the Anti-Leader of Occupy Wall Street" *BusinessWeek*, October 26, 2011. http://www.businessweek.com/printer/magazine/david-graeber-the-antileader-of-occupy-wall-street-10262011.html

Ellen Evans and Jon Moses. "Interview with David Graeber" *White Review*, December 7, 2011. http://www.thewhitereview.org/interviews/interview-with-david-graeber/

Larry Gambone. "Why the Dominators Hate Direct Democracy" *Porcupine Blog*, May 25, 2014. http://porkupineblog.blogspot.com/2014/05/why-dominators-hate-direct-democracy.html

David Graeber. "Are You an Anarchist? The Answer May Surprise You" (Anarchist Library, 2000). http://theanarchistlibrary.org/library/david-graeber-are-you-an-anarchist-the-answer-may-surprise-you

Graeber. *Beyond Power/Knowledge: An Exploration of the Relation of Power, Ignorance, and Stupidity.* (Malinowski Memorial Lecture: Thu-rsday 25 May 2006).

Graeber. *Debt: The First 5,000 Years* (Brooklyn and London: Melville House, 2011).

Graeber. *The Democracy Project: A History, a Crisis, a Movement* (Spiegel & Grau, 2013).

Graeber. *Fragments of an Anarchist Anthropology* (Chicago: Prickly Paradigm Press, 2004).

Graeber. "The Machinery of Hopelessness" *Adbusters*, April 29, 2009. http://www.nytimes.co

m/2012/12/14/business/colleges-debt-falls-on-students-after-construction-binges.html

Graeber. "The New Anarchists" *New Left Review* 13 (January-February 2002). http://newleftreview.org/II/13/david-graeber-the-new-anarchists

Graeber. "On Playing By The Rules—The Strange Success of OccupyWallStreet" *Countercurrents.org*, October 23, 2011. http://www.countercurrents.org/graeber241011l.htm

Graeber. "A Practical Utopian's Guide to the Coming Collapse" *The Baffler* 23 (2013). http://www.thebaffler.com/past/practical_utopians_guide

Andrej Grubacic and David Graeber. "Anarchism, or the Revolutionary Movement of the Twenty-first Century" (2004). In *David Graeber: Collection of Essays* (The Anarchist Library. Anti-Copyright February 5, 2012).

Charles Johnson. "Counter-Economic Optimism" *Rad Geek People's Daily*, February 7, 2009. http://radgeek.com/gt/2009/02/07/countereconomic_optimism/

John Robb. *Brave New War: The Next Stage of Terrorism and the End of Globalization* (Hoboken: John Wiley & Sons, Inc., 2007).

Robb. "THE SYSTEMPUNKT," *Global Guerrillas*, December 19, 2004. http://globalguerrillas.typepad.com/globalguerrillas/2004/12/the_systempunkt.html

James Scott. *The Art of Not Being Governed: An Anarchist History of Upland Southeast Asia* (New Haven and London: Yale University Press, 2009).

Scott. *Seeing Like a State* (New Haven and London: Yale University Press, 1998).

CHAPTER
NINE

"PUBLIC" VS. "PRIVATE" SECTOR

KEVIN CARSON

The distinction between the state, or "public" sector, and the "private" sector economy is universal in commentary and policy analysis. But in the case of the corporate economy, it's almost meaningless. First of all, the large corporation cannot be called "private property" in any meaningful sense. And second, the relationship between the corporate economy and the state resembles nothing so much as an interlocking directorate.

1. *The idea of the large corporation as the "private property" of its shareholders is, in most cases, utter nonsense.*

Berle and Means, in *The Modern Corporation and Private Property*,[1] pointed this out as long ago as 1932. Even right-leaning libertarian defenders of the corporation are forced, against their instincts, to minimize the shareholder's real ownership ties to the corporation.

---

c4ss.org/content/12941

[1] http://books.google.com/books?id=mLdLHhqxUb4C&printsec=frontcover&source=gbs_atb#v=onepage&q&f=false

The orthodox teaching among Mises's followers is that of the "entrepreneurial corporation": the corporation is not a managerial bureaucracy, but a simple extension of the entrepreneur's will, subject to his absolute control through the magic of double-entry bookkeeping. For instance, in "Sean Gabb's Thoughts on Limited Liability,"[2] Stephan Kinsella started out by citing Hessen's defense of the corporation as a simple contractual device by which the owners of capital manage their joint property, no different in principle from a partnership.

But in the same article Kinsella, in order to justify shareholder limited liability, suggested that the difference between shareholder and lender was only one of degree, and that the shareholder was simply another class of contractual claimant (as opposed to residual claimant, or owner). He was forced, in fact, to retreat to an argument very like that of Berle and Means: that the shareholder's "property" in the corporation is largely fictitious, and that real ownership is associated with control.

> What are the basic rights of a shareholder? What is he "buying" when he buys the "share"? Well, he has the right to vote—to elect directors, basically. He has the right to attend shareholder meetings. He has the right to a certain share of the net remaining assets of the company in the event it winds up or dissolves, after it pays off creditors, etc. He has the right to receive a certain share of dividends paid IF the company decides to pay dividends—that is, he has a right to be treated on some kind of equal footing with other shareholders—he has no absolute right to get a dividend (even if the company has profits), but only a conditional, relative one. He has (usually) the right to sell his shares to someone else. Why assume this bundle of rights is tantamount to "natural ownership"—of what? Of the company's assets? But

---

[2] http://archive.mises.org/005679/

he has no right to (directly) control the assets. He has no right to use the corporate jet or even enter the company's facilities, without permission of the management. Surely the right to attend meetings is not all that relevant. Nor the right to receive part of the company's assets upon winding up or upon payment of dividends—this could be characterized as the right a type of lender or creditor has.

In the comments below, he added:

I think the manager is more analogous to a sole proprietor. They have similar control in making policy, hiring, and directing employees. You [quasibill] think the shareholder and proprietor have more in common—because they are both "owners."

And in a comment[3] at my blog,[4] he wrote:

It is bizarre that there is this notion that owners of property are automatically liable for crimes done with their property... Moreover, property just means the right to control. This right to control can be divided in varied and complex ways. If you think shareholders are "owners" of corporate property just like they own their homes or cars—well, just buy a share of Exxon stock and try to walk into the boardroom without permission.

In fact even the right to elect the Board of Directors, the only real right of control possessed by shareholders, is largely symbolic. Corporations are generally controlled by inside directors who engage in mutual logrolling with the CEO, and a proxy fight by shareholders is usually doomed from the outset.

---

[3]http://mutualist.blogspot.com/2006/04/corporate-personhood.html #c115877811800163664

[4]http://mutualist.blogspot.com/2006/04/corporate-personhood.html

The threat of hostile takeover, of which corporate defenders have made so much in their arguments for "a market in corporate control,"[5] was in fact a significant threat only for a limited time in the early- and mid-'80s, immediately following the junk bond innovation in corporate finance. Even then, arguably, the hostile takeover was the action, not of investors, but of the management of the acquiring corporation acting in their own interests. In any case, corporate management quickly altered the internal rules of corporate governance to make hostile takeover extremely difficult through such devices as "poison pills," "greenmail," and "shark repellent." As a result, from the late '80s on, most takeovers were friendly actions, made *in collusion with* the management of the acquired firm.

The dominant model of MBA behavior since the 1980s, arguably, amounts to management promoting its own interests at the expense of the shareholder: starving, milking, and asset-stripping, and generally gutting the long-term productivity of the enterprise, in order to inflate artificially high short-term numbers, and game their own bonuses and stock options.

That's why the big retailers have essentially stripped themselves of human capital. Thirty years ago if you walked into a store, you were likely to be served by career employees who knew the product lines and customer tastes inside and out. Today if you go into Lowe's and need help, the likely response from the minimum-wage high school kid is "I dunno. I guess if you don't see it, we ain't got it." That's why, when you go into a hospital, your nurse is likely to have eight patients (and your orderly ten, fifteen, or even thirty patients), and you can expect to go five days without a bath or linen change, and shit the bed waiting forty-five minutes for a bedpan. And you'd better count on getting an MRSA infection before you get out. An MBA is someone who would break up all the furniture in his house and burn it in the

---

[5] http://web.archive.org/web/20080725052342/; http://www.mises.org/story/2786

fireplace, and then brag about how much he'd saved on the heating bill this month.

Generally speaking, Michels's *Iron Law of Oligarchy*[6] operates in the corporation: corporate management will always have an advantage over those on the outside it allegedly "represents," in gaming the internal rules to thwart outside control.

To summarize this portion, the corporation in practice is simply a free-floating aggregation of unowned capital, controlled by a self-perpetuating managerial oligarchy which exercises all the material rights of control without ever having acquired an "ownership" right by any legitimate means (i.e., by actually buying into the equity it controls and uses to feather its own nest).

The obvious comparison is to the thousands of industrial enterprises in the Soviet state economy. They were theoretically the "property" of the people or the workers, who exercised no actual control over them. In practice, they were controlled by the upper levels of the Party and state apparatus, a self-perpetuating managerial oligarchy which milked the state economy to support their lavish lifestyle of dachas, fancy cars, and GUM department store privileges.

The modern corporate enterprise is not the legitimate property of *anyone*. It isn't the "property" of the shareholders at all, in any meaningful sense. And although it's the de facto property of the managers who loot it for their own benefit, it doesn't belong to them in any *legitimate* sense.

2. *The boundary between the corporate economy and the centralized state, likewise, is largely fictitious.*

If we went back in time seven hundred years, it would be meaningless to ask whether some great feudal lord was a "private" landowner or part of the state. In that society, the landowning classes *were* the state, and the state was

---

[6]https://en.wikipedia.org/wiki/Iron_law_of_oligarchy

the landowning classes' rent collection agency. The great landlords, under the Old Regime, controlled the commanding heights of the state apparatus; the king and his nobles owned the land of the entire realm in feudal legal theory, and used the state's coercive power to extract rents from the people actually living on and working the land.

Under modern state capitalism, likewise, the management of the corporate economy and the management of the state apparatus consist largely of the same rotating pool of personnel.

A typical pattern is for the same individual to go from being a director or vice president in some large corporation, to being an under-secretary or assistant secretary or deputy agency chief appointed under some administration, and then back to being a director or senior manager in a large corporation. The interlocking directorate system, that ties together the large banks and industrial corporations, also includes the state. It's hard not to think of Marx's catchy little phrase: "executive committee of the ruling class."

At the same time, the several hundred dominant firms in the corporate economy, and the structure of power they constitute, depend on ongoing state intervention for their continued existence. The state subsidizes their operating costs, to the extent that for many of the Fortune 500 the total sum of direct and indirect corporate welfare exceeds their profit margin; if state subsidies and differential tax advantages were eliminated, they would immediately start bleeding red ink and sell off subsidiary enterprises at fire sale prices until we had a Fortune 50,000. And with the collapse of profitability and share value that would result from the extraction of the government teat, it's likely that many of those enterprises would be bought up at pennies on the dollar by their own workers, or simply abandoned to workers (like the recuperated enterprises of Argentina).

The stability of corporate oligopoly markets, and the administered (or "cost-plus markup") pricing that they make possible, depend on the cartelizing effect of state regulations in protecting the large corporations from full-blown market competition.

This is true, especially, of so-called "intellectual property," which is the biggest single tool for cartelizing industry. AT&T was built on the foundation of the Bell Patent Association. Numerous industries have created cartels by the exchange or pooling of patents (for example, Westinghouse and GE cartelized the home appliance industry in the 1920s by pooling their patents). The American chemical industry was created almost from scratch during WWI, when the Justice Department seized German chemical patents and distributed them among the fledgling American chemical firms. Alfred Chandler's account of the dominant firms in the early consumer electronics industry consists almost entirely of which patents were owned by which firm.

The dominant sectors in the global corporate economy depend almost entirely on a business model based not just on copyright and patent ownership, but on the draconian upward ratcheting of IP law under the Uruguay Round of GATT and the Digital Millennium Copyright Act: entertainment, software, electronics, biotech, and pharmaceuticals. They would not exist in a remotely recognizable form without these state-enforced monopolies.

International IP law, specifically the long terms of patents, locks transnational corporations into control of the latest generation of production technology, and effectively relegates Third World countries to the supply of sweatshop labor for Western-owned capital.

Intellectual property plays the same central protectionist role in today's corporate global economy that tariffs did for the old national corporate economies.

Most safety and quality regulations serve in practice to limit competition in terms of the features covered by those regulations. The minimum standards enforced by the regulations usually become a maximum. Their effect is exactly the same as if all the firms in an industry got together to formulate an industry quality and safety code in order to reduce quality and safety competition to a manageable level, except that by acting through the state they avoid the destabilizing possibility of defection by individual firms. And in practice, safety and quality regulations absolve the corporation from meeting any standard of civil liability higher than the state's dumbed-down, lowest common denominator regulatory standard. Under the common law of nuisance, as it existed into the early nineteenth century before the courts eviscerated it to make it more "business-friendly," a firm was liable for any harm it caused—period. Today, if a firm pollutes the air or water in a manner that causes objective harm, but falls within the limits set by the EPA, it can use those limits as a fig-leaf to escape tort liability for the harm it does. Monsanto has attempted to use FDA standards as a club to suppress commercial free speech, arguing that it should be illegal to advertise milk as free from recombinant Bovine Growth Hormone; it is libelous, they say with a straight face, to suggest there is something deficient in practices which fully meet FDA standards.

On the most general scale, Gabriel Kolko argued that it was the *Clayton Antitrust Act*[7] which first made stable oligopoly markets possible. Its prohibition of "unfair competition" made destabilizing price wars illegal for the first time, and for all intents and purposes placed each industry under a government-sponsored trade association.

The best analogy I've ever seen for understanding the close ties between the state and the corporate economy, and their conjunction in a single state capitalist ruling class, was thought up by Brad Spangler, in "Recognizing Faux Private Interests that are Actually Part of the State":

> Let's postulate two sorts of robbery scenarios.

---

[7]https://en.wikipedia.org/wiki/Clayton_Antitrust_Act

- In one, a lone robber points a gun at you and takes your cash. All libertarians would recognize this as a micro-example of any kind of government at work, resembling most closely State Socialism.

- In the second, depicting State Capitalism, one robber (the literal apparatus of government) keeps you covered with a pistol while the second (representing State-allied corporations) just holds the bag that you have to drop your wristwatch, wallet, and car keys in. To say that your interaction with the bagman was a "voluntary transaction" is an absurdity. Such nonsense should be condemned by all libertarians.

Both gunman and bagman together are the true State.[8]

The implication of this, he followed up elsewhere,[9] is that "the true state is the entire political class, the parasitic net beneficiaries of the coercive apparatus of government." And more specifically, "corrupt government 'privatization' schemes that benefit large corporations are thus seen as mere transfer of assets to a different arm of the political class..." In fact, he cited Murray Rothbard's argument, which I plan to treat more fully in a future post, that corporations that get the majority of their profits from state intervention should simply be regarded as state enterprises and expropriated by their own workers, transformed into "genuine" private property in the form of worker cooperatives.

Update: TGGP,[10] in a comment to another thread, posted a link to an excellent piece at *2Blowhards* I'd forgotten about:

---

[8] http://c4ss.org/content/15324
[9] http://web.archive.org/web/20080409192320/; http://www.rationalreview.com/content/5266
[10] http://entitledtoanopinion.wordpress.com/

"The New Class and Its Government Nexus, Part I."[11] It described the New Middle Class as a collection of

> financiers, senior corporate and government bureaucrats, and professionals (doctors, lawyers, accountants, etc.), all of whom collect high incomes without being required to put their own money at risk. These people make up most of the people in the top 10% of the income distribution, and a very high percentage indeed of people in the top 1% of the income distribution. (Another, much smaller chunk, of the people in the top 10% and the top 1% are entrepreneurs, who are assuredly not members of the New Class; they are economic experimenters and risk takers, as their high bankruptcy rate demonstrates.)

This ties in with what I said above. Corporate management, through its control of organizations, collects all the benefits of actual property ownership. But because what it exercises is mere *control* over property that really isn't owned by anybody, it has none of the risk of personal loss that comes from having actually invested their own resources by buying into the property (holding, at best, stock options that are a tiny fraction of the equity they control).

I believe this was one of Mises's criticisms of the Lange model of market socialism: the manager of a state-owned enterprise was not a genuine entrepreneur, even when he had administrative incentives to maximize the profits of the enterprise, because all he risked was loss of future income; he didn't risk the value of the enterprise itself, because he hadn't invested his personal wealth in it.

---

[11] http://c4ss.org/content/13791

CHAPTER
TEN

GEOGRAPHY AND ANARCHY: A LIBERTARIAN SOCIAL ORDER AS GOAL

THOM HOLTERMAN

The earth's surface, the natural environment, human, animal, and plant life, but also the culture, have all been mapped out for centuries. Old cartography and engravings often show this with striking images. How one understands and interprets this mapping and imaging will depend largely upon the state of scientific development at the time. The reasons why people begin this activity can differ greatly.

Can the space be exploited? What about the possibility of trade, industry, and traffic, which logistical problems will incur? These questions relate to imperialist objectives. There are geographers who offer their services to answer these questions. In the nineteenth century the objectives of imperialist nations such as England, France, and Germany contributed to the development of a nationalist geography.

Not every geographer, just as every economist, sociologist, or lawyer, is willing to serve the development or application of nationalist, imperialist objectives. The rejection is due to the difference in ideological perspective, which is chosen. This approach simultaneously determines scientific development. Because the ideas of the French geographer Élisée Reclus (1830-1905)[1] will be central here, it is not so strange to choose anarchy as the ideological perspective.

Anarchy refers to a state of order without an imposed government and without imposed rules. It is about order, which is self-chosen or has a freely accepted structure. The question now is, what is the possible link between geography and anarchy? It is this question that is formulated by the French social geographer Philippe Pelletier in his recently published book *Géographie et anarchie: Reclus, Kropotkine, Metchnikoff et d'autres*.

The author, besides teaching geography at one of the universities in Lyon, is active in the anarchist movement. He publishes regularly on both subjects.

* Introduction

For the purpose of answering the question of the possible link between geography and anarchy, it is necessary to discuss a number of previous questions. Pelletier does this especially in the first part of his book. Then it should be clarified that there are several choices to be made, depending on the ideological "spectacles" that one uses. It matters greatly whether personal presuppositions are being influenced by anarchist elements or ideological elements of a capitalist and nationalist kind. Pelletier maps these differences out relevant to the kind of geography that is developed, in the second part of his book.

Although Élisée Reclus plays a leading part in Pelletier's

---

[1] The most Élisée Reclus has published about geography is his unprecedented *La Nouvelle Géographie universelle, la terre et les hommes*, Hachette, Paris, 1876-1894, 19 volumes. Towards the end of his life he completed *L'Homme et la Terre*, Librairie Universelle, Paris, 1905-1908, 6 parts, in which he explicitly elaborated on his "social geography."

book, it has not become a Reclus biography. Significantly he puts in the title of his book, next to Reclus, the geographers/anarchists and his friends, Peter Kropotkin (1842-1921) and Leon Metchnikoff (1838-1888). Reclus does have a distinct stamp on the kind of geography that he operates. He has called this "social geography." In addition, Pelletier also speaks of "Reclusian geography." In short, Reclus has claimed attention in many ways.

This makes a person vulnerable to insults. But are these indeed justified? Did Reclus defend colonialism, which is asserted, and would he not be free of anti-semitism? In the third part of his book Pelletier responds to such insults and he makes it clear that these are without any foundation. In this part he also deals with some themes that are dear to Reclus, such as the development of the social phenomenon: the city.

The work of Reclus has influenced both geography and anarchism. Each continuously overlaps the other. In order to provide an insight into the heart of those thoughts, I will first discuss some concepts or phenomena in pairs, taking Pelletier's text as a point of reference.

The first pair concerns "geography and anarchy": to what do these concepts refer? This then leads to the pair "anarchists and geography": why are anarchists interested in geography? After that we come to the "anarchist position and science." Anarchism (and anarchy) is not a science, but some anarchists are called scientists. Does the one have an impact on the other?

If this has repercussions, is this reflected in the type of geography in which one is engaged? This question refers to the following theme, in which the core is formed by the phenomenon of "border." The accumulated sum of knowledge leads Reclus, towards the end of his life, to what he calls "social geography." Finally, one can find here a summary by Pelletier successfully defending Reclus against unjust criticism.

✻ *Geography and Anarchy*

Previously, Pelletier notes in his book that when we wander through the countryside, then we engage with geography. This is what I call a functional description of the object of study. What purpose does geography serve? It can be used for diplomacy and warfare (geography serves in the making of topographic maps for commanders) and for discovering areas that can be exploited (colonialism, imperialism).

Such a functional description, as opposed to an essentialist definition (what is geography?), is an open description. So geography can also be used for the creation of "peace." In that case, it is possible to connect it to irenology[2] (the science of peace), for which I refer to the Dutch libertarian social critic and antimilitarist Bart de Ligt (1883-1938).

A functional description can be instrumentalized. Through the course of time this can also be done with geography, as Pelletier has outlined in detail. This is exactly what the geographers among the anarchists have done. They have instrumentalized their geography using anarchy. This created the goal of a social order other than the existing one.

Anarchy is a term used in anarchist circles to indicate simultaneously a state of affairs, a perspective, and a set of principles. Pelletier explains that one should not confuse anarchy with anomie. The latter term refers to the absence of rules in social life. Such absence is not characteristic of anarchy. A characteristic of anarchy is the rejection of heteronomy. So in summary, anarchy does not preclude the existence of freely expressed, social rules. Anarchy includes order and structuring, freely agreed by free people. It also reflects, Pelletier argues, the recognition of scientific and natural laws

---

[2]It is the libertarian social critic and antimilitarist Bart de Ligt (1883-1938) who deals explicitly with irenology between the two world wars; see his "Introduction to the science of peace" (written by De Ligt for the first summer course at the Academie de la Paix in 1938), included in the anthology *Bart de Ligt 1883-1938*, Arnhem, 1939.

(so it is absurd to resist the law of gravity) and presupposes a multitude of principles. The principles referred to are considered to include mutualism and libertarian federalism, other elements of the social order as the goal.

* Anarchists and Geography

The descriptions of geography and anarchy do not clarify by themselves which links exist between the two. Therefore Pelletier poses the question: why would anarchists involve themselves with geography? Furthermore, why should geographers engage themselves with anarchy? In short, there is a whole mélange of links to investigate. That is the task that Pelletier has set himself.

The practice of geography to the extent that occurred in the last quarter of the nineteenth century within anarchist circles involved three main characters: Reclus, Kropotkin, and Metchnikoff. In addition, it is striking that in the work of some of the anarchists who preceded them, such as Proudhon (1809-1865) and Bakunin (1814-1876), geographical dimensions can be distinguished. And in our period the work of Paul Goodman (1911-1972) and Murray Bookchin (1921-2006) refers back to the geographical dimensions of the previous ideas of Reclus and his contemporaries.

In this way, Pelletier develops an order of people who, on the one hand, held libertarian views, and on the other hand gave their work geographical dimensions (such as Patrick Geddes, Ebenezer Howard, Lewis Mumford, and Colin Ward). It is also striking that the development of the Reclusian network of anarchist geographers coincides with the development of the anarchist, socialist, and syndicalist movement. From the beginning of the nineteenth century, socialism is known as an intellectual and social project. It gets rid, as noted by Pelletier, of mysticism and irrationality. It is then possible to connect it with various social sciences.

Thus, in Proudhon one can see an "announcer" of sociology (following Auguste Comte [1798-1857], who was one of its founders). Proudhon is the first one to theorise mutualism and the premises of anarchism. Pelletier then sees Bakunin building, "on the rubble of the romantic nationalism," the theory of revolutionary and libertarian socialism.

In fact, here we find the "personal touch" of scientification of the libertarian project: some scientists (like geographers) began to instrumentalize their ideological principles (anarchy) within their scientific work. Can this be justified methodologically? That is the question, which is discussed in the following topic.

* *The Anarchist Position and Science*

In the practice of science it is inevitable that a "personal touch" plays a role. Strict positivism in this regard is a pacifier. "Facts are not facts," I learned from the Dutch legal philosopher J. F. Glastra van Loon (1920-2001) in his critique of positivist science. The personal element provides subjectivity in science. Is there then, in that case, any science possible, as objectivity is presupposed?

I would think so. For that purpose, I derived from Helmut Schreiner (1942-2001) two minimum requirements proposed to be able to rise above a purely subjective moment.

These concern:

- The requirement of intersubjective possibility of reconstruction, and

- The requirement of intersubjective acceptability.

Possibility of reconstruction refers in this regard to the possibility of a person, other than its author, to develop not at random certain reasoning of the author. The reader must therefore be able to follow and to check the data in use by the author (verifiability requirement). The requirement of reconstruction thus presupposes the existence of mutual communication and open communication channels.

Acceptability demands the accounting with regard to the conformity to the principles contained within a thought. The agreement about the principles can be realised voluntarily and/or by convention (conventional legitimacy) or procedural (procedural legitimacy). Thus an intersubjective level can be achieved by using well-known methods, such as to analyse, systematise, and abstract, to apply logical reasoning, coherence, and transparency.

It is clear that especially the requirement of acceptability places a clamp on the open end of the anarchistic epistemology, which was pleaded at the time by Paul Feyerabend (1924-1994).[3] "Anarchy" is reflected in his slogan: *anything goes.* The

---

[3]For my observations on Paul Feyerabend, I used his *Against Method: Outline of an Anarchistic Theory of Knowledge*, London, 1975; furthermore, I based my comment on his "Outline of a Pluralistic Theory of Knowledge and Action," in S. Anderson (ed.), *Planning for Diversity and Choice: Possible Futures and Their Relations to the Man-controlled Environment*, Cambridge, Mass., 1968, p. 275-284.

My thoughts on scholarship I justified in my book *Argumentative Arbitrariness and the Practice of Constitutional Science* (Zwolle, 1988), as well as in "Scholarly and Public Law" in the collection: Thom Holterman, C. Riezebos (eds.), *General Constitutional Concepts* (Zwolle, 1991, third edition; p. 281-317). Both texts are only available in Dutch.

The "facts are not facts" of J. F. Glastra van Loon is included in his collection *The Unity of Action: Drawing on Law and Philosophy* (Boom, Meppel/Amsterdam, 1980). With regard to intersubjectivity I worked from H. Schreiner, who wrote *Die Intersubjektivität von Wertungen, Zur Begründbarkeit von Wertungen im Rechtsdenken durch ethisch verpflichtetes Argumentieren*, Berlin, 1980.

On the position of Paul Feyerabend within the anarchist movement, I suggest the following information. In the years 1974-1985 appeared the anarchist cultural magazine *Unter dem Pflaster liegt der Strand*, edited by Hans Peter Duerr, published by the libertarian Karin Kramer Verlag, Berlin. It appeared in fifteen parts (in the form of yearbooks). In almost every part a contribution of Paul Feyerabend is included.

De AS, a Dutch anarchist three-monthly, devoted considerable attention to Feyerabend in the special issue "Anarchism and Science" (No. 37, January/February 1979).

latter should be understood as a methodological challenge. I refer here to this point, because Pelletier expresses a different vision regarding Feyerabend, as do I.

With Pelletier, I am of the opinion that Feyerabend is frankly nearsighted in his book *Against Method*, with regard to his observations on Lenin and the neutrality of the state. Feyerabend also uses the term anarchy in a different way to both Pelletier and myself. He disconnects it from the anarchist movement and uses the term anarchy to describe the unconditioned practice of science. He rejects the compulsion and pressure in science. And this, for me, is an acceptable use of the term anarchy. However, at the same time, Feyerabend consigns the history and continuity of classical anarchism and anarchist philosophy to the dunghill. As with Pelletier, I do not agree with this. Whilst this whole discussion can be ignored, the methodological approach of Feyerabend can still be appreciated.

So I am of the opinion that the methodological meaning of "anything goes" with regard to Feyerabend has a fundamental, a procedural, and a conditional character. It is fundamental because it requires the channels through which the communication takes place to be kept open. It is procedural because it works by hearing both sides: it is accepted that it is possible to introduce all arguments, to voice opposition (principle of contradiction). It is conditional because it is free to look at a completely different way beyond current levels. It is quite possible that what is accepted as a "normal" position or vision should or can be surpassed.

All of this can lead to the discovery of facts or to acquire insights that are contrary to those previously considered being part of a "well-established position." The methodological posi-

---

On YouTube one can find an interview with Feyerabend, a year before his death, recorded in Rome, from a balcony overlooking the Vatican. The opening refers to it when the interviewer rhetorically comments on its grandeur. Feyerabend reacted by declaring "Es kann nicht gros sein!" For the interview: http://www.youtube.com/watch?v=nr-Q6pfXSPo.

tion, which has the potential to enable contrarian discoveries, I am willing to defend as an "anarchistic position." Without such a methodological commitment, the earth would still be flat, the sun would still revolve around the earth (Galileo Galilei, 1564-1642); evolution would still be objective, linear, directed, and executed according to a certain (divine) design (Charles Darwin, 1809-1882).

The opposition (of Galilei, Darwin) would under no circumstances be made public, as for example where the power has lain entirely within the Roman Catholic Church. These are the thoughts, which Feyerabend has provoked under his slogan "anything goes." It is therefore completely incomprehensible why precisely he extols Lenin and his state as "neutral." On this point he must have been blind. Perhaps his aim was to antagonise people; to that end, his approach was masterly.

* Different Types of Geography

So far, Pelletier has outlined different starting positions on geography and geographers, anarchy and anarchism, and the study of science and their mutual relationship. Now it is possible for him to concentrate more on the Reclusian geography and the Reclusian network in particular. In addition, he can now also clarify what other types of geography occur or develop. In the context of this discussion I will focus primarily on the Reclusian view. But for creating a contrast it is good to pay some attention to the other views.

Two leading geographers in the late nineteenth century are, alongside Élisée Reclus, the Frenchman Vidal de la Blache (1845-1918) and the German Friedrich Ratzel (1844-1904). Politically, we find here very different personalities. Reclus takes on the side of Bakunin and the Paris Commune (1871), in which he also participated. He will be sentenced for that (ultimately to ten years exile from France). Reclusian geography has its roots in Proudhon and Bakunin and develops by the cooperation of Reclus with Kropotkin and Metchnikoff. They are anarchist and anti-capitalist in character.

In contrast, Vidal takes the side of "Versailles" (the right-wing government that also bloodily pounds the Paris Commune). He will be the first to occupy the chair of historical geography (1891). Pelletier describes him as a nationalist intellectual who elaborates on an economic imperialism within a territorial one. This is influenced by the vision of Ratzel. Ratzelian geography serves the state apparatus and provides support for colonialism. This view permeates through Vidal into the Vidalian School. This school will preach pétainism (derived from the French commander Pétain), so too the Vichyist doctrine "back to nature," explains Pelletier. It is the line along which the "Géopolitique nazifiée" develops.

Thus Pelletier outlines two orientations, each with their own "ideology" and diametrically different results. Who can thus pretend that an objective study of science is possible? In my opinion nobody can (the question of the personal touch arises; we are always at the level of statistical objectivity and/or in intersubjective situations). So it is clear that whomever is engaged alongside that of power, it is his conception that will be recognized as "objective" and will be selected for use. Thus, those on the one hand in order to preserve "the power" purge out those on the other hand who have a "desire for change." Reclus, spokesman for the second position, holds that a libertarian social order is the goal.

In short, it does matter to pose the question, along with German jurist Joseph Esser (1910-1999), with which kind of "Vorverständnis" (premise, prejudice) one works. This is not only so in jurisprudence—compare Esser's *Vorverständnis und Methodenwahl in der Rechtsfindung* (1970)—but also in geography. In that science it is not about "law" that one thinks, but about "borders." It appears that our perception of borders is equally as influenced by our different presuppositions, as we shall see from Pelletier.

* Border

We saw above that Ratzel and Vidal take nationalist positions, whilst Reclus takes a "communalist" position. The nationalist positions are grafted onto state law and the communalist manifests as anti-state law. The first two geographers focus on defending state borders, the latter rejects state borders. Pelletier argues that it is from this rejection of borders that the federalist proposals by Proudhon, Bakunin, and Reclus come into being.

In the context of the ideas of Reclus, he takes a real break from predefined, legally guaranteed, territorial boundaries just like the so-called "natural" borders. What applies to national state borders can, I think, also be applied to municipal and provincial boundaries. In this case a functional approach can play an important role, concerning—current—boundaries. My suggestion here is derived from the role it also plays in jurisprudence. Two examples:

When the Dutch lawyer J. In't Veld was searching (for his thesis in 1929) for new forms of decentralization (also the title of his thesis), he did not begin by describing a legal order; instead, he places value on thinking in terms of dynamic forces: centripetal forces (centralizing) and centrifugal forces (decentralizing). The problems analysed by In't Veld were mainly related to the growth of the harbour of Rotterdam and the question of whether or not the expanding harbour activity "reflects" the need in that area of Rotterdam for a new type of administrative authority of their own.

In a different way, considering (current) boundaries comes up for discussion via the expression of the immanent law of the functional structure, a conception by the Dutch legal theorist Jack ter Heide (1923-1988), elaborated in his doctrine of functional law. I took this from him, but applied it in a broad geographical perspective. The phrase indicates the relationship between a concrete means and the (direct and indirect) effects of the use of that means.

For example, an operating windmill (let's say for grinding grain or sawing wood) can be used. Such a mill can only work if it can catch the wind freely and surely, which I call the *immanent law*. This means that within a certain radius around the mill no high constructions may arise. The mill itself can be seen as a *functional structure*. The interdiction of erecting high-rise constructions within the indicated radius does not depend on legal regulations (the ban), but the immanent law of that mill, which is contained within itself as a functional structure. Here the functional structure dictates the "law" (the border), and not a legislator.

Pelletier reminds us that borders are markers of dominance. They are determined by or after warfare—by conquest. I would add that dominance also comes into play when determining municipal and county borders.

Borders are associated with geography, which is partly reflected in geopolitics. Theoretical anarchists, who are interested in politics by definition, engage consciously or not in geography, even though it is not their area of activity (such as Proudhon and Bakunin). Obviously the reverse is also true. A geographer, who is carrying anarchy as his *Vorverständnis*, will develop geography with an anarchist appearance. We meet this as far as it concerns Reclus in his "social geography."

✲ Social Geography

Pelletier points out that the geography as practiced by Reclus rests on the dialectics of environment-space and environment-time. Space is a social construct; environment-space is studied in a synchronous approach to the complex structures of interactions ("horizontal" consideration). It involves attention to phenomena that coexist in the same period. Environment-time is studied by means of a diachronic, evolutionary approach. Here the attention is paid to phenomena that follow each other in time ("vertical" consideration). This provides a dynamic vision. So, as Pelletier concludes, Reclus has no static views of nature.

A difficulty arises when translating the term "environment." Reclus has given that term a wider range than usual. The "environment" simultaneously indicates a middle position: *median* (Reclus also speaks about *mesology*; "meso" indicates the place between *micro* and *macro*). In my discussion with the author we found that the term, representing the inclusive character of "environment" in Reclus's notion, should be *ambience*: the material and moral atmosphere that surrounds a person or a group of people.[4]

Toward the end of his life, Reclus defines three "laws" and uses the term "social geography." The three laws are "orders of facts" which must be studied, namely: (1) class struggle, (2) search for balance, and (3) the sovereign decision of the individual. In the chaos of things, these orders of facts show themselves as sufficiently constant to talk about in terms of "laws," believes Reclus.

It is not about legal but sociological laws, which are characterized in sociology as "conventional laws." This involves groups of no more than partial regularity. This is also apparent in the explanation by Pelletier. The first law is a reference to socialist issues: human history can be understood as a long story of struggle between two differently resourced groups, of which one group consists of rulers.

The second law is now known by the term "homeostasis." In relation to the first law, the second refers to seeking a balance in the struggle for justice. The third law refers to the idea that society cannot function properly and cannot move forward if it is not based on the free cooperation of the individual (for which the individual should be sovereign).

The three laws mentioned by Reclus make it clear where the differences can be found in relation to the view of Marx. For Marx the course of history is derived from determinism. Therefore predictions about the future possess levels of

---

[4] See the French explanatory dictionary *Le Petit Robert*.

certainty (following the phases of capitalism, socialism will occur in the world). It is, as Pelletier indicates, an approach to history rejected by anarchists. Namely it upholds a vision in which phenomena are approached, linear, teleological, and fatalistic (based in part on the dialectics of Hegel). In history, it is proclaimed as necessary for the different phases to proceed. We now know that nothing remains of the predictive value of these Marxian dialectics.

Insofar as one can speak of dialectics in anarchism, they take a serial form. So Proudhon speaks about "dialectique sérielle" (sérielle—serial—is here: bipolar). One is seeking balance (Reclus). That's to say, there are "fields of tension," for example, between freedom on the one side and justice on the other side. The contradictions have no "synthesis" in which they are released (as in the Hegelian, Marxist conception). It just runs to "unstable equilibrium" (Reclus).

This manner of Reclusian observation also determines how one reacts in discussions about, for example, Darwinism, nature, and ecology. Pelletier discusses all of this and takes the opportunity in his magnum opus to treat the themes. Whenever something is presented as transcendent, a non-correctable determinism, an inevitable fatalistic and an eschatological end, then this exasperates both Reclusian geographers and anarchists. Tirelessly Pelletier explains why this is so.

✻ *Criticism of Reclus*

It almost goes without saying that certain views, or views of a scientist more than a century ago, will be outdated. Pelletier points this out regularly as he discusses Reclusian views. However, these observations do not diminish the value of the aforementioned scientist. This is not the purpose of the criticism mentioned here.

The criticism here has been expressed within recent years, namely that Reclus has been accused of being a racist, that he would have approved of colonialism, and would have espoused anti-semitism. Pelletier rejects these criticisms, the basis for them being in one case a vague reference and in another literally nonsensical. The reason why such anachronistic accusations are made is completely unclear. The only thing I can think of is that one wishes to bring Reclusian anarchist thought into disrepute.

Pelletier pays most attention to the anti-semitism reproach. He refers to texts by Henriette Chardak and Jean-Didier Vincent. These two authors do not mention documented sources from where they get their idea. Beatrice Giblin recently joined them. She notes that Reclus always refers to Jews in a certain discriminatory manner, but for this accusation she gives no textual reference. Pelletier takes some thirty pages for citing sources to disprove these damaging allegations.

Pelletier does not waste words answering the burning question of where this desire to discredit someone like Reclus comes from. I return to this question because in the Netherlands a similar anachronistic issue is at stake concerning the figure of Ferdinand Domela Nieuwenhuis (1846-1919). Domela is one of the nineteenth-century founders of socialism and, later on, an anarchist. It is the contemporary Dutch biographer Jan Willem Stutje who, not so long ago, seized upon anti-semitism within Domela's work. Historians such as the Dutch Bert Altena and Rudolf de Jong then skillfully parried these complaints. Nevertheless, such a reproach remains and is not easily silenced.

To another author, Robin te Slaa, these facts lead to the disfiguring comment that some fascists have derived their anti-semitic conceptions from some anarchists. On what does he base his view? Among other things, on a number of remarks about Domela found by Stutje. Hans Ramaer, editor of the Dutch anarchist three-monthly *De AS*, notes in his commentary on te Slaa's book that this is how myths develop and go on to lead their own lives.

✷ Sociability First

What is the overarching doctrine of Reclusian geography? This is difficult to summarize in one word, but with sociability, or mutual aid, we are pointing in the right direction. It can be reasoned as follows.

The space, as we saw, is a social construction. A plurality of spaces is to be found. Also the "environment" is characterized by Reclus in multiple forms. The human himself he called *an environment for human beings*. This multiplicity of spaces and environments are thought of as being in motion, hence the use of dynamic thought in relation to geographical and historical determinism. Determinism is in fact immediately counterbalanced by *variation*.

Plurality is therefore essential for Reclus, says Pelletier. That struggle therefore is a factor in evolution, as Darwin worked out, is not denied. Darwin, however, forgot some factors—namely those of solidarity and cooperation—contained in one term: *entraide* (mutual aid). On this the anarchist geographers expound unrelentingly. It is one of the effects of people (and animals) that live in social relationships. The reference to the use of the term *sociability* proves it.

Mutual aid, *entraide*, plays a role in Reclus's thoughts but it is put on the map by another anarchist and geographer, Kropotkin (with whom he was a friend) in his book *Mutual Aid, a Factor of Evolution* (1902). It should be noted that Leon Metchnikoff, the third geographer and anarchist, has played a major role in this. In fact it is he who in 1886 put forward the material base for the theory of mutual aid.

Pelletier has mapped out all of this in his book. He has consistently pointed out how concrete situations and social structures—in other words, concrete sociability—produce composite human forces. These forces contribute to define the quality of emancipation and revolt of collective unity. But without the presence of the sovereign individual this collective unity would deflate. The dynamics must be guaranteed.

Pelletier has delivered a book to study and to use as reference. It is also one of the rare French books with particular keywords and index!

PELLETIER, Philippe. *Géographie et anarchie: Reclus, Kropotkine, Metchnikoff et d'autres.* Éditions du Monde libertaire & Éditions libertaires, Paris, 2013, 632 p., price 24 euros.

CHAPTER
ELEVEN

POWER AND PROPERTY: A COROLLARY

GRANT MINCY

The concept of property is widely discussed by social theorists and is a hot-button issue within political circles. This is mostly because property is somewhat of an abstract concept. Property is a possession—it belongs to someone or something. Seems simple enough, but the social ramifications of how property is acquired, distributed, and managed are rather complex. Beyond the abstract, when investigating the concept, property quickly becomes a central theme in the politics we address. Property is incredibly important to economic systems, with far-reaching implications into our social organization, distributions of wealth, and management of resources—both manufactured and natural.

As property is a possession it must have an owner. But who has a right to property? How should property be distributed, managed, and utilized? Should property be rivalrous and/or excludable, or perhaps not? If these considerations are not yet enough, the most important question remains: To whom should power be granted to make these decisions?

c4ss.org/content/31680

As property and property rights are fundamentally important to social organization it logically follows that with property comes the burden, responsibility, and privilege of power. In this study I wish to investigate three prominent forms of property as they exist today: public (read state), private, and common. It is my desire to deconstruct the legitimacy of state property rights while leaving the options of both private and common ownership intact.

There has been much work conducted over private property rights in libertarian circles; therefore, I will briefly discuss private property and its legitimacy. It is my intent to focus the efforts of my labor on common property rights and the benefits they grant society in social and natural settings.

❋ *Three Prominent Forms of Property*

Property can take many forms and functions, ranging from the tangible to the intangible. Property can relate to land and resources on one hand, and on the other one's own person, intellectual privileges, and financial interests. Though there is much to be said about property in all its forms and functions, I wish to focus on land—space that can be, or is, utilized for the purposes of resource extraction, conservation, financial interests, or fellowship.

In determining how space is used, managed, and owned there are three primary ideas on how rights should be distributed over said property—each is unique and distinct from one another. The owners, or players, of this property regime game are government(s) in the form of "public property," an individual entity in the form of private property, and individuals or associations in the form of common control.

❋ *I. Public Property (State Territory and the Corporate Sector)*

The term "public property" takes on many different forms. Simply put, the wide use of the term public property today refers to government, or more precisely, state ownership of property. Under these conditions we find the term is rather misleading. These lands are not really "public" at all as they are fully managed by state authority. Any individual or collective use of "public" property is granted solely by the state apparatus—these rights of use are not transmissible.

National parks in the United States, along with national forests and seashores, even city parks, represent land that is state territory. Here, the state allows resources to be used by the populace with terms and conditions. The public can be excluded from these territories by executive decree, however, as we saw in previous government shutdowns.[1] Due to political gridlock in Washington, D.C., the public was barred from all lands under government management. There also exist other government institutions funded by public tax dollars that are either closed to the public entirely, such as national laboratories, or where one must pay a (often hefty) fee for access, such as public universities.

It is also important to note how far state property rights extend. In the current capitalist economy of Western nation-states, government regulation has worked to produce a neoliberal corporate-state nexus. In the United States, specifically, state-sanctioned economic privilege has been granted to big business and the financial sector under the premise that these institutions are necessary for social organization. The corporate sector is separate from, but intimately related with, the state. The state bestows corporate charter and grants the corporate sector legal privileges and favorable regulation that it actively denies individuals. This prevents competition and affords monopoly status to many in the corporate sector. Independent scholar Kevin Carson, in his piece *Why Corporate Capitalism is Unsustainable*,[2] explains:

---

[1] https://www.huffingtonpost.com/topic/government-shutdown
[2] c4ss.org/content/10498

Capitalism as a historic system is five hundred or more years old, and the state was intimately involved in its formation and its ongoing preservation from the very beginning. But the state has been far more involved, if such a thing is possible, in the model of corporate capitalism that's prevailed over the past 150 years. The corporate titans that dominate our economic and political life could hardly survive for a year without the continuing intervention of the state in the market to sustain them through subsidies and monopoly protections.

As such, the economy of the nation-state is directly linked to these institutions, forging a corporatist political economy where the state has direct interest in the success of these now "too big to fail" concentrations of capital. Proliferation of the corporate state results in the exploitation of thousands of hectares of wilderness area for resource extraction and enhanced neo-liberalism in our urban corridors. For this reason, it is prudent to step up simultaneous deconstruction of actually existing capitalism *and* the state, as further explained[3] by philosopher Roderick T. Long:

> But surely the way for libertarians, Austrian or otherwise, to win over those who mistrust concentrations of power both corporate and governmental is to increase our critical scrutiny of corporate power, not to relax our critical scrutiny of governmental power. After all, empirical research—including Austrian empirical research—has shown that these two forms of power are mutually reinforcing far more than they are mutually antagonistic.

Virtually all tiers of government are involved in either outright property ownership or partial ownership by an economic

---

[3] aaeblog.com/2014/07/07/cordial-and-sanguine-part-63-from-the-unthinking-depths/

interest that favors corporatist institutions. For instance, nearly 25% of the territory of the United States is owned by the federal government. Additionally, the use of powers such as eminent domain, paid for by government contracts, and compulsory (forced) pooling, often used to obtain private property for oil and gas drilling, are just two among many examples of how government uses its privilege of coercion to obtain territory and simultaneously benefit the corporate sector.

Of particular concern about monopoly capitalism is how it advances the state's economic agenda outside of its geographic restrictions. With the rise of multinationals, economies around the globe have been centralized under state capitalism. This is rather dangerous because it allows states to expand their power without military conquest and it is an effective way to obtain new territory. Military imperialism still exists, of course, but it is not as popular as it used to be within political circles. Corporate colonialism, however, is rarely discussed if not outright dismissed by the power structure—it has redefined global economics, changing the course of individual labor nearly everywhere.

The corporate sector is polycentric in the sense that different corporations must coordinate and often compete with one another, but they all have monocentric agendas and hegemonic tendencies. Consider the differences in capitalism across the nation states. There exist differences in the corporate sector's relationship with their host state—United States capitalism differs from the capitalist practices of other nations. Capitalists and state officials from all over the world, however, come together at economic summits such as G20, discuss best management practices, and advance monopoly capitalism on world economic systems. Capitalism is thus dynamic while simultaneously centralizing. Actually existing capitalism is a dangerous current of state power.

State power lies in its monopoly of the "legitimate" use of physical force, commonly known as the monopoly of violence.

Sociologist Max Weber first defined the state in this way in his essay *Politics as a Vocation* (1919)[4] where he argues "the modern state is a compulsory association which organizes domination." One is beholden to question the legitimacy of such power as it has been evoked to claim property and resources for itself or close allies in the name of the "common good."

Arguments for state authority are many, but the root of them all adhere to the long-held fallacy: "We are the state." If one lives in a neo-democratic state or a representative republic, such as the United States, then the fallacy concludes: we are all represented by the institution which will in turn carry out policies that reflect our interests. But we are not the state. The state, as noted by Murray Rothbard, in his essay *Anatomy of the State*,[5] is the systematization of the predatory process over a given territory. The state is a rational actor that works in its own self-interest—the interest of the ruling caste and its allies. The state never has, nor will it ever, allow for the spontaneous development of society. We are not the state, its property does not belong to us all in common; to call such spaces "public" is a linguistic deceit. It is not our heritage; it can be torn from us by government decree. The exclusion of the public from national parks and the caging of *Plow Shares*[6] peace activists at the Oak Ridge National Laboratory in Tennessee, who dared to protest nuclear proliferation, are testament to this.

By using terms like "public domain" in reference to public universities that are in fact closed to the public, the state works to socialize a major input of the corporate economy at common expense, thus privatizing wealth. The state sells the idea of "public" property as well as "legitimate" force and the "we are the government" fallacy to legitimize a common

---

[4] anthropos-lab.net/wp/wp-content/uploads/2011/12/Weber-Politics-as-a-Vocation.pdf

[5] mises.org/document/1011/Anatomy-of-the-State

[6] appalachianson.wordpress.com/2014/02/22/the-oak-ridge-three/

"national interest" that we all share—though no such interest exists. The state is incredibly dangerous. Rest assured, every sacred piece of land or space available for, or currently utilized by, human labor inside government borders are territories of the state that may be taken at will—this is a power that must be abolished. Agrarian Wendell Berry, in his essay "The Long Legged House,"[7] further elaborates:

> Since there is no government of which the concern or the discipline is primarily the health of either households or of the Earth, since it is in the nature of any state to be concerned first of all with its own preservation and only second with the cost, the dependable, clear response to man's moral circumstance is not that of law, but that of conscience. The Highest moral behavior is not obedience to law, but obedience to the informed conscience even in spite of law.

Large mistrust of, and dissociation from, centralized institutions has been a noticeable trend in human history since the rise of such hierarchies in the age of the ancients. Rudolph Rocker[8] explains:

> ...a fixed, self-enclosed social system but rather a definite trend in the historic development of mankind, which, in contrast with the intellectual guardianship of all clerical and governmental institutions, strives for the free unhindered unfolding of all the individual and social forces in life. Even freedom is only a relative, not an absolute concept, since it tends constantly to become broader and to affect wider circles in more manifold ways. For the anarchist, freedom is not an abstract philosophical concept, but the vital concrete possibility for every human being to bring

---

[7] amazon.com/The-Long-Legged-House-Wendell-Berry/dp/1593760132

[8] marxists.org/reference/archive/rocker-rudolf/misc/anarchism-anarcho-syndicalism.htm

> to full development all the powers, capacities, and talents with which nature has endowed him, and turn them to social account. The less this natural development of man is influenced by ecclesiastical or political guardianship, the more efficient and harmonious will human personality become, the more will it become the measure of the intellectual culture of the society in which it has grown.

It is important to continue this trend and follow the principles behind such democratization to their only logical conclusion—absolute liberty. In the stateless society property will be available for inclined labor,[9] conserved for leisure and, most importantly, preserved in its natural state. Property will be boundless, democratic, and liberated.

✱ *II. Private Property*

Private property may easily be defined as the ownership of land or space by non-governmental entities. Private property is not state territory, nor is it any kind of public aggregation of land—rights to private property belong solely to the owner or owners. Much has been written about private property rights in libertarian (and other) socio-economic circles. I do not wish to re-invent the wheel, but instead give a broad overview of private property ownership, defend its legitimacy, and briefly discuss private property in a (social) free market economic system.

Many who identify as libertarians, market anarchists, or advocates of laissez-faire principles (especially those hailing from the Austrian or Chicago schools of economic theory) consider private property key to building a free and prosperous society. Many in these aforementioned traditions would argue land in the hands of private entities ensures the productive use and protected value of the property. In fact, Austrian economists Ludwig von Mises and F. A. Hayek up the ante

[9] appalachianson.wordpress.com/2014/04/04/inclined-labor/

and claim private control of property is the only legitimate form of ownership (a claim with which I disagree). Of all the defenders of private property, however, one would be hard pressed to find a more ardent and boisterous proponent of associated rights than Murray Rothbard.

Rothbard is famous for noting that property rights are human rights.[10] Rothbard believed it to be the right of the individual to "find and transform resources." Production is key for property here because the ability to produce allows life to be sustained and advanced. Rothbard's anarchism and heterodox academics mold nicely with his view of property. The state, as a coercive body with a monopoly on violence, can restrict the labor of individuals, thus denying production and our civilization's sustainability—the state is an enemy of private property. I do not consider myself a Rothbardian in any way, but I feel his argument here, much like those made in the same vein by Benjamin Tucker, Josiah Warren, and other individualist anarchists, is correct.

Governments often steal private property, either by eminent domain or compulsory (forced) pooling. Much of this theft has not been for the purpose of "public" use or any common good, but for development of the corporate sector—an extension of the arm of the state. Private property—homes, land, businesses—have been demolished to be replaced by the will of the affluent and politically connected. Furthermore, the state's conquest of territory has restricted homesteading, a valuable way for individuals to mix their labor with the land. It is not private property that is illegitimate, but rather the strong-arm of the corporate state reigning over the market. Private property is not to be confused with the corporate, for it belongs to individuals.

In a liberated society all property under private control would be legitimate as it would be obtained and managed without economic privilege, central planning, or "too big

---

[10] mises.org/daily/2569

to fail" corporate institutions. The current deformation of markets exists not because of property ownership, but from centralized authority—free markets do not exist, rather state-sanctioned economic privilege exists. The current system is not the result of property ownership (private or common), competition, or even profit, but rather the captive market form. This system exists because legal privilege is granted to those with the most capital. The development of this economic and social order is indeed political, as opposed to free and participatory.

For this reason it is necessary to liberate property from the state. The libertarian argues that the free market, by its very definition, must resist domination, violence, and privilege because these societal attributes are violations of liberty and human dignity. Free markets, then, based on the spontaneous order of human ingenuity are a fundamental aspect of a free and more egalitarian society. In *Markets Freed From Capitalism*,[11] Charles W. Johnson describes poignantly the possibility of what may rise in market liberation:

> A fully freed market means the liberation of vital command posts in the economy, reclaiming them from points of state control to nexuses of market and social entrepreneurship—transformations from which a market would emerge that would look profoundly different from anything we have now. That so profound a change cannot easily fit into traditional categories of thought, e.g. "libertarian" or "left-wing," "laissez-faire," or "socialist," "entrepreneurial" or "anti-capitalist," is not because these categories do not apply but because they are not big enough: radically free markets burst through them. If there were another word more all-embracing than revolutionary, we would use it.

In this socio-economic order individuals would be free to labor. In a rather Lockean tradition, as labor is owned by the

---

[11] c4ss.org/content/27171

individual, the land or space with which labor is mixed is free to be claimed. In this sense, private property ownership can take on a number of different traits, each expressed differently by the free will of those involved, as explained by individualist anarchist Benjamin R. Tucker:[12]

> Anarchism is a word without meaning, unless it includes the liberty of the individual to control his product or whatever his product has brought him through exchange in a free market—that is, private property. Whoever denies private property is of necessity an Archist. This excludes from Anarchism all believers in compulsory Communism. As for the believers in voluntary Communism (of whom there are precious few), they are of necessity believers in the liberty to hold private property, for to pool one's possessions with those of others is nothing more or less than an exercise of proprietorship.

The concept of private property is both simple and complex—land in private hands with seemingly infinite possibilities for its organization. Fundamental to private property, however, is its voluntary nature. Whether acquired from homesteading or the exchange of goods and services, private property resists violence in its acquisition. So long as its acquisition does not infringe on the rights of other individuals, private property will hold a respectable place in the markets of a libertarian society.

✼ III. Common Property

Common property is land or space in which all members of a given community hold equal rights over said territory—power is equally distributed. Here there is no coercive body delegating property management or use, as in state territory, nor is there exclusive ownership given to an individual or

---

[12]library.libertarian-labyrinth.org/items/show/318

isolated group, as in private property. Common property is liberated of enclosure movements—the cultural and natural resources remain accessible and managed by all stakeholders. This is not to say there is no governance of these resources. To the contrary, a highly ordered, decentralized, adaptive governance manages common property.

It is prudent in this discussion to differentiate between the property regime and the types of property. A regime is defined as a management system or a planned method for executing tasks. In the commons, regimes work to protect and conserve resources, usually by consensus decision-making and adaptive management. Common types of property include natural or man-made resources such as water, the atmosphere, fish, or an irrigation system in a community garden. The regime is a social arrangement that regulates utility of common pool resources.

In such a system, place is an integrating concept. Land is easily associated with the community and the individual in the commons—land is legacy as space is place. For this reason, as well as the efficiency of adaptive systems found in the commons, the true public arena labors for best management practices. Sense of place and place attachments are very powerful—and with them come the tragic beauty of human emotion. Being connected to land, or place, is very moving. Perhaps Wendell Berry describes the feeling best in his essay, *Mat Feltner's World*,[13] about an aging farmer and his land. Berry writes:

> As we watch Mat lean against the tree, we sense how like the tree he has become. They are kindred spirits, the two of them, equal enough in age and coming, finally, to the same spot. By the life he has led, standing erect in the light, Mat too, has stood "outside

---

[13] http://books.google.com/books?id=_S8J65xgF6sC&lpg=PA82&ots=BBslOeFjq-&dq=MatFeltnersWorldwendellberry&pg=PA78#v=onepage&q=as%20we%20watch%20Mat%20lean&f=false

> the woods." Just as the walnut has relinquished its
> nuts, so Mat has given freely of himself, nourishing
> the land and giving rise to new life. Like the tree,
> Mat has sunk deep and lasting roots.

The statement, "Mat has sunk deep and lasting roots," speaks volumes about the attachment people have to place. Sense of place can resemble a host of things such as: memories with family and friends, coming of age, solace, comfort, etc. The concept of a human being having lasting roots and an area of land representing those roots exhibits deep human bonds and connections to the Earth. In many cases, respect for the land one lives on adds to the importance of place attachments. Oftentimes people equate their land with their legacy. The commons are tied to land and space through unique historical and cultural traditions. Furthermore, economic benefits, pride, and a moral or spiritual relationship with land is experienced by many people. Respect of the commons is a demand of place attachment and, in said commons, governance and management of place takes on an exciting, dynamic, and libertarian form.

Incredibly important to the commons is adaptive governance, where all stakeholders are free to participate in democratic decision-making. Governance of this type utilizes Adaptive Collaborative Management (ACM) to determine the use and regulation of common pool resources. ACM is an effective instrument in bringing competing interests together to make these difficult decisions. The work of economist and Nobel Laureate Elinor Ostrom[14] demonstrates the success of horizontal property management and the conservation of common pool resources.

As common property has now been defined and management of such property has been introduced, I will now explore, in detail, adaptive governance and its consequences for our cultural and natural heritage. In this discussion I will

---

[14] en.wikipedia.org/wiki/Elinor_Ostrom

focus on the human dimensions of governance, institutions, and science. I will examine decentralized regimes and their use of natural resources.

* Adaptive Governance

Adaptive Collaborative Management (ACM) is an approach to conflict resolution developed to resolve complex problems requiring collective action. Going beyond personal points of view, this governance style implores science, politics, and underlying interests to come together to confront conflict. ACM develops resolutions to benefit all points of view. Though there are some very real challenges to achieving these resolutions, it is increasingly clear that the hurdles we face in the twenty-first century will require common action. These challenges thus require differing ideologies to make difficult compromises to ensure sustainability. ACM is an effective instrument in bringing competing interests together to make these difficult decisions.

ACM can best be described by a simple model composed of four levels. The ACM model promotes collaborative resolutions during conflict management. Each level of this approach is designed to alleviate disagreement and promote compromise among opposing sides of conflict. The model of adaptive governance is as follows:

1. ACM first distinguishes what the conflict is about,

2. followed by why the conflict exists,

3. the model then implores individuals to develop options for a plan of action,

4. and finally establishes an action plan to potentially end the conflict.

Determining what the conflict is about allows each party to voice their perspectives and concerns. This allows all members of the ACM process to state their positions while allowing interests, motives, and feelings to be heard by the entire group. The groundwork for collaboration is laid by discussing why the conflict exists. First, this process calls for focusing on the problem at hand while considering all underlying interests. This allows the participants to then examine and understand the emotional link to all involved in the conflict, thus humanizing the argument. While examining different points of view, practitioners may begin to find common ground. The model then shifts to a more progressive approach to resolve the conflict at hand.

Adaptive governance utilizes collaboration to explore possible options to resolve conflict. This pro-active approach allows the development of resolutions to promote mutual gains for all involved. Elevating compromise as a goal ensures that the interests of all parties are left in a much better position than their previous state. After options are thoroughly discussed, an action plan is then implemented to ensure real-world success of the collaboration. Once in motion, it is important to note what part of the plan is working and what needs re-calculation. This allows for the continual assessment of the practice to yield maximum beneficial results to all parties.

There exist great challenges in the successful implementation of the four-step model. In practice, the determination of what conflict is about and why it exists is usually rather easy. The challenge of ACM lies in the final two steps. Reaching a consensus able to benefit everyone in a natural resource conflict is a rather daunting task. Equally daunting is the development of a fair assessment of these decisions. An intricate study of the mechanisms leading to periodic failure of ACM is a must, especially in the wake of the ominous global challenges of the twenty-first century, so that the approach can adapt and mitigate conflict. It is the decentralized nature of ACM that allows it to be so dynamic. This is perhaps its greatest benefit: it can adapt, where sweeping policy cannot.

There are many consequences involved in both succeeding at ACM and in failing. Success in the process leads to a number of desirable outcomes. The most important may be the emergence of pragmatic, decentralized leadership. In regard to natural resource management, this is important because it merges differing opinions together to promote sustainable resource use. This, in turn, promotes environmental stewardship and practices beneficial to natural resource management. This new sense of stewardship will positively benefit the development of a community and reduce impacts to the environment. On the other hand, failure to reach collaboration may result in prolonged harmful effects to the environment and halt sustainable community development.

Practitioners of natural resource management in the twenty-first century have their work cut out for them. We are approaching a point in Earth's history where all of humanity will be forced to deal with anthropocentric impacts to the biosphere. We now live in a time where we can physically see and experience the impact of civilization's ecological footprint. There is a true human dominance of all global systems. This dominance is now affecting a range of topics from human health to the politics we address. As we further encroach on natural systems, the transmission of new diseases to humans from animals and insects is growing rapidly (Shah 2009). A hotbed political issue in the United States right now is immigration reform. New studies suggest that a number of Latin American farmers will start migrating north due to the effects of climate change on their crop yields (Cattan 2010). There are many more examples of the connection between human impacts to the biosphere and current affairs. The question is: how should society address these issues?

The implications of these challenges require the science of resource management to rapidly change in the face of great uncertainty for the future. This uncertainty has been created by global environmental change and the globalization of the world economy—it is a product of the corporate state. A reevaluation of the long-term implications of the use of our natural resources, while paying attention to societal demands and well-being in a globalized market, becomes more and more urgent with each passing day (Franklin 2008). Natural scientists, social scientists, politicians, the private sector, and the public are in need of a resource-use paradigm shift. There exists a great need to restore the biosphere, protect bio-diversity, and promote sustainability. It is in our best interest to remain honest about, and aware of, the limitations of our natural ecosystems. It then follows we should implement policies that best fit the needs, health, and demands of an informed society. In doing so, the commons can sustain the long-term health of the biosphere—of which human beings are included (Franklin 2008). ACM is one mechanism that, if used openly and responsibly, can merge competing interests together to better our ecology.

Perhaps the most important attribute of ACM is the insistent inclusiveness and diversity of ideas. This allows practitioners to move forward with the best plans possible. This diversity, however, has very large implications for traditional leadership. ACM is our instrument to promote and achieve the redistribution of power, to champion ideas that benefit people, markets, and the environment. This idea of collaborative governance will bring people and common institutions together to build on the adaptive capacities and capabilities of the true public arena.

ACM, then, is a tool of transition. Its power lies in its decentralised structure—as it becomes implemented, state power will recede. It is this reclamation of power that makes common governance so important, especially in regard to common pool resources. We live in an era of anthropocentric use of the biosphere. Human consumption trends and, moreover, the nation state's consumption of resources are at an all-time high, and with a globalized market show no sign of slowing down. The harsh reality of today is that instead of preserving nature for nature's sake we may achieve more for the biosphere if we begin preserving nature for our own well-being (Armsworth 2007). This idea is the basis for market-based solutions to conserve the biosphere. The idea that human beings are separate from, or above, the rules of nature is not only dated, but dangerous. A popular trend among ecologists and conservation biologists is to promote ecosystem services to save biodiversity. This has the potential to revolutionize the market system.

American libertarian and political philosopher Karl Hess, Jr., in his book *Visions Upon the Land: Man and Nature on the Western Range*,[15] attributes the decline in health of natural lands to inherent problems in government policy, ecological destabilization due to government intrusion and the destructiveness of sweeping land use policies. Hess argues that instead of looking for more laws and regulations to manage natural resources (inevitably enhancing state economic power), we should instead seek an economic system based on voluntary market interactions without the involvement of the state.

This adaptive approach to ecological protection yields incredible results. Environmental sustainability is not the product of government intervention, but instead a result of self-organized institutions where key management decisions are made as organically as possible. It is also wise to remember that community-based, sustainable management of village lands was prevalent for much of human history until suppressed by the great landlords, the communist state, and the neoliberal state in succession. Nature and human civilization are incredibly complex and dynamic—neither will be sustained by sweeping ideas of natural resource management.

---

[15] http://books.google.com/books?id=UuUXOxomAPAC&pg=PP3&lpg=PP3&dq=karl+hess+environment&source=bl&ots=gCKovfldrH&sig=Xn7LK-slpLW_mT7P326DW5%E2%80%93B58&hl=en&sa=X&ei=y42pU7mTI4PNsQTd74CgBw&ved=0CFYQ6AEwBw#v=onepage&q=karl%20hess%20environment&f=false

Ecological systems and free markets share an affinity for diversity and both long for sustainability. The dissolution of power and control will advance best management practices. For this reason, we should not look vertically to state institutions, but horizontally to one another in the market. The goal should not be the expansion of the floor of the cage, to borrow from Noam Chomsky; the goal should be its abolition. Neighborhood environmentalism will build sustainable markets—and markets are beautiful.

Though the future is uncertain and an uphill battle awaits the public, ACM gives us the tools necessary to effectively manage our future. If used responsibly, in a sustained effort, the four-step model can be used to resolve conflict and promote sustainability practices. ACM is also rather inspiring in that the concept demands an informed and engaged public. A people's movement to become actively involved in collaboration is central to the model's idea of diversity and inclusiveness. Though there are severe challenges in achieving collaboration, we must closely examine our shortcomings to ensure a growing rate of progress. ACM can continually be improved upon to ensure challenges are met and actions are set in motion to better every aspect of health and life on Earth. We will succeed because we must—we all inherit this small, wonderful blue planet.

✳ *Human Dimensions: Reclaiming Governance*

As National Resource Management (NRM) has evolved over the years, traditional views of the environment and human relationships between nature and sense of place have also evolved. Today, NRM is characterized by certain "wicked" problems. The dynamic and often aggressive nature of these problems creates difficulty for management policy. It has become apparent we can no longer utilize the one-dimensional approach of centralized, private decision-making (Hunter 2007). The complexity of resource problems today often fall outside the realm of traditional policy analysis and centralized legislation. This has paved the way for more adaptive management styles which utilize alternative stakeholder approaches to NRM (Hunter 2007). These new approaches formally redistribute power from centralized authority to neighborhoods. This new style of adaptive governance actively educates stakeholders about the challenges and demands of NRM today. As societies' ethical considerations of the environment and property continually grow, so too do our considerations of governance. Today, as more people relate to their communities, and thus the commons, collaborative management between stakeholders and institutions work for a more sustainable world—we decentralize all the time.

❋ I. Methods of Governance

The adaptive governance and alternative stakeholder approach to NRM addresses the past failures of government and emphasizes the development of partnerships between all people involved in resource conflict (Decker 1997). The process of building alliances between private and common interest requires all parties to network with each other. This broadens consultation with community members who will most likely be responsible for—and experience the consequences of—resource management (Decker 1997). Governance is currently monopolized by the state, but it is important to explore and advance existing alternatives. To reclaim our governance, I find it beneficial to note that we will not simply wake up in liberty one day. Transition from the state requires civic participation. Though governance is still monopolized by authority, there are emerging orders within currently existing institutions that have the goal to defuse power to the commons. In regard to common pool resources, there are five prevalent methods of governance:

Expert Authority. (DAD approach: Decide, Announce, and Defend). This is a traditional approach largely practiced by the state.

Passive/Receptive. This approach is based on awareness and involves keeping one's eyes and ears open.

Inquisitive. This involves actively seeking information to understand stakeholder views, needs, wants, etc. Utilizes surveys, focus groups, and other things of this nature to gain information.

Transactional. (Involve, Negotiate, and Implement). Often has multiple objectives of involvement. This approach strives to develop trust and build relationships to reach implementable decisions. Stakeholders involved in some/many aspects of decision-making though their input is not binding.

Co-Managerial. This approach involves shared decision-making, action, and accountability (Ostermeier 2010).

The DAD approach is a traditional approach that remains in wide use today, especially in terms of crisis-oriented conservation events (Decker 1997). DAD is the simple solution. Hierarchies make decisions and sweeping resource policy is the result. The problem is, no matter how simple an ecological concept, the natural system behind it is incredibly complex. Simple solutions cannot mitigate complex systems— but evolving, dynamic systems can continually shift policy to meet public and environmental health demands. This is why there is a need for greater community involvement, free association, and a stakeholder approach that allows equal participation among all. The goal of such collaboration is resilience[16]—for both communities and ecosystems. In ecology, resilience is a property that reflects the ability of a system to withstand perturbations or shocks; of course, we want this for our social systems as well. Resilience theory suggests that

---

[16] en.wikipedia.org/wiki/Resilience_(ecology)

managed ecological systems are dynamic and unpredictable. Moreover, strategic top-down management tends to erode resilience, making the system vulnerable to dramatic and surprising change.

Lucky for us, collaboration is in demand and the market is growing. Today, in the ACM setting, the authoritative approach seems to be outdated. Stakeholder interest in NRM continues to grow. These interests are diverse and stakeholders often demand desirable management policy. This can cause a great rift between a resource practitioner and stakeholders; thus the "I know what's best for you" approach to NRM is being met with criticism (Decker 1997). For example, in the Adirondack Mountains region of New York, stakeholders greatly disagreed with what biologists deemed to be acceptable deer populations. Resource managers wanted to uphold their decision and refused to change existing policies (Decker 1997). In response, local hunters contacted their representatives who eventually took authority away from the resource agency. As a result, one-third of New York's deer population was mismanaged for over a quarter of a century (Decker 1997). It was not until power was redistributed, with the populace given equal footing, that the crisis was ameliorated—a common trend I will discuss in more detail in the upcoming section "Common Property: An Ecological Consideration."

The passive/receptive approach to NRM requires resource managers to listen to concerns of different stakeholders and place weight on these concerns prior to making decisions (Decker 1997). In this approach, managers listen to the concerns of stakeholders but do not actively seek public input. Furthermore, resource managers decide what is the most important of these concerns, not the stakeholder. The result is that stakeholder concerns have little impact on the policy-making process. Initiative in the collaboration process is solely the responsibility of the stakeholder, as resource managers do not actively seek advice (Decker et al. 1997). During some instances, managers may interact with stakeholder groups, but generally interaction is avoided. At best the manager will take into account concerns of the public when making decisions with this approach (Decker et al. 1997). Clearly this management style does not fit the ACM model.

The inquisitive approach may be described as the antithesis of the passive/receptive approach. Here, resource practitioners (note: no longer managers) seek input from stakeholders, are engaged with the public during the decision-making process, and place a lot of weight on public concerns when helping stakeholders develop policy (Decker 1997). With this approach, resource managers often utilize "systematic surveys" to gain a uniquely scientific understanding of stakeholder interests. This may be the most commonly used management style today, and has produced a great many benefits (Decker 1997). This is closer, but the goal we seek is horizontal, dynamic adaptive governance.

The transactional approach to policy development greatly represents ACM. This approach requires practitioners to create and facilitate events in which stakeholders talk with one another about their concerns (Decker 1997). Traditionally, stakeholders met with resource managers separately; this transactional approach brings everyone together to address issues. Additionally, transaction allows stakeholders to identify common ground in their conflicts, thus allowing negotiations to occur (Decker et al. 1997). More often than not, stakeholders reach a consensus on a management plan that suits the interests of involved parties. The role of the resource manager is to educate all stakeholders on the challenges that face resource management, facilitate discussion over complex issues, mediate debate between invested parties, and allow collaboration to solve resource conflicts (Decker 1997).

The New York Department of Environmental Conservation (NY DEC) practiced the transactional stakeholder approach to NRM in response to hunter discontent of New York's deer management program (Nelson 1992). In 1990, the NY DEC created citizen task forces (CTFs) to heavily influence policy. New York deer managers developed a forum and ground rules to allow various stakeholders to collaborate with one another (Nelson 1992). Stakeholder discussions, with resource practitioners playing the role of resource experts, allowed citizens to negotiate the respective weight of their stakes throughout the process. The overall goal of the CTFs was to reach a consensus on deer population (Nelson 1992). All important stakeholders were included, the resource managers discussed and informed these stakeholders about the challenges of resource management, and a facilitator handled the meetings. Discussion among stakeholders was encouraged and everyone involved in the process had a clear understanding of each others' interests (Nelson 1992). Wildlife managers then helped participants determine management objectives. Overall, the transactional approach implored by the NY DEC has had resounding success (Nelson 1992).

Finally, the co-managerial approach places great responsibility in the hands of the general public (Decker 1997). This approach recognizes the need for, and difficulty of, making resource decisions that meet the demands of stakeholders. To meet these challenges, this approach develops operational guidelines for managers and stakeholders while providing oversight, accountability, and evaluation of the entire process (Decker 1997). This approach employs educational communication programs for all participants. This fully informs stakeholders about the process and challenge of NRM (Decker 1997). The resource practitioners provide expertise on what NRM is and establishes a management process to be followed by stakeholders. Furthermore, resource practitioners train community members in NRM, approve community management plans, and monitor programs put in place (Decker 1997). The co-managerial approach requires resource agencies to work directly with stakeholders in local communities. The practice of adaptive governance promotes collaboration with community members, while developing, implementing, and monitoring management plans. The co-managerial stakeholder approach is a new and emerging practice in resource management as it is an evolution of the transactional approach (Decker 1997).

Of these alternative stakeholder approaches, the transactional and co-managerial traditions of NRM are best suited to tackle the complex, wicked problems facing resource management today. Human dimensions are growing continually important to the decision-making process. The two described stakeholder approaches work to redistribute power between resource agencies and the communities they serve. By practicing ACM, resource managers are able to make scientifically informed and community supported resource decisions. Human dimension considerations also provide a forum for honest communication among professionals, stakeholders, and the community members who will be affected by management policies (Decker 1997). These approaches work to promote collaboration between agencies and people, thus promoting democratic decision-making. Engaging the citizenry while calling for public discourse and reasoned debate brings consensus and legitimacy to management decisions (Ostermeier 2010). The public process also has the power to either expose or avoid agency capture, insuring the people's needs are being reflected, not the interests of state institutions or industry (Ostermeier 2010). In the current environment, this approach assists a reclaiming of the commons because it redistributes power away from institutionalized authority only to labor towards a democratic alternative. The transactional and co-managerial stakeholder approaches consider and reflect upon public concerns when crafting resource policy.

A closer look at the NY DEC engagement of stakeholders to resolve the deer population conflict furthers the case for ACM to tackle today's wicked problems. The NY DEC, due to public anger over deer management policies, needed to involve the community in the management process (Nelson 1992). The old management model put the wildlife manager at the heart of decision-making. After listening to everyone's concerns, and reviewing available data, the wildlife manager alone dictated policy. The NY DEC promoted public hearings and interactions with stakeholders to develop policy. In a public hearing, each stakeholder would learn other concerns and positions (Nelson 1992). Stakeholders would also see how their input was used in the process. Furthermore, stakeholders would know the underlying interests of their opposition, find areas of common ground, and be part of a collaborative process (Nelson 1992).

The NY DEC, in conjunction with the Human Dimensions Research Unit at Cornell University, developed their CTFs. The CTFs were used to bring opposing interests together and compile stakeholder recommendations to create management policy (Nelson 1992). This approach takes the manager out of the middle of decision-making and places stakeholders at the heart of the process. The group determined what the deer population should be (Nelson 1992). Group decision-making negates the idea of the agency pitted against the stakeholder. In addition, this eliminates the possibility of the loudest stakeholders dominating an entire hearing (Nelson 1992).

Aside from community input on deer management, the NY DEC also wanted to build relationships with stakeholders and the general public (Nelson 1992). The agency also desired to educate the public on deer biology and the challenges of deer management. These goals too were obtained through outreach and the development of CTFs.

The formation of the CTFs is groundbreaking. The process places the power of decision-making in the hands of those who will be directly affected by policy decisions. The resource practitioners have been able to educate the public about the issues of deer management, thus allowing an informed and engaged citizenry to develop policy. The CTFs allow a direct and honest communication between all stakeholders and democratic decision-making follows. Opposing views are equally considered during these public meetings, compromises are made, and ACM follows. Though challenges may certainly arise with this type of conflict resolution, the NY DEC has experienced great success with this process. By ceding power back to the people, the agency built relationships throughout the community and involved the public in the resource management process (Ostermeier 2010).

In a time of increasing complexity of the challenges facing NRM, it is imperative that the public at large and resource professionals practice ACM. In our current social order the trend of resource practitioners to educate and inform the public about issues facing their communities should be championed. We live in a time of wicked problems, but with power continually growing in the commons, resource practitioners can utilize public values, recommendations, and preferences in their decision-making. Resource professionals also need to build working relationships with their communities. This relationship will foster greater stakeholder interest in the collaborative process and will promote consensus building around issues, along with support for policy decisions. In conjunction with relationship building, it is imperative that resource practitioners are able to defuse conflicts among stakeholder groups. Resolving conflict and moving collaboration forward is essential to respond effectively to resource problems. Practitioners of ACM need to increase the quality of decision-making, offer advice when necessary, and implement effective policies (Ostermeier 2010).

Following the method of ACM, it is easy to note the public also claims responsibility in the process. Stakeholders must take an active role in educating themselves about new challenges in resource management. It is beneficial for the public to address resource challenges in a civil manner and have honest communication with other stakeholders and resource specialists. Conflict would be better resolved if approached in a responsible and effective way. Stakeholders, with their new leadership role, are willing to build on common ground and compromise to develop a best management practice. The public is needed to fill the role of discussing management issues while reaching consensus on sound resource policies (Ostermeier 2010).

The role of the commons stands out, utilization of stakeholder approaches in policy-making is now a necessity for the development of management plans. This requires stakeholders to effectively engage the management process. The human dimensions of NRM are of growing importance. If this trend continues, full participation and power in the commons is the logical conclusion of such practice.

❊ II. *Conflict and Resolution*

ACM would be incredibly successful under a common regime because diverse human values and perspectives would be taken into consideration. Over the years, there has been a shift in our institutions as they move away from anthropocentric utilitarian ideals towards a more sustainable ethic. Utility still plays a major role in society, but the recent shift to the ecosystem services approach of resource management reflects an emerging intrinsic value perspective. As Western values change, at the personal level, society is beginning to relate more to place. Policy of state is still unsustainable, but the trend of adaptive governance is real—we are living in the period of transition. But how did we get here, and how can we push ourselves ever more forward?

Power systems view natural resources as a means of maximizing utility (Wilson 2010). This anthropocentric outlook over resources expanded throughout the early history of the United States at the behest of imperialism and capitalism. As the United States gained power in the world, the nation continually waged military campaigns to acquire more land and resources (Zinn 2003). Early U.S. history (from events such as the Trail of Tears, the War of 1812, manifest destiny, and others) reflects the conquering of land from indigenous people or weaker nation states to obtain large tracts of land, enclosed property, and new resources (Zinn 2003). As time progressed and the Industrial Revolution occurred unchecked, capitalism viewed land as a commodity (Wilson 2010). As the natural world suffered from this unchecked capitalism, so too did the commons. Capitalism ensures the populace has little or no control over their individual labor or the means of production. Take Appalachia for example. In my C4SS commentary, *Wild, Wonderful, and Free*, I explain the impact of capital and industry on common governance:

> Before industry came to the mountains, a unique form of common governance existed. Communities obtained subsistence from the surrounding old growth forest. Everyone understood not to claim more than necessary from the commons. This governance naturally produced the maximum sustainable yield of resources. Locals labored, bartered, and brought goods to market together.
>
> As European expansion claimed the new world, land became the ultimate commodity and all eyes were fixed on the pristine forests of Appalachia. Enclosure movements commenced as a cash economy developed in the region for the first time. By the early nineteenth century, violent confrontations ruined native populations. The mass slaughter of indigenous people culminated in the Trail of Tears, eradicating tribes from Appalachian governance.
>
> Decades later, in post-Civil War America, mountain settlers were coaxed into selling mineral rights to would-be industry barons. Broad form deeds were developed to acquire local lands. Mineral rights were obtained for less than a dollar an acre as mountaineers maintained surface rights. Clauses in these deeds, however, allowed industrialists to take over the land at the company's discretion for resource extraction—even if such acquisition would surprise grandchildren decades later. Locals were forced off of their property to line the pockets of absentee capital-

ists, often by rights that had been sold generations before. By the end of the Industrial Revolution coal reigned as king.

Industry came to own a vast amount of property in the Central and Southern Appalachians, affording barons incredible power over mountain communities. Company towns popped up near mining operations. Workers lived in company barracks, were paid in company scrip, and were required to purchase goods at the company store. Mono-economies developed across the coalfields that still persist today.

The rise of industrial capitalism deeply scarred landscapes as vast areas of land were managed for maximum utility. This rise has been long, but at the turn of the industrial revolution a growing social consciousness and awareness of the socio-economic divide—the many poor and the few wealthy—gave rise to alternative movements. There is much history to discuss, far outside the boundaries of this study, but in regard to place, society developed an idea that all human beings' culture and natural heritage deserved moral consideration. This idea of cautionary utility for all then began to consider future generations. The thought of preservation of the natural world and saving resources for posterity sparked a political and environmental movement throughout the West (Wilson 2010).

In the twentieth century there also emerged non-anthropocentric views of the natural world—property management could yield a mutualist relationship between human civilization and the surrounding ecology (Wilson 2010). This emerging consensus extended moral standing to organisms other than human beings. A humane movement has evolved, re-emerging views about the intrinsic value of the entire biosphere and ecosystems became again part of the national conscience. The environmental movement throughout the twentieth—and on into the twenty-first—century has reached great heights and is discussed regularly in social, economic, and political arenas. The environmental movement today remains deeply political as western values continue to evolve. Climate change, environmental justice, sustainability, and other issues are common dinner table discussions for many.

This evolution of western values has unique consequences for NRM. In an era of state-controlled institutions, laboring to understand the worldview and personal relationship community members have with the natural world can help reduce conflict and further democratic decision-making (Morford 2003). By understanding the public's relationship with nature, both resource practitioners and stakeholders can mitigate conflict. Actively pursuing a cultural awareness will help community members feel comfortable with the ACM process (Morford 2003). Public hearings can be very personal; both resource practitioners and stakeholders must become aware of cultural values and worldviews. It is also important to note how opposing viewpoints can exacerbate conflict (Morford 2003). Practitioners will have to respect opposing views and continually clarify what others have said to ensure collaboration. For public participation to be successful, resource practitioners, along with stakeholders, will have to learn, understand, and respect differing ideas (Morford 2003). For resource practitioners, understanding the evolution of values will help develop the ACM process by bringing the public's idea of the natural world, sense of place, and social views together (Morford 2003).

The importance of place and the attachments people share with them directly affects NRM. Sense of place re-enforces the need of NRM to continue the transformation from anthropocentrism to a sustainable property management ethic. Respect of the land is a demand of place attachment; furthermore, sustainable land use practices, along with community involvement in the land use process, is of growing importance (Freyfogle 1998). Land use utilizes both the public and private realms of our institutions. When this is realized, new visions of our landscapes will evolve to benefit individuals, communities, and the natural world. NRM, with respect for land and the people attached to it, will maximize benefits to the environment, ecological communities, and our neighborhoods (Freyfogle 1998).

In terms of resource use, place conflicts are unavoidable. The role of the resource practitioner is to minimize these impacts (Ostermeier 2010). To be successful at this, in recent years professionals have labored to understand the place they are working in. This means understanding community members and obtaining information on their cultural and natural ties to property (Ostermeier 2010). These resource managers now take time to learn about land and space that is significant to people. This new development encourages practitioners to labor and leave as little impact on place connections as possible. To do so, common interests are discovered and collaborative management plans are developed to protect special areas (Ostermeier 2010). Under the traditional DAD approach to governance this was not the case. A paradigm shift has occurred.

Many professionals now learn cultural ties to the land, the history between land and people, and the connectedness local stakeholders share with their land. If the decentralised theme continues, resource decisions will be based on the interaction between property and the sociopolitical processes that act upon it. Professionals today need to share their decision-making power with stakeholders. Because of recent paradigm shifts this is a growing trend. ACM is essential to the resource management process, allowing experts to educate stakeholders and take careful consideration of connectedness to place (Cheng 2003). In an ever-changing world, the human dimensions of NRM are growing increasingly important to policy, conflict resolution, and the achievement of a more just and sustainable world. Furthermore, to the libertarian, trends of adaptive governance underlie a more important current: one of changing institutions and a reclaiming of the commons.

✢ Human Dimensions: Changing Institutions

There are a growing number of complex problems facing NRM and society. In the face of these problems it has become apparent that a reevaluation of the relationship between the public at large with the state, market, and civic institutions is necessary to meet the challenges of the twenty-first century. Effective communication is imperative to uphold public welfare, seek justice, and solve the issues confronting civilization. Furthermore, the public needs to continually challenge institutions to ensure their practices are legitimate. If a power structure wields illegitimate authority (which is usually the case), then it should be dismantled. This power, once institutionalized, will be liberated and reclaimed in common. The growing importance and successes of collaboration and partnerships in NRM indicates the need for an informed and engaged citizenry to work with each other in the public arena to develop sustainable resource policies that protect both the land and biosphere.

There are a number of institutions involved in NRM. Being that natural resources are a public good and that said resources are neither rival nor excludable, in the current market state institutions perhaps hold the most authority in regard to resource management (Armsworth 2010). In recent decades, the environmental movement has been strengthened greatly by the formation of both large and small non-profit organizations (Armsworth 2010). The civic sector has become a viable environmental force. The non-profit movement has been very efficient in promoting the sustainable use of resources at the local level. Their subsistence is imperative to the changing world of resource management. As these institutions become well-known and respected in their communities this will allow non-profits to implement conservation strategies more effective than the state—another transition of power. Finally, market institutions greatly affect resource policy as well. In recent years, the emerging idea of investing in ecosystem services has prompted an economic movement to sustainably manage resources. However, under the corporate state, there also remain very powerful capitalist institutions with enough political clout to ensure the continuance of exploitative, often hegemonic, resource policies.

✽ I. *Systems of Governance*

With a wide range of astounding resources all tiers of government have become involved in environmental policy (Armsworth 2010). Institutions at the multilateral (World bank, IMF, UN, EU, etc), national (federal government), regional (state governments), and local (city council, municipalities) levels all work to manage natural resource issues. In the United States, all branches of government are also involved in NRM. The legislative branch creates resource policy and authors laws that dictate the use of our resources (Armsworth 2010). The judicial branch interprets and decides how these laws are to be applied. Finally, the executive branch and its multiple environmental agencies practice and enforce resource policy (Armsworth 2010). Just a few examples of major federal reforms are the Clean Water Act (CWA), Endangered Species Act (ESA), and the Surface Mining Control and Reclamation Act (SMCRA). These policies, along with many others, directly affect NRM.

There are three principal tools governments utilize in NRM. First, government defines the rules of resource management for both the civic and private sector. One example of government mitigation is the establishment of acceptable conductivity for groundwater; this is a concern for extractive resource industries that introduce heavy metals to watersheds. The federal government also enforces laws regulating the legal limit of environmental impact allowed. Again, examples of this are the ESA and the CWA. Also, through conservation easements and exempting non-profits from taxes, government utilizes the tax system to allow others to move forward with resource-related issues. The state also purchases and manages public lands. The federal government owns 650 million acres of land in the United States. This is approximately 25% of the country's total landscape (Armsworth 2010). This has major implications for NRM.

Government institutions also exercise the authority to buy resource management responsibilities from other parties. A recent practice of the U.S. Department of Agriculture under the Farm Bill has distributed 1.6 billion dollars a year to farmers to establish ten-year agreements to manage conservation initiatives on their land (Armsworth 2010). As a result, the government manages resources on 31 million acres of privately owned property. The federal government also outsources NRM responsibilities to non-profit organizations. This is done by awarding numerous grants to civic sector institutions along with establishing a tax exempt status for these organizations (Armsworth 2010).

For all the hype, government policies do not always garnish desirable results. Conflict currently exists between the regulatory state and the elite, but it is latent. Utility monopolies such as Duke-Progress Energy and the Tennessee Valley Authority (among others), coupled with industry giants King Coal, Big Oil, and Fracked Gas, have a lock on the energy market. Because of the state-capitalist system, other market players (and people like you and I) remain economically dependent on these elites. The state knows this and is loyal to them. Its economic strength is fueled by the energy industry. Take, for example, the Environmental Protection Agency (EPA) under the Bush Administration. In 2002, the Administration reclassified mining waste as permissible fill material under section 404 of the CWA. Because of this redefinition, the process of valley fill has been deemed legal for coal surface mine operations and dangerous pollutants such as arsenic, sulfates, and selenium found in mine waste have made their way into the streams, tributaries, and wetlands of Appalachia. This change in the interpretation of the law has allowed the massive acceleration of mountaintop removal permits and requires mining waste to be dumped into Appalachian waters. Aside from the environmental concerns, this has devastated the Appalachian rural poor by creating a mono-economy, controlled by the coal industry, all with a negative effect on public health. The relationship between our government and corporate special interest has a history of exploiting innocent people and our natural resources. People's movements across the country have been evoked due to this relationship.

Counter to the state, the non-profit sector has gained considerable power in the past few years as more organizations develop. Environmentally oriented non-profits are growing at a larger rate than any other civic sector initiative (Armsworth 2010). These organizations have affected many aspects of NRM. This is because there are multiple organizations with diverse management objectives. The result is an eclectic set of institutions with diverse management strategies. The civic sector is composed of large organizations such as the Nature Conservancy which operates both internationally and nationally, to local organizations such as the West Virginia Highlands Conservancy and my previous employer Clean Water for North Carolina.

The growing importance of the civic sector cannot be ignored. Bill Bradley, a former democratic congressman, repeatedly stresses this point. In a 1998 article to the National Civic Review, Bradley states: "Never has a real vision come out of Washington and never has a real vision stemmed from just one of our political parties." Bradley stresses the civic sector is more effective in defining a common purpose with local community members and stakeholders. This allows non-profits to negotiate consensus on, and agreements to, resource management issues at the local level. Non-profit organizations are effective because of their independence from the corporate sector and their ability to work on the ground in communities (Bradley 1998). The ethos of these organizations have greatly prompted public trust in their approach to NRM and has made them an effective force in the environmental movement (Bradley 1998).

The rise of non-profits are also very important politically. These organizations, especially at the local level, are composed of everyday citizens that are concerned about the well-being of their cultural and natural heritage. This allows for organization at the grassroots, alleviating restrictions over the discussion of NRM in terms of environmental sustainability, public health, and the concept of environmental justice. Many non-profits are products of, and continue to build, people's movements against destructive resource agendas while advocating smart management initiatives to protect our environment, place, and people.

Though there have been many accomplishments achieved by the civic sector, these institutions too must be closely monitored by society. New reports suggest that a number of Non-Governmental Organizations (NGOs) are in fact not actually NGOs (Schott 2010). Instead, these organizations have been classified as GONGOs, or rather *Government Organized Non-Governmental Organizations*. These particular groups are not only funded by, but are fully staffed and supported by, government (Schott 2010). What is most striking about GONGOs is that, being a government operation, they do not seek to bring change to the system, but to control and manage change (Schott 2010). The ethics and motivations of these institutions must be gauged to ensure that their interests positively affect humanity.

Market institutions also heavily influence NRM. The market system includes small businesses and large multinational companies that have corporate policies that directly affect our resources. Some of these institutions consider sustainable resource management as a social responsibility, others use their relationship with the state to enforce policies that are detrimental to our land, water, and air. The emerging idea of investing in ecosystem services is gaining the attention of some market institutions, and environmental restoration and conservation initiatives have developed. Rio Tinto, for example, is one of the world's largest mining and mineral companies (Armsworth 2010). The company operates in some of the most sensitive areas of the world in terms of biodiversity. Corporate policy dictates that their mining operations must be offset by a net-positive gain in biodiversity in another area (Armsworth 2010).

Though investment in sustainable NRM is on the rise, economic globalization has had detrimental impacts to natural resources around the planet. Wendell Berry often explains how the growth of factory farms and agribusiness has taken jobs away from local farmers. As industrialization continually forces locally owned farms and businesses closed, it removes the ability for communities to produce their own food and other necessities (Berry 2002). In terms of natural resources, Berry explains that rules imposed on farmland from mega-corporations result in soil loss, genetic impoverishment of our crops, and contamination of our groundwater. In many cases, industrial economies impoverish communities they move into (Berry 2002). As natural resources in an area are exploited by large industries, the local uniqueness and cultural heritage of the area simultaneously diminishes (Berry 2002). Furthermore, there still remain state-enforced laws such as compulsory pooling and eminent domain that serve to allow big polluters to disregard property rights and wreck natural habitats that naturally offer the ecosystem service of carbon sequestration. There still remain intellectual property laws that permit patent monopoly, producing a barrier to competition in the market. As argued previously, the current captured market is undesirable.

"Growth at any cost" economics, the dogma of neoliberalism and government institutions, utilizes precious landscapes and resources needed for ecological subsistence. Even programs that seek mechanisms for conservation, such as the United Nation's REDD (Reduced Emissions from Deforestation and Forest Degradation), inadvertently promote the total exploitation of natural areas simply because regulation diverts resource extraction to unprotected land/seascapes. Enclosure movements (acquisition of territories for the state or private capital) more often than not exploit natural landscapes. To the contrary, democratic management of natural areas has resulted in best sustainability practices.

The freed market, operating underneath the spontaneous order, is categorically different, however. The work of Nobel Prize recipient Elinor Ostrom demonstrates environmental protection increases with Common Pool Resource Institutions. Arun Agrawal, in his work *Environmentality*, notes sustainable forest policy emerged in the Kumoan region of the Himalayas as a result of decentralized, democratically controlled resource management. In our cities, the establishment of urban wilderness areas popping up around the globe, from the labor of civic sector institutions and private citizens, are protecting large expanses of forest and crucial habitat from economic exploitation—my favorite example hails from the Scruffy City of Knoxville, Tennessee, where over 1,000 acres of forested habitat is preserved. I will explore all of these in more detail in a later section.

There are many more examples of freed markets protecting wilderness and ecosystem services. This protection simultaneously provides ancillary benefits to all flora and fauna—including humans. Government institutions and concentrations of private capital are all too often hurdles to the implementation of policies that can ease the current biodiversity crisis.

* *II. Common Institutions*

Institutions administer both positive and negative impacts to society. Perhaps their greatest benefit is their openness—in the true public arena, the commons, people have the power to sway the opinion of their institutions as they are democratically operated. The public's ability to change policy is very empowering because this responsibility calls for everyday people to become an active force in the advancement of their communities. The question then becomes: what is the best way to ensure our civic participation? The answer lies in responsible and just policy crafted by common regimes. At the local or regional level, people advance non-profits they believe in via philanthropy, donations, or becoming members or volunteers. As more citizens become active and engaged, true grassroots movements develop. People's movements have the power to alter all of their institutions, ensuring they work to better society and use natural resources sustainably. Put simply, power is best when shared in common.

A reconstruction of both public and private institutions is necessary to allow future generations to inherit a world of social responsibility and environmental sustainability. History is full of people's movements achieving great victories against institutional oppression. Social movements must progress society towards an economic system that does not seek to achieve maximum profit; instead, economic systems should utilize their capital to provide for the public good. This is the mutualist political economy, where decentralized communities own their labor and influence the means of production, thus advancing civil and individual liberty.

Perhaps the most important deconstruction of power to be made is that of imperialism. Wars are fought for the attainment of natural resources, not the absurd notion of a national interest. There is no greater conflict between people and their institutions than that of war because war ends lives. Utilizing natural resources to build weapons of war for the conquest of more natural resources can no longer be accepted. War as a means of resolving conflict must be eliminated because technology today allows for the indiscriminate killing of mass amounts of innocent people. No longer can a "just" war be waged because human beings cannot protect themselves from armed forces in possession of great machines and weapons of war. In regard to the commons, governments will not protect natural resources. Nation-states work as rational actors to advance their own self interests and expand their power, largely through exploitation of natural resources. There is an inherent conflict of interest among states—the state with the most territory has the most resources for consumption. States will not share a territory or resource for too long. This is why war (be it military or economic) is the health of the state—it provides a monopoly over a territory and thus its resources. The state will only enhance the complex problems facing the world today. Progress, development, growth, and industry are the objectives of states. States and their supported industries are rapidly using up the common pool resource base to enhance their own power. It is the name of the game. Nation-states are large, bloated structures that require tons of resources—they will never protect the commons.

Free people will develop alternative federations and institutions to protect resources, however. It happens every day. People are becoming more aware of what burdens their societies. Education and awareness of public and environmental health are fostering concern for natural resources. Though markets are still largely controlled by the corporate state, liberation is coming. Contrary to the state, the liberated market, controlled and crafted by free human beings, will build the sustainable communities of tomorrow. Indeed, only in a liberated society, with no political boundaries, will human civilization realize its relationship with the environment. States can only destroy, never create. It is individual labor and initiative that enriches the commons, not executive decree. Common power would ensure best use of finite resources, beneficial ecosystem services, and property, thus ending the vicious cycle of global warfare for the attainment of more resources.

It is wise to be continually suspicious of authority—such suspicion allows the public to reclaim illegitimate institutions. This can create a world in which individuals are truly free—liberated from the ill effects of concentrated power.

This is worthy, and I would argue necessary, of our labor. Perhaps the closing paragraphs of Arthur C. Clarke's *Profiles of the Future*[17] best describe why:

> One thing seems certain. Our galaxy is now in the brief springtime of its life—a springtime made glorious by such brilliant blue-white stars as Vega and Sirius, and, on a more humble scale, our own Sun. Not until all these have flamed through their incandescent youth, in a few fleeting billions of years, will the real history of the universe begin.
>
> It will be a history illuminated only by the reds and infrareds of dully glowing stars that would be almost invisible to our eyes; yet the sombre hues of that all-but-eternal universe may be full of colour and beauty to whatever strange beings have adapted to it. They will know that before them lie, not the millions of years in which we measure eras of geology, nor the billions of years which span the past lives of the stars, but years to be counted literally in the trillions.
>
> They will have time enough, in those endless aeons, to attempt all things, and to gather all knowledge. They will be like gods, because no gods imagined by our minds have ever possessed the powers they will command. But for all that, they may envy us, basking in the bright afterglow of creation; for we knew the universe when it was young.

As a species, one day humankind will cease to exist. Whether there exists an opportunity to evolve, or if the rules of nature or hegemony force our extinction, in time, humanity will be realized as nothing more than a fleeting moment in the history of space. Perhaps the rise of our civilizations will remain a silent memory for all the eons that follow. For all

---

[17]http://books.google.com/books?id=ch19NjEERFMC&dq=Profiles+of+the+Future&hl=en&sa=X&ei=o8puVNzdEZD6iAK1mYHgBg&ved=0CCgQ6AEwAA

of that, here we are, with one another, basking in the bright afterglow of creation. We have but one bright and shining moment, such a precious space, for our inclined labor to craft a beautiful existence. If we achieve such a feat, we will know what it means to be free—such grandeur is only attainable in liberty.

✻ *Common Property: A Neighborhood Consideration*

Henri Lefebvre,[18] a French sociologist, is most famous for his observation that there are no neutral spaces in the city. The city center should be rich in places that can be occupied by the public. Most venues, however, are spaces of capital exclusions, and barriers exist everywhere. Even the geography of the city is affected by this power system, creating spaces of privilege and spaces of disparity, blocked apart by neighborhoods, zoning laws, and manipulated by the gentry.

Lefebvre strongly believed in the commons, holding, however, that the public had the right to common utilization of city space without restriction. In this view, being an agent in the city is not dependent on wealth or property ownership, but by participation in one's community—an idea deemed the "right to the city."

In the same tradition, political economist Elinor Ostrom, in her groundbreaking work, *Governing the Commons*[19] (1990), showed that common management led to more democratic and far more efficient systems of governance than that of private capital or state control. It is important to note that this is the result of action—reclaiming the commons requires an active, participatory populace. In his piece in *Aeon* magazine, *Cities Belong to Us*,[20] urban historian Leo

[18] en.wikipedia.org/wiki/Henri_Lefebvre

[19] http://www.kuhlen.name/MATERIALIEN/eDok/governing_the_commons1.pdf

[20] http://aeon.co/magazine/society/cities-thrive-when-public-space-is-really-public/

Hollis explains:

> Through violent and defiant protests, provocative performances, citizen action, even unsolicited horticulture, the battle for civic space continues to reinvent itself. Sometimes, the action starts in reaction to the state. Other times, it kicks off because the powers-that-be are too slow to react to events, and local residents or campaigners take matters into their own hands, taking the urban domain to be a common realm rather than "someone else's problem."

People are proud of their communities; they long for clean, safe neighborhoods and a healthy environment to live out their lives. It is also a desire of many to feel connected to their community. This longing is why social power and common property are so important—place and action are connected. Common property ownership demands the inclined labor of the citizenry.

"This place is our place." This is the mantra of the commons. The ramifications of this statement are revolutionary. As such, the state and concentrations of capital seek its destruction—but the people do rise. In this section, I wish to discuss state violence against the commons and growth coalitions in the city that threaten common stewardship of property. I will then identify ACM as praxis for moving forward.

* I. People's Park—Then and Now

The University of California, Berkeley, was a hotbed of political activity in the 1960s. The civil rights movement, anti-Vietnam War movement, and the feminist movement were all forces on campus—movement participants were ready colleagues who assisted each other in their respective causes. On the Berkeley campus, libertarians and the New Left worked together and squared off against the state, corporate interests, and the newly elected Governor of California, Ronald Reagan.

Dissent persisted throughout the decade of change, but perhaps the greatest confrontation between state and social power occurred at the People's Park in 1969. Here in the People's Park, dedicated students, members of the "public" university, took control of corporate land on their campus that was held under the dominion of the state of California.

The existing property was muddy and dormant. The space lied in the hands of absentee landowners to, one day, become a for-profit parking lot. The student activists turned it into a park. Using a wide variety of tools, after days of manual labor, the students dug up the earth and transformed the land into a student commons—access was open to the Berkeley community. The space became a gathering ground for students and a safe haven for the city's homeless. The students argued (at this public university) that they had every right to reclaim the corporate-controlled property for common use. The creation of the People's Park represented a new way of looking at property and looking at the distribution of power throughout the Berkeley community. The park resembled an image of a new society—a decentralized participatory system, as opposed to a space for capital.

The University did not take the acquisition lightly—college administrators and corporate bureaucrats turned to the state. Supporters of the park argued that the university was a public institution, and thus the will of the student body should be upheld. Reagan instead put his support behind state property under private contract.

Reagan called in the National Guard; as they marched onto campus fully loaded in combat gear, violence soon followed. In a violent clash with the student body, riots ensued. Images of tear gas and batons soon filled the news. When questioned about the use of force on the student body, Reagan noted: "We cannot choose the laws we obey just because of social protest." The state took control of the park and fenced it in. The military presence occupied Berkeley for a month—and the movement changed.

To raise awareness about state violence and the closure of the park, a peaceful demonstration was planned for the campus. Students and community members gathered at the university plaza to denounce the police treatment of students, the National Guard occupation of the campus and town of Berkeley, as well as the hostility the university displayed towards the park. The gathering was a typical non-violent demonstration—full of cheers, jeers, and chants. Jentri Anders, a student at Berkeley, attended the rally that day. In the documentary film, *Berkeley in the Sixties*,[21] she describes the violent actions taken by the state to kill the demonstrations:

> Everybody on the outside of the police line was running to try and get away from the gas. Everybody on the inside of the police line was trying to get out and police were beating people as they tried to get out. We went back to Grover Hall and waited for my friend to show up. She had been through the mill. She had been throwing up, it was nausea gas. So we drove up to the rose garden. We were standing up there at the rose garden looking out across the campus and the helicopters were still circling around.... I said I don't think we can stay here anymore. It was a very poignant moment. We all felt very defeated.

The response was indeed incredibly violent. The state police and the National Guard set their sights on unarmed student activists. Endorsed by Reagan, these state officials moved into the plaza and attacked the populace with fixed bayonets. They shot into the defenseless crowd, wounded seventy people, and murdered James Rector—all of this as helicopters flew over the student body, who were caged in the plaza by police and sprayed with burning mace. Karl Hess and Murray Rothbard, in their piece *Massacre at People's Park*[22] condemn

---

[21] imdb.com/title/tt0099121/
[22] mises.org/journals/lf/1969/1969_06_15.pdf

the action:

> The issues are crystal-clear: the armed, brutal, oppressive forces of the State stomping upon peaceful, unarmed, homesteading citizens. Anyone who fails to raise his voice in absolute condemnation of this reign of terror, anyone who equivocates or excuses or condones, can no longer call himself a libertarian. On the contrary, he thereby ranges himself with the forces of despotism; he becomes part of the Enemy.

The violent actions taken to disrupt the commons in 1969 still exist today. The events in Ferguson, Missouri, following the shooting death of teenager Michael Brown, offer a corollary to the events of Berkeley.

Following a vigil for the slain teen, community members squared off against police. What started as a protest regarding police brutality was soon met with military force. The police in Ferguson ascended on the town dressed in military garb, with M-4 carbine automatic rifles, sound machines, tear gas, and military vehicles. What has evolved in the time since this first confrontation is the "Hands Up, Don't Shoot"[23] movement.

Central to the story of Ferguson is the local QuikTrip gas station. On the second night of protests the store was looted and burned, but in the days that followed, the property was reclaimed and served as a space for organizing and the exchange of information. The front of the store lot even bore the sign "QT People's Park." As in Berkeley, police power soon peppered those gathering in the lot with tear gas. Just three short days after the park was occupied as public space, the police fenced off the lot. There are no longer social gatherings on the property, no demonstrations, no music or dance, and no organizing. A story in the *Washington Post* covering the QT People's Park closes with the following:

---

[23]appalachianson.wordpress.com/2014/08/19/hands-up-dont-shoot/

On the large metal post that once displayed the red-and-white QT logo, one person spray-painted "The QT People's Park. Liberated 8/10/14." But on Monday, police cleared the lot, removing the dozens of people who had been gathered there for days. The signs were torn down. And on Tuesday morning, a newly constructed wire fence protected the gas station at the corner. A group of men in hard hats and yellow vests worked to pick up debris and drain the gasoline from tanks beneath the pavement. They moved quickly, and silently. A single news crew shot a stand-up on the corner. But after a few takes, they left. Nothing happening here anymore. The lot is private property, so the protesters had no right to assemble there. As rapidly as it had sprouted, it was gone.

Is it that open-and-shut, however? It is proper to question the legitimacy of the statement: "The lot is private property, so the protesters had no right to assemble there." The lot had become a rallying point for the community of Ferguson. State senator Maria Chappelle-Nadal, a central figure of the Ferguson protests, told the *Washington Post* that the lot became a point of pride for the community: "These people have no other place, so they've made it their own." The common control of property is legitimate, the coercive state justifies its use of force in closing off the park as necessary for protecting private property.

The lot still lies vacant, however, and no individual for some time will labor on the space. The lot was reclaimed; even if it was private property, the gassing and clubbing of the new occupiers by state agents was brutal, unnecessary, and criminal. The state sanctioned violence far worse than behavior given a simple charge of "failure to disperse."

The state does not want common control of property. When the true public arena is discovered, nothing but massive decentralization is sure to follow. As seen in Berkeley nearly six decades ago, and in Ferguson today, the state will deploy brutal and violent tactics to remain in control of the public sector.

A revolutionary moment is inevitable, however, and such a moment will allow us to reclaim the commons—it is a cause that is just and it begins simply through civic participation. Protest is just one example of engaging the power structure; there are many more. The emergence of new technologies and our global connectedness has an incredible liberating capacity. There exists a constant push throughout human history to decentralize when the time is optimal. The emergence of democracy, for example, shows off this trait. We are connected. With each social movement that results in the abolition of illegitimate authority we take one step closer to the commons and the mutualist political economy[24] that awaits.

✣ II. The Growth Machine

In 1976, urban sociologist Harvey Molotch published his landmark paper *The City as a Growth Machine: Toward a Political Economy of Place*.[25] In his work, Molotch turned the prevailing dogma of urban space on its head. Molotch objects to the idea that cities are the product of competition between rational actors for property. In short, the prevailing idea of his time was that the spatial construct of urban systems were developed from market competition—this idea was wrong and Molotch knew it.

Our urban spaces are as complex as the power structures that govern them. It is important to remember, though, that the power structures of local governance are different from the halls of power of the nation-state. Local power structures exist as land-based growth coalitions—they wish to enclose

---

[24] mutualist.org/sitebuildercontent/sitebuilderfiles/MPE.pdf
[25] phobos.ramapo.edu/~vasishth/Readings/Molotch-City_As_Growth_Machine.pdf

property for maximum utility. This utility often leaves them at odds with local neighborhoods, as they are invaded, stolen via eminent domain or compulsory pooling, polluted, and/or developed (Domhoff 2005). Growth, the urban mentality, does not benefit everyone—it is largely the affluent coalitions that profit off of the current distribution of property. As sociologist William Domhoff (2005) explains:

> A local power structure is at its core an aggregate of land-based interests that profit from increasingly intensive use of land. It is a set of property owners who see their futures as linked together because of a common desire to increase the value of their individual parcels. Wishing to avoid any land uses on adjacent parcels that might decrease the value of their properties, they come to believe that working together is to the benefit of each and every one of them. Starting from the level of individual ownership of pieces of land, a "growth coalition" arises that develops a "we" feeling among its members even if they differ on other kinds of political and social issues.

The "we" feeling Domhoff describes is exacerbated when pro-growth land interests attract opponents to property development. These challengers are community members—neighborhoods and civic sector institutions with common interests. It is conflict that arises out of these competing interests that determine the spatial geography of the city. The power structure is responsible for increased suburbanization and gentrification for the affluent, urban renewal for spaces of capital and the disenfranchised parts of town—namely ghettoization and working class neighborhoods cut off from the urban center (Domhoff 2005). Spaces of capital invade the city, thus human labor, especially of the working poor and working class, is trapped in these spaces. Property is carefully divided in the city and usually benefits the growth coalitions who wish to obtain rent from property (land or developed space), as Harvey Molotch (1987) explains:

> Unlike the capitalist, the place entrepreneur's goal is not profit from production, but rent from trapping human activity in place. Besides sale prices and regular payments made by tenants to landlords, we take rent to include, more broadly, outlays made to realtors, mortgage lenders, title companies, and so forth. The people who are involved in generating rent are the investors in land and buildings and the professionals who serve them. We think of them as a special class among the privileged, analogous to the classic "rentiers" of a former age in a modern urban form. Not merely a residue of a disappearing social group, rentiers persist as a dynamic social force.

As capital is produced from rent, growth coalitions often look to government to create an environment friendly for capitalist control of space. There exists tension between the corporate sector, government, and these growth coalitions. The relationship is certainly not a healthy one. However, in the neoliberal era, a favorable relationship does exist for spaces of capital, as opposed to spaces to be owned in common. Of course profit is not the argument made by these institutions in their self-justification—the appropriations create jobs. In actuality their appropriations are thefts of property and common labor. Molotch (1976) describes the situation:

> Perhaps the key ideological prop for the growth machine, especially in terms of sustaining support from the working-class majority, is the claim that growth "makes jobs." This claim is aggressively promulgated by developers, builders, and local chambers of commerce. It becomes part of the statesman talk of editorialists and political officials. Such people do not speak of growth as useful to profits—rather, they speak of it as necessary for making jobs.

This structure of growth and the political forces within the city exemplify the importance of advancing the ideas of adaptive governance and ACM. Property (space) and land are resources of utmost importance in the city. With increased stakeholder involvement in the decisions over how such resources will be utilized, policy that reflects the common good will be more prevalent in our urban landscapes. The goal of ACM, as mentioned in previous sections of this study, is to redistribute power equally among all stakeholders—ending domination of the policy process. There is political success in common, however, as social movements develop and claim their right to governance; as Domhoff illustrates in this list from his publication *Power at the Local Level: Growth Coalition Theory*[26](2005):

1. Urban renewal increased tensions rather than resolving them, leaving cities in a greater state of fear and uncertainty.
2. Demands by African-Americans to integrate neighborhoods and schools put the growth coalitions in a bind because they feared increased white flight if the demands were met. Most growth coalitions tried to walk a tightrope, some more successfully than others.
3. Many local banks and corporations were bought up by even larger corporations from outside the city, or moved their headquarters to even larger cities, leaving the growth coalitions holding the bag. Some growth coalitions then fragmented.
4. Up-scale neighborhoods, environmentalists, left-wing activists fresh from Civil Rights and anti-war struggles, and well-educated high-tech workers passed slow-growth legislation or blocked specific projects in some cities.
5. Low-income people in small towns and urban neighborhoods, often led by women and minorities, became part of an environmental justice movement that resisted the creation of chemi-

---

[26] http://http/www2.ucsc.edu/whorulesamerica/local/growth_coalition_theory.html

cal dumps and waste treatment plants in their areas (Szasz 1994).
6. Unions based in service workers and government employees later joined the slow-growth, pro-neighborhood coalitions in some major cities.

With increased civic participation in the ACM process, it follows logically that challenges to these growth coalitions and spaces of capital would result in a true commons. In our urban areas, the commons would be a space communities understand as open to all for public benefit. Enclosure of the commons for capital or monopoly, as championed by absentee landlords and those who appropriate rent for profit, would be considered aggression against the entire community. This is not to say private property should not, or cannot, exist in the city—it is a legitimate form of property and thus permitted. This is to say, however, that along with private property there would also exist robust common space.

Common property within urban political boundaries would mean common ownership of production, usage of factories, and the wealth produced from these activities. It would also mean the conservation of space, as the freed-market mechanism would naturally provide economic incentive to protect and conserve the ancillary benefits awarded to the commons from ecosystem services. Decisions pertaining to urban space would follow the ACM model, thus liberating the populace from growth coalitions, concentrations of private capital, and the theft of space.

❋ *Common Property: An Ecological Consideration*

We are living through Earth's sixth great mass extinction crisis—on par with the rate that ended the reign of the dinosaurs, thus terminating the Mesozoic. As flora and fauna continue their precipitous decline, geologists and ecologists are again looking at the geologic timescale—a system of chronological measurements that relate rock strata with time. The timescale is divided by major moments in Earth's history—the most common divisions are in recognition of mass extinctions and the subsequent great radiations of life. As we experience this modern biodiversity crisis a new epoch is being contemplated, and it is already (unofficially) in wide use—welcome to the Anthropocene.

The Anthropocene marks the complete human dominance of the Earth system. This dominance affects a range of topics from human health to the politics we address. Our dominance raises important questions: how, and perhaps more importantly, by whom, did this dominance arise and how, and by whom, should these ever-important issues be addressed?

This ecological challenge requires constant revision of natural resource management/policy. If we are honest about the limitations of our natural ecosystems, however, and implement policies that best fit the needs, health, and demands of an informed society and its natural heritage, then we also need to take conversations about the nature of governance very seriously. What is governance? Where should its power lie? How can its influence best support a healthy, sustainable, ordered biosphere?

This final question has often been used to once again argue the great fallacy that state power is legitimate—it is not. The state's property monopoly has yielded a continual process of compromise between conservationists, big business, and government courts resulting in ever more encroachment on needed habitat. Government and industry continually sacrifice natural lands for development to fuel its consumption, which makes it necessary for the state and industry to sacrifice more natural areas.

Common property management, however, works to find maximum sustainable yields as opposed to maximum utility. In the commons, land is not a commodity, but a connection— a place of labor and heritage. This is true of wilderness areas, but also rural counties and urban environments. Adaptive governance offers unique ecological considerations—respect for cultural and natural heritage along with sustainable management of common pool resources.

✳ I. Urban Ecology

When most folks think of ecosystems they probably envision natural wilderness landscapes. This need not always be the case, however, as urban landscapes are in and of themselves ecosystems. Urban landscapes may even be home to large forest tracts and aquatic systems that provide habitat for many different species. Urban ecology is a biological science in its own right. The subject not only deals with human beings living in neighborhoods, towns, and cities but also with other organisms, how they relate to the urban landscape, and what habitats are available to them (Rebele 1994). Even a single city park can be divided into various different types of communities, such as lawns, meadows, woodlands, and aquatic habitats that all interact with one another (Rebele 1994).

Ecosystems are evolving landscapes that direct the development of species (Tansley 1935). Management of urban space, then, has rather far-reaching implications for biodiversity. Construction and urban development[27] destroys habitat and can eliminate local populations (Rebele 1994). Use of groundwater, eutrophication from nutrient loading of local aquatic systems, waste dispersal, and a host of other activities normal to the neoliberal city can have negative impacts on local biota (Sukopp 1981). Poor planning can exacerbate the effects of anthropogenic activity, impacting species richness and diversity, ecosystem complexity, stability, and equilibrium.

The most unique feature of urban ecosystems is absolute human dominance over the landscape—the urban environment is manufactured by politicians, concentrations of capital, and developers to support public needs and wants in the local economy. But is this desirable? People care about where

---

[27] en.wikipedia.org/wiki/Urban_planning

they live and hope for the best for their communities. New markets are beginning to emerge in cities as local business begins to network and scale up production against corporate institutions. People care about place—the neighborhood and the town—more with each passing day. The local movement is alive and well, and this feeds into the "this place is our place" mentality—it is important to extend that feeling towards our urban ecosystems as well. Feeding off of these human dimensions and sense of place connections, a healthy urban ecology can foster desire to protect local biodiversity. Through different mediums, the urban ecological movement can help people become aware of (and thus more concerned about) both their cultural and their natural heritage. This will naturally lead to a populace that is more concerned about conservation—urbanites will invest in the natural world to protect their commons. This is an important point because there currently exists a dilemma between urbanization and conservation.

Over 50% of the human population now lives in cities, and as populations expand, so too does urbanization. This creates an incredible challenge to species conservation, as the total size of urban space in the United States now exceeds the total size of areas protected for conservation (McKinney 2002). It is important, then, for markets to develop that encourage biodiversity conservation. Urban landscapes are very large and thus are very important for local, regional, and even global biodiversity (Dearborn and Clark 2009). It is here where the case for reclaiming the commons in urban space is particularly strong. The halls of power in the capitalist city seek maximum utility of land and space to create places of wealth. Elinor Ostrom has demonstrated the commons are managed as a net neutral—common regimes seek conservation of heritage and thus the maximum sustainable yield of available resources.

The dilemma is conserving biodiversity while creating a habitable environment for human beings. The aforementioned place connections, however, coupled with common property, create a liberating space for both human flourishing and habitat conservation. Our connections to place, after all, are dependent on our communities and our natural heritage. Civic participation is necessary for the public to gain control of the urban ecosystem. This participatory engagement would also encompass the entirety of an ecological system. Ideas of urban wilderness have been popping up in cities recently. An example near and dear to my heart, the Knoxville Urban Wilderness (KUW), is not a perfect reclaiming of the commons, but it is a start. Here, civic sector institutions, community members, and private land owners donated property, time, and labor to work with the city government to establish the largest urban wilderness corridor in the United States.

Two miles from Knoxville's (Tennessee) urban center there is a large patch of interconnected wilderness areas that offer recreational activities for all trail enthusiasts and valuable (now protected) habitat for a number of plant and animal species (LPF 2013). The south-side of this wilderness system is defined by thirty-five miles' worth of surface trails that connect city parks and natural areas with public and private lands. In all, the KUW is estimated to be over 1000 acres. The project was championed by the Legacy Parks Foundation and is the result of partnerships among Ijams Nature Center, the Appalachian Mountain Bike Club (all civic sector institutions), Tennessee Wildlife Resources Agency (state agency), and both the City and County of Knoxville (LPF 2013). Many individual Knoxvillians dedicated time to the wilderness project, offering their labor to build trails and bridges. Others donated their money, property, and even their legal advice to see the project through. Of course, all volunteer labor built the system—there was no help from any other source.

How does the urban wilderness support biodiversity? Urban ecosystems have usually been examined in how they *neg-*

atively impact species diversity—this is not the case in urban *wilderness*, however. The KUW provides 1000 acres of natural habitat to a variety of species in Knoxville. The spatial heterogeneity, complex structure and function, and diverse species composition of vegetation greatly helps the fitness of other living biological organisms such as mammals and birds (Tilgham 1987). The KUW just existing enhances biodiversity in the city. For birds alone there are great benefits of the wilderness area: trees and shrubs provide viable habitat; they provide nesting structures, places to feed, and now enhance civic participation and common governance.

An example of this community governance is noted in the popular uprising against a road project in the city. In 2013, the Tennessee Department of Transportation (TDOT) looked to use eminent domain to build yet another highway across East Tennessee. This highway, the James White Parkway, would have bored through crucial habitat in the Knoxville wilderness and destroyed part of the trail system that so many had labored over—and even more had come to enjoy. What followed was a fury of protest, and massive turnouts to public forums, all denouncing the land grab. In August of that year, due to public outrage and significant participation in public forums, TDOT scrapped its plans for construction, noting explicitly the wilderness system and common objection. This preserved the benefits of the wilderness for a host of other species living in Knoxville.

A feedback loop exists here, too: enhancement of biodiversity as a result of the KUW has increased the quality of life for Knoxvillians, and this alone will indirectly facilitate the preservation of biodiversity in urban centers and natural ecosystems. In short, urban wilderness is essential for promoting and preserving biodiversity in the urban forest. It is this type of participation that is needed to reclaim property in our urban space. In the years since the establishment of the KUW, civic sector institutions, private landholders, and disparate user groups have all come together to acquire even more territory. The system continues to grow, providing crucial habitat for all flora and fauna and true public places for city dwellers. Social power has spurted ahead of state power. This place is our place—mountain heritage and a true public commons are on the way.

This is a particularly interesting point in regard to the commons. Power lies with the decision makers. Adhering to the rules of adaptive collaborative management, places like Knoxville are in a unique position to advance common property. The labor of locals built the system. In South Knoxville in particular, there is a large sense of community pride in the ability to host the wilderness system. It has enhanced sense of place and, with it, civic participation. Halting TDOT, a state agency, and the capital to be made off of a new highway system is no feat to casually overlook. It is an advancement of social power and thus a reduction in state power. If movements such as this, reclaiming wilderness areas, installing community gardens, open access farms, etc. become a trend, then social power will continually advance—all while the grip of the state over our inclined labor is reduced and (hopefully) eventually forgotten.

This is the true beauty of the commons and decentralization movements. These liberating ideas open markets, allowing spontaneous order, as opposed to top-down decree, to build the communities we live in. The market mechanism and common regimes naturally look to the economic incentive of resource conservation. The ecosystem services awarded to the public from natural landscapes far outweigh maximum utility of land and roll-with-it development. Ecosystem services are for human beings. The more an urban populace realizes the economic and social benefits of natural areas, the more return investment ecological systems will receive from human populations.

Just a few examples of these market incentives: wetlands in urban areas improve urban hydrology by absorbing containments and mitigating flood hazards (Pankratz et al. 2007).

Increased vegetation can reduce the heat island effect during hot summer months—the more green space, the more comfortable urban dwellers live (DeNardo et al. 2005). These green areas also enhance local biodiversity for plants and woodland species, plus beetles, birds, spiders, and other species that colonize the area (Brenneisen 2006). These insects and birds may also help as pollinators supporting another growing industry: urban agriculture. With the growing local food scene, there is enormous potential for more small-scale farms that provide local food to the public. Another incredible ecosystem service is the regulation of air quality—which is notoriously bad during the summer months in many places across the country. In the United States, urban trees annually remove 711,000 tons of air pollutants—an economic value of nearly $3.8 billion (Nowak et al. 2006). Urban wilderness systems would be/are instrumental in providing a cost-effective way to reduce pollution in the city. Another service of urban trees, often overlooked, is their capacity for carbon sequestration. The more trees there are in an urban area, the more carbon is sequestered. This is particularly important in the age of climate change—especially interesting is the fact that urban trees may have a larger effect on climate regulation than trees in wild landscapes (Akbari 2002).

Perhaps the most pertinent ecosystem service provided is how natural landscapes improve the health and well-being of the human population. There exist, of course, physical benefits of air quality regulation from wilderness flora and water quality regulation from aquatic species, but there is also encouragement to get out and play. There are many psychological benefits to having a green escape near the city: it enhances leisure. Fuller et al. (2007) shows something particularly amazing about urban greenscapes: psychological and emotional benefits awarded to the human population from urban wildernesses actually increase with the amount of biodiversity in the ecosystem, as measured by species richness of plants, birds, and butterflies. The mutual feedback loop exists; conservation enhances urban life.

There are many more incentives for conservation in urban ecological systems, but they will only be actualized in the market. Because of its presence, future development must be mindful of the human dimensions of urban green space—providing ancillary benefits for the public arena, biodiversity, and surrounding landscape—otherwise known as the whole of the commons.

✣ II. Natural Resource Management

As adaptive governance is the name of the game in managing common property, it is necessary to investigate how such a mechanism would manage the resources we need to sustain and progress society. Here, the commons really get a chance to shine. Beyond the liberating qualities innate to decentralization, there also comes sustainable management of natural resources.

This of course makes perfect sense. Contrary to arguments made in *The Tragedy of the Commons*, Elinor Ostrom and other horizontalists such as Arun Agrawal have demonstrated in the economic literature that adaptive governance yields the best results. The reason is rather simple: when the populace is not included in the process of conservation, often enough, individuals feel like they can dismiss the relevance of executive decree. Authority alienates the individual, leaving a sentiment that not only does public dissent not matter, but any destruction or mismanagement of resources wrought upon a natural system is perhaps unfortunate, but justifiable. However, when individuals are brought into the process of governance there is a transformation: individuals become responsible collective actors. When ACM is applied to natural resource management, transition economies move away from centralized policy-making toward adaptive, dynamic governance—from state to neighborhood.

This trend holds rather large implications for traditional

leadership. The success of decentralized policies can be used as an argument to promote the redistribution of power, to rethink the common perception of authority, and, perhaps of most importance, to rethink property. This success builds the case for public, as opposed to state, ownership of the commons. Collaborative governance ultimately empowers the populace; it takes power from authority and promotes the concept of democratic governance.

The commons experiences this success because those in an environment, as opposed to a displaced authority, better understand human impacts to said environment and how subsistence is bettered/tied to natural resources. This makes sense; humans are part of nature, but nature continues to exist outside of human civilization. It is reckless and ill-informed human actions that pose a great risk to natural areas. The conclusion of many, that in order to protect our ecology there must be a strong government to oversee our natural areas, is refuted by poor land management at the hands of the state—excessive road construction, dams, surface mining, clear cuts, and much more. The state views land as a commodity, first and foremost, but the commons view land as their cultural and natural heritage.

A real-world case study of the benefits of ACM can be found in the Applegate Partnership. The partnership is a result of competing interests of environmental groups, farmers, the timber industry, the Bureau of Land Management, and the Forest Service. The conflict began in regard to management of the Applegate watershed in southern Oregon. Accelerated logging and road building after World War II raised great public concern for the local environment. In the 1990s, the Spotted Owl, whose habitat range is within the boundaries of southern Oregon, was listed as an endangered species. This was cheered as a victory for environmental groups as it halted a majority of the logging operations. Fires became a grave concern for southern Oregon, however, as a result of decreased logging. All the major players in this struggle remained greatly autonomous until the partnership was formed (Rolle 2002).

The conflict is a consequence of unique interests of natural resources, industry, and environmental quality. The very existence of this conflict is based on the perception that these entities are mutually exclusive. The Applegate Partnership examined and sought to end this conflict with a distinct mission (Rolle 2002):

> The Applegate Partnership is a community-based project involving industry, conservation groups, natural resource agencies, and residents cooperating to encourage and facilitate the use of natural resource principles that promote ecosystem health and diversity. Through community involvement and education, this partnership supports management of all land within the watershed in a manner that sustains natural resources and that will, in turn, contribute to economic and community well-being within the Applegate Valley.

The partnership explored collaborative options to bring all interests together and "encourage and facilitate the use of natural resource principles that promote ecosystem health and diversity" (Rolle 2002). Furthermore, their mission allows for the development of an action plan to support "management of all land within the watershed in a manner that sustains natural resources and that will, in turn, contribute to economic and community well-being within the Applegate Valley" (Rolle 2002). Though the conflict is ongoing, the Applegate Partnership is working because the organization is utilizing the principles of ACM. Sustainable forestry practices have helped industry and preserved forest tracts from fires and over-harvesting.

The success of Applegate has greatly depended on the partnerships' insistent inclusiveness and diversity of all parties on all sides of issues pertaining to the valley. Members are also continually successful at creating a forum of diverse ideas for mutual education. Due to this effort, over the last few years, community trust in the partnership has grown as problems are solved. Furthermore, the relationships between all parties corresponding with the partnership have greatly improved. Another success of the partnership is, through continual outreach and education, enormous benefits to the environmental and economic health of their community. Perhaps most important for the commons, Big Timber and the BLM are subject to the same rules as the other stakeholders—they hold equal, not greater, power within the partnership. This is another example of the reduction of state power, placing more in the hands of our social order.

To examine a true example of common governance creating best management practices, one may look to the Kumoan villagers who reside in the foothills of the Himalayan mountains. Their natural heritage is enriched by tremendous valleys and expansive rivers—the product of tectonic forces that continue to mold the region. Of incredible importance to the villagers is the bio-region's forest tracts. The ecosystem services the Kumoan forests offer the villagers are immeasurable. These forest tracts were, at one time, very beneficial to the colonial British state as well. Often at odds, the Kumoan people and the British state had very different ideas as to how the forests should be managed. Arun Agrawal, a political scientist who studies natural resource management, in his book *Environmentality*, discusses the history of intense conflict between the colonialist and villager. As his book progresses, it becomes a story of decentralization, community empowerment, and best management practices. Agrawal provides readers with a historical overview of natural resource management in the Kumoan region and explains the emergence of collaborative management, environmental identity, sense of place, and changes in the relationship between the state and the local.

The story of the Kumoan people is one of reclaiming the commons. Agrawal's book is a great example of how the cost of bureaucratic control always falls on locals. This burden forces democratic change. The regulatory mechanisms separated the Kumoan villagers from their natural heritage. The burdens of regulation and revolt led to a decline in ecological health which manifested itself throughout the population. As a result, the Kumoan villagers began to organize—the principles of democracy and the ideas of self governance led to the development of forest councils. It is during this stage of transition, from revolt to organization, that the state was forced into ceding its power. The entire relationship between the state and community was transformed—there were more channels for the flow of power. This empowerment caused stakeholder participation to increase and best management practices shifted from the centralized state to communities.

Agrawal's book echoes a theme prevalent everywhere today. As natural resource management has evolved over the years, traditional views of the environment and human relationships between nature and sense of place have also evolved. The trend is indeed welcome to libertarians and environmentalists. States tend to view natural resources as a means for maximizing utility—especially when considering military strength (as is the case in Agrawal's book) and neoliberal economics. As nation-states rise to power they continually wage campaigns to acquire more land and resources. The concept of collaborative management offers an alternative to the states' view of natural resources. Furthermore, this collaborative approach offers the method of achieving sustainability—reclaim the commons, understand the nature of power and the making of subjects, and dismantle illegitimate authority. It is this unique intersection of common property, political ecology, and environmental sustainability that is an incredibly concise argument for decentralized governance.

The conclusion of many, that in order to protect our ecology there must be a strong government to oversee our natural areas, is refuted when examining common resources and regimes. The state views landscapes as a commodity, first and foremost, but the commons views the places as natural heritage—a place for labor and preservation. It is decentralization, not authority, that will produced sustainable management of resources.

✻ III. Wilderness and Wildness

Ecology, the study of the living environment, has a rather interesting etymology. It is derived from the Greek *oikos*, meaning the home, and *logia*, meaning the discourse or study of. Ecology: the study of our home. Our home has its origins in wilderness, wildness, and place. Reclaiming our home, by reclaiming the commons, would allow for the emergence of a new but all-too-familiar order—one that asserts wildness in the human condition. As naturalist Gary Snyder states: "Wild doesn't mean disorderly; it means a different kind of order." A different kind of order is what all living species desperately need.

Thus far this has been a rather anthropocentric argument for the commons. The history of land and space includes not just people, politics, and economics, but also the biodiversity and environment of a given region. Every piece of land on this Earth has been shaped by the forces of deep time. Every living organism, all flora and fauna, landscapes, and seascapes are products of evolutionary adaptation. The world as we know it is the result of countless selection pressures, changing landscapes, restless seas, and vastly different climates. The land and resources that are subject to our civilization exist because of 4.6 billion years of natural history. Though ecosystem services offer a market mechanism for the preservation of natural areas, it is important to remember the moral imperative of treading lightly on the land. Nature for nature's sake has become somewhat of a forgotten ethic, but its importance is extraordinary.

All biomes are unique. Landscapes and seascapes are incredibly vast, and depending on one's travels, place connections, and experiences, favorites are made. We truly are a bounded people on boundless land, but my favorite area of the world lies in the humble, weeping mountains of the Appalachians. Humble because of eons of geologic time weathering majestic peaks to form the valley and ridge we know today. Weeping, because they have been subjugated to so much trespass.

When thinking of Appalachia, I am amazed by the sheer amount of water in the region. Imagine a drop of water falling from the sky over the rolling mountain ecosystem. As it plummets towards the Earth, a vast green valley and ridge awaits it. The water may land on a mountaintop, perhaps on the limbs of a great Eastern Hemlock, only to join with countless other molecules and make its way to the topsoil. The water would either provide nutrients to the local plant community or make its way into the ground where millions of microbes and bacteria await to naturally filter the precious resource. Water could escape to fresh mountain springs, to be lapped up by a number of animals or perhaps travel further still—until a great turn in the rocky slope takes it to the beginnings of a trickling stream. Here, the water will travel along the river continuum, passing vast aquatic communities, providing habitat for some of the region's incredible, endemic biodiversity. The water will carve and erode ancient rock, just to lay the sediments that will one day tell future travelers about our unique place in history. Water is nourishment, and it is incredibly important to this region's ecology.

The Appalachian Mountain chain is a mixed temperate rainforest. The Appalachians, at one point in their history, were the largest mountain chain in Earth history, dwarfing the Himalayas of today. The chain currently exists as a great cradle of biodiversity, home to over 100,000 species. The Eastern deciduous forest boasts incredible trees including oak, hickory, maple, birch, and the great poplar. The canopy of this forest provides habitat for numerous species of animals, and the peak of this succession also assists shrubs, fungus, aquatic systems, and even the soil. Maximum diversity has been reached in the Appalachians. The magnificent landscape is the product of the labor of snails, fungi, birds, salamanders, frogs, freshwater mussels, bears, and countless others. These mountains, often purple across the horizon, have had hundreds of millions of years to evolve a complex ecological community—among the most complex that currently exists. Perhaps Charles Darwin, in his groundbreaking work *The Origin of Species*,[28] best describes this phenomenon:

> It is interesting to contemplate an entangled bank, clothed with many plants of many kinds, with birds singing on the bushes, with various insects flitting about, and with worms crawling through the damp earth, and to reflect that these elaborately constructed forms, so different from each other, and dependent on each other in so complex a manner, have all been produced by laws acting around us.... There is grandeur in this view of life, with its several powers, having been originally breathed into a few forms or into one; and that, whilst this planet has gone cycling on according to the fixed law of gravity, from so simple a beginning endless forms most beautiful and most wonderful have been, and are being, evolved.

The Appalachian region is the oldest habitat in North America. These ancient mountains rose out of the Earth 200 million years before life evolved to occupy them. The first inhabitants of the land were plants. It is here plants developed vascular systems for the transport of water and essential nutrients. Evergreens soon marched across the ancient land creating one of the greatest forests in Earth's long history. Today, just one acre of forest in the Great Smoky Mountains National Park is home to more plant species than the whole of Europe.

---

[28] darwin-online.org.uk/Variorum/1860/1860-490-c-1859.html

Ecological succession on the continents began in the ancient Appalachians, allowing the formation of an array of microclimates that in turn provided an environment for enhanced species radiation. There were suddenly new niches for all flora and fauna to develop. This process of deep time was absent of human beings until just 12,000 years ago. At the end of the last ice age, humans came to the Appalachians for the first time.

Human history has taken its toll on Appalachia. To tell the story in its entirety is perhaps impossible, thus beyond the boundaries of this study. But perhaps the greatest agents of change in the Appalachians came in the 1750s when Europeans first colonized the land. Life on the frontier, prior to this point, was occupied by Native American tribes and early settlers of Scots-Irish, English, and German descent. Frontier life was radically different from life in the mountains today: everyone enjoyed the land. There was a true commons in the mountains; homesteading demanded sustainable control of resources. It was ill practice to take more than the forest could replenish. This changed when the Europeans came to the mountain communities: they sought to change both the natural and social order.

The communal use of land was at odds with state and private ownership of property. The affluent soon sought conquest and the race for resources was on. The newcomers soon began enclosure movements. Looking into the vast forest, the colonialists saw only commodities for exploitation. Missing from such a short-sighted view is the work of the soil microbes, fixing nitrogen to nourish an incredible array of plant species. These plants, as the base of the food web, from grasses and ferns to the hemlocks and the towering poplars, provide habitat to a truly remarkable succession of avian, terrestrial, and aquatic species. Conquest of land was devastating to this ecological community. These early enclosure movements were incredibly dangerous to human inhabitants as well because they gave rise to the iron fist of capital over the region. Timber and coal became king.

In just a few fleeting centuries, the result of over 200 million years of evolution was, and is still being, changed forever. The timber industry effectively logged the majority of Appalachia. The coal industry evolved, came to prominence in the late 1800s, and became king during the Industrial Revolution. This industry eventually developed coal surface mining which has leveled over 520 mountains to date throughout the region via mountaintop removal valley fill operations. These industries, coupled with others, are owned and operated by absentee landowners. The reign of capital over the mountains has spawned ecological tragedy. It is estimated that 700,000 acres of temperate Appalachian forests throughout West Virginia, Virginia, Kentucky, and Tennessee have been destroyed by coal surface mining (ilovemountains.org). As a result, more than 7% of Appalachian forests have been timbered and over 1,200 miles of streams across the region have been buried and polluted.

The cost of losing the commons has been great. The human story of what has been lost in Appalachia alone is troubling, but the plunder of this ancient landscape is a story of incredible tragedy. It is a story that is not isolated to this region, either. What has plundered Appalachia is centralized authority, and this is a global phenomenon. Across the world, wilderness destruction and biodiversity loss is managed, even desired, by top-down decree—power requires maximum utility of resources.

Kevin Carson, in his studies *The Great Domain of Cost-Plus: The Waste Production Economy*[29] and *Energy and Transportation Issues: A Libertarian Analysis*[30] expertly tells the story of how our manufactured economy utilizes far more energy per unit of output than necessary. The state does this because it makes energy inputs artificially cheap—this is why coal is so cheap—we do not pay the high price of losing

---

[29] c4ss.org/content/5580
[30] c4ss.org/content/11542

a mountain ecosystem. This, in turn, provides extractive resource industries preferential access to land: space enclosed by the state. The corporate arm of the state then heavily subsidizes resource extraction, highway transport, and, let us not forget, the war campaigns to secure, enclose, and exploit even more natural lands.

Management in the commons, however, was, and would again be, incredibly different. Liberated of state-sanctioned economic privilege, the market would equilibrate. Communities would purchase goods produced in smaller factories in the towns they live. Good benefits for us, but even better for landscapes, watersheds, and biodiversity. Such an order would ensure that vast landscapes will rarely, if ever, be occupied by our bodies. Liberty and wilderness are necessary for each others' survival, as American environmentalist Edward Abbey writes in *Desert Solitaire*[31]:

> A man could be a lover and defender of the wilderness without ever in his lifetime leaving the boundaries of asphalt, powerlines, and right-angled surfaces. We need wilderness whether or not we ever set foot in it. We need a refuge even though we may never need to set foot in it. We need the possibility of escape as surely as we need hope... Wilderness is not a luxury but a necessity of the human spirit, and as vital to our lives as water and good bread. A civilization which destroys what little remains of the wild, the spare, the original, is cutting itself off from its origins and betraying the principle of civilization itself.

Natural habitats, absent of human beings, are communities in their own right. In every corner of the Earth, species and resources interact to form the living environment. There are associations among these populations, they work in competition with one another, while simultaneously living in

---

[31] booksjadore.com/2016/05/26/desert-solitaire-a-season-in-the-wilderness-edward-abbey/

incredibly mutualistic relationships with one another. Some species are so connected, in fact, that an evolutionary change in one will lead to a change in the other. The natural world is home to a wonderfully complex order. This order does not deserve to be subjugated to the Anthropocene, but liberated from it.

✻ *Power and Property*

In the final analysis, any individual or institution with a claim to property wields power. When the libertarian examines property rights, they must consider systems of power, domination, enclosure, and assimilation. If one is to mix labor with land, the individual(s) hold dominion over it. A claim to property is a claim to power, but where should such power lie? If we wish for a society rooted in liberty, then there exists a necessary reclaiming of the commons. Full commitment to liberty demands both the individual and the collective.

In many libertarian circles the idea of individual liberty is well championed, while all too often collective liberty is shunned. But these ideas are one and the same. The commons are built and sustained by individuals—empowering the commons, by default, empowers all individuals. This is the true beauty of the freed market. A society operating under the principles of liberty necessarily rejects the concentration of power and coercive claims to property. Such an order thus champions individual labor, place connections, and civic participation in the political economy. Individual achievement exists not in spite of, but due to liberty. The commons are not coercive in any fashion, and thus meet the standards of appropriate property for a libertarian society as laid out by Benjamin R. Tucker[32]:

---

[32] fair-use.org/benjamin-tucker/instead-of-a-book/rights-and-duties-under-anarchy

> Anarchism being neither more nor less than the principle of equal liberty, property, in an Anarchistic society, must accord with this principle. The only form of property which meets this condition is that which secures each in the possession of his own products, or of such products of others as he may have obtained unconditionally without the use of fraud or force, and in the realization of all titles to such products which he may hold by virtue of free contract with others. Possession, unvitiated by fraud or force, of values to which no one else holds a title unvitiated by fraud or force, and the possession of similarly unvitiated titles to values, constitute the Anarchistic criterion of ownership.

A libertarian economic system would fully support common governance of property. In such a system, collective labor would be free to mix with the land. The possibilities such a society could achieve are endless; the spontaneous order is awe-inspiring. What can we craft together during our time under the sun? What will our property gift future generations? It is exciting to think of the prospects. To get there we will need to reclaim the commons. When control of property, and the power over it, is decentralized, our lives will fully be ours to craft—individually and collectively, in liberty.

LITERATURE CITED & WORKS REFERENCED

Abbey, Edward (1990). *Desert Solitaire*. McGraw Hill Book Company.

Agrawal, Arun (2005). *Environmentality: Technologies of Government and the Making of Subjects*. Duke University Press.

Akbari, H. (2002). "Shade Trees Reduce Building Energy Use and CO_2 Emissions From Power Plants." *Environmental Pollution*, Vol. 116, S119-S126.

Armsworth, Paul (2010). *Conservation Biology.* University of Tennessee, Knoxville.

Armsworth, Paul (2007). "Ecosystem Service Science and the Way Forward for Conservation." *Conservation Biology*, Vol. 21, No. 6. Society for Conservation Biology.

Berry, Wendell (2002). "The Agrarian Standard." *Orion Magazine.*

Berry, Wendell (1965). *The Long-Legged House.* Harcourt, Brace & World, Inc. United States of America.

Berry, Wendell (1998). *Mat Feltner's World.* Island Press.

Bradly, Bill (1998). "The Importance of the Civic Sector." *National Civic Review*, Vol. 87, No. 2.

Brenneisen, S. (2006) "Space for Urban Wildlife: Designing Green Roofs as Habitat in Switzerland." *Urban Habitats*, Vol. 4, 27-36.

Butler, Rhett (2007). "As Rain Forests Disappear, A Market Solution Emerges." *Yale Environment* 360. Yale University.

Carson, Kevin (2010). "The Great Domain of Cost-Plus: The Waste Production Economy." *The Center for a Stateless Society* (c4ss.org).

Carson, Kevin (2012). "Energy and Transportation Issues: A Libertarian Analysis." *The Center for a Stateless Society* (c4ss.org).

Carson, Kevin (2012). "Why Corporate Capitalism is Unsustainable." *The Center for a Stateless Society* (c4ss.org).

Cattan, Nacha (2010). "Climate Change Set to Boost Mexican Immigration to the US, Says Study." *The Christian Science Monitor.*

Cheng, S. Atony (2003). "Place as an Integrating Concept in Natural Resource Politics." *Propositions for a Social Science Research Agenda.*

Taylor and Francis. *Society and Natural Resources*.

Clark, Arthur C. *Profiles of the Future* (1963). Harper & Row, New York.

Dearborn, Donald C. & Salit Kark (2009). "Motivations for Conserving Urban Biodiversity." *Conservation Biology*.

Decker, Daniel J. and Lisa C. Chase (1997). "Human Dimension Approaches to Citizen Input: Keys for Successful Policy." *Deer as Public Goods and Public Nuisance: Issues and Policy Options in Maryland*, ed. Bruce L. Gardner, pp. 95-106. College Park, MD: Center for Agricultural and Natural Resource Policy.

Denardo, J.C., A. R. Jarrett, H. B. Manbeck. D. J. Beattie & R. D. Berghage (2005). "Storm Water Mitigation and Surface Temperature Reduction by Green Roofs." *Transactions of the ASAE*, Vol. 48, 1491-1496.

Domhoff, William G. (2005). *Power at the Local Level: Growth Coalition Theory*.

Freyfogle, Eric T (1998). *Bounded People, Boundless Land: Stewardship Across Boundaries*, ed. Richard Night and Peter Landues. Island Press.

Fuller, R. A., K. N. Irvine, P. Devine-Wright, P. H. Warren and K. J. Gaston (2007). "Psychological Benefits of Green Space Increase with Biodiversity." *Biology Letters*, Vol.3, 390-394.

Heifetz, Ronald (2005). *Leadership Without Easy Answers*. The Belknap Press of Harvard University Press. Cambridge, Massachusetts. London, England.

Hess, Karl and Murray N. Rothbard ed (1969). "Massacre at People's Park." *The Libertarian Forum*. Vol. I, No. VI

Hess, Karl Jr. *Visions Upon the Land: Man and*

Nature on the Western Range.

Hollis, Leo (2013). "Cities Belong to Us: Reclaiming the Streets Through Civic Participation Does More Than Change the City: It Creates Citizens." *Aeon Magazine.*

Hunter, Boyd (2007). "Conspicuous Compassion and Wicked Problems." Australian National University Electronic Press. *Agenda*, Vol. 14, No. 3.

Johnson, Charles W. (2011). "Markets Freed From Capitalism." *Markets Not Capitalism: Individualist Anarchism Against Bosses, Inequality, Corporate Power and Structural Poverty.*

Kitchell, Mark (1990). *Berkeley in the Sixties.* Kitchell Films and P. O. V. Theatricals.

Legacy Parks Foundation. (2013) *Knoxville's Urban Wilderness.*

Logan, J. R., & Molotch, H. (1987). *Urban Fortunes: The Political Economy of Place.* Berkeley: University of California Press.

Long, Roderick (2014). "From the Unthinking Depths." Bleeding Heart Libertarians.

Lowery, Wesley (2014). "The QuickTrip Gas Station, Ferguson Protestor's Staging Ground, Is Now Silent."

McKinney, M. L. (2002) "Urbanization, Biodiversity and Conservation." *BioScience*, Vol. 52, 883-890.

McKinney, M. L. (2008) "Effects of Urbanization on Species Richness: A Review of Plants and Animals." *Urban Ecosystems*, Vol. 11, 161-176.

Molotch, H. (1976). "The City as a Growth Machine." *American Journal of Sociology*, 82, 309-330.

Nelson, David H. (1992). *Citizen Task Forces on Deer Management: A Case Study.* Department of Environmental Conservation, New York.

Nibset, Matthew C. (2010). "Ecologist Says Scientists Need to Re-Evaluate Approach to Communication." Big Think.

Nowak, D. J., D. E. Crane, and J. C. Stevens (2006). "Air Pollution Removal by Urban Trees and Shrubs in the United States." *Urban Forestry and Urban Greening*, Vol. 4, 115-123.

Ostermeier, David (2010). "Human Dimensions of Natural Resource Management." *FWF* 412 Lecture Notes.

Ostrom, Eleanor (1990). *Governing the Commons*. Cambridge University Press.

Pankratz, S., T. Young, H. Cuevas-Arellano, R. Kumar, R. F. Ambrose & I. H. Suffet (2007). "The Ecological Value of Constructed Wetlands for Treating Urban Runoff." *Water Science and Technology,* Vol. 55, 63-69.

Rebele, Franz. (1994) "Urban Ecology and Special Features of Urban Ecosystems." *Global Ecology and Biogeography Letters*, Vol. 4 173-187.

Rothbard, Murray (2009). *Anatomy of the State*. Ludwig von Mises Institute.

Rolle, Su (2002). *Measure of Progress for Collaboration: Case Study of the Applegate Partnership*. United States Forest Service. Ashland, OR.

Schott, Ben (2010). *GONGO: Government Organized Non-Governmental Organization*.

Shah, Sonia. (2009) "The Spread of New Diseases: The Climate Connection." *Yale Environment 360*.

Soule, Michael E. (1985). *What Is Conservation Biology?* American Institute of Biological Sciences.

Sukopp, H. (1981). Translated: *Grundwasserab-*

senkungen. 239-272. Berlin, West.

Tansley, A. G. (1935). "The Use and Abuse of Vegetational Concepts and Terms." *Ecology,* Vol. 16, 284-307.

The University of Tennessee, Knoxville (1995). "Little Book of Conflict Resolution." UTK Conflict Resolution Program.

Tilghman, N. G. (1987). "Characteristics of Urban Woodlands Affecting Breeding Bird Diversity and Abundance." *Landscape and Urban Planning,* Vol. 14, 481-95.

Wagner, Melinda B. (2002). *Space and Place, Land and Legacy. Culture, Environment and Conservation in the Appalachian South.* Ed. Benita Howell. University of Ih Press.

Weber, Max (1919). *Politics as a Vocation.*

Wilson, Chad (2010). *Evolution of Western Values Toward the Environment.*

Zinn, Howard (2003). *A Peoples' History of the United States.* HarperCollins Publishers, New York, NY.

CHAPTER
TWELVE

ANY (GOOD) THING THE STATE CAN DO, WE CAN DO BETTER

GARY CHARTIER

The question whether people in a stateless society could respond satisfactorily to a disaster like the BP oil spill is really just a special case of the general question whether people without the state can do the things people attempt to do through the state. It seems to me that the answer is "yes."

That's because everything the state purportedly does is actually done by people. Sometimes they act out of fear; sometimes out of the perception that the state is legitimate; sometimes what the state commands turns out to be just what they want to do anyway; and sometimes because they believe that what the state is asking them to do is just what they are morally required to do anyway. But, for whatever reason, they do it.

This fact ought to be sufficient to make us confident that ordinary people, cooperating peacefully, can deal with environmental or other disasters in a stateless society. In what follows, I briefly discuss the purported advantages the state might be thought to possess in dealing with large-scale problems before noting some ways in which people in

c4ss.org/content/17899

a stateless society could cooperate to prevent or remedy a disaster like the one currently taking place in the Gulf.

✷ *The State's Supposed Advantages*

What might be thought to give the state an advantage over the various non-state institutions of a stateless society? Statists are most likely to point to two kinds of factors: information and force. A third, concerned with a potential difficulty faced by a non-state legal system relying on tort law to deal with environmental harms, might also be highlighted by some statists.

✷ *Informational Advantages?*

Statists often think the state has information that ordinary people lack. But to the extent that this information concerns optimal production levels and distribution patterns for goods and services, we know as confidently as we know anything about economics that more information is distributed throughout a given economic environment, possessed by various actors as a matter of "local knowledge." Polycentric processes that mobilize this local knowledge will ultimately prove more effective than top-down, hierarchical ones at aggregating relevant information.

Statists might suggest that the state had an important role to play, not so much because it possessed information relevant to consumption and production, but because it possessed access to expert information. The assumption here seems to be that experts know just what needs to be done about a given problem but, because ordinary people aren't convinced, the options are either to let nothing be done about a serious problem or to impose the will of the experts. Clearly, there are problems here related both to the ignorance of experts and to the right of people to make mistakes.

But here the question is how information comes to be

classified as expert, and how it is used by the state. Political processes clearly affect the selection of experts and the assessment of the information they provide. Further, given both the potential abuse of expertise as a rationalization for authoritarianism, and the inherent value of personal autonomy, it does not seem as if the conclusions of particular experts ought to be imposed on people without their consent. There are, it seems, side constraints on the use of expert authority, whatever its potential value. Finally, if expert claims are accurate, why can they not be winnowed by public evaluation—in the course of conversations in which other experts from outside the political process, as well as ordinary people able to employ their common sense, are free to participate?

* Advantages Reflective of the State's Monopoly of Force?

If purported informational advantages provide no reason to think that the state is better equipped to aid us in, for instance, responding to natural disasters, what about its capacity to use force to compel people to cooperate? As I've already suggested, the vast majority of instances of cooperation with or under the direction of the state do not reflect any immediate threat or application of force. Instead, they reflect people's sense of the moral or prudential appropriateness of doing as the state directs.

Sometimes, of course, people may cooperate voluntarily, but only because they believe that others will do so, too, under the background threat of compulsion by the state. But there is no reason not to think that a combination of social norms and advance agreements (cp. David Schmidtz's discussion of "assurance contracts") could not in many cases foster the needed cooperation in the absence of threatened force.

I'm inclined to think that there are very few, if any, pure public goods, and it's not clear to me that any environmental good we could currently affect would count as one. But, if there are any, it seems to me both that (i) as Schmidtz suggests, there are interesting market-based ways of providing at least some of them and (ii) the difficulties associated with alternatives mean that there's no good reason to prefer coercive solutions to market-based ones. For if worthwhile cooperation is not forthcoming in some cases in which we wish it might be, we must still recall that the state is not, never has been, and never will be directed by angels, that instituting an organization with monopolistic control over the use of force in a given region opens up enormous possibilities for violence, abuse, cronyism, depredation, and dispossession. In short, while there may be failures of cooperation, the costs associated with these failures must be compared to the costs associated with failures on the part of monopolistic states.

Sometimes, of course, people will grudgingly obey the state only because of its threats of violence. The fact that these threats would not be available in a stateless society does not seem like a particular loss. For it is almost certain that, in cases in which people only obey out of fear, they see little or no independent reason to do whatever it is the state wants them to do, and we have good reason to be glad, therefore, that they will not be forced to do similar things in the state's absence.

✤ *The Advantage of Being Able to Bypass the Need to Delineate Lines of Causal Responsibility in Dealing with Environmental Problems?*

One final reason that might be advanced for adopting the view that the state was better positioned to deal with certain kinds of environmental problems than free people engaged in peaceful cooperation is the difficulty of identifying relevant causal connections between particular actions and environmental harms. If something like tort law is to be used to compensate victims of harms (as many anarchists suppose it should be) and if the prospect of compensation is expected to play a key role in deterring violators, but if there is no clear way of identifying the actual cause of a harm, will numerous harms go undeterred and uncompensated?

Suppose, for instance, that anthropogenic global warming is occurring and poses a serious hazard to present and future generations. Suppose, too, that we can be reasonably sure that certain classes of human actions contribute in a general way to AGW. It is hard to see how we might identify particular actors as liable for causing particular AGW-related harms, so it's unclear how an ordinary tort regime would help here.

There are, I think, at least three non-exclusive possibilities open to us here. First, something like an expanded class action lawsuit could be permitted exclusively in such cases, in which classes of plaintiffs could sue classes of potential perpetrators. It would still be necessary to demonstrate a causal connection between a class of actions and a class of harms, and to demonstrate the extent of the harms. Second, while a full-blown tort regime treating environmental pollution and similar phenomena as common-law nuisances, combined with specific property rights in particular regions and ecosystems now claimed en masse by the state, might not (if the first option just mentioned were ruled out as unjust) provide compensation for past harms, it could perfectly well make possible a thoroughgoing system of restraint on pollutants imposed by newly empowered property owners. Third, a thoroughgoing system of social norms could limit the activity of polluters and secure compensation for victims (especially in cases in which harm was clear but causation impossible clearly to demonstrate, but in which demonstrating causation was required for legal liability). Thus, if there was widespread agreement on the reality and causes of AGW, or any other environmental harm, people freely and peacefully cooperating could identify ways of stopping or slowing the occurrence of the relevant causes and compensating victims.

In short, any good thing the state can do, we can do better.

What we do will be done more efficiently, because we can draw on bottom-up knowledge. And we will also spend our resources efficiently because the decision whether to employ them at all will be ours, not that of a group of economic and political elites who can externalize the costs of satisfying their preferences onto ordinary people.

✻ *Large-Scale Environmental Disaster in a Stateless Society*

How could people in a stateless society deal with challenges like those caused by the BP disaster?

✻ *The Importance of Property Rights or Their Equivalent*

The first thing to do, clearly, is to assign responsibility—to assign particular places to particular people. This needn't mean assigning those rights to individuals for commercial exploitation; it just means that something like the Gulf—a place, a region, an ecosystem—needs to be in someone's hands. Someone might be seeking to develop the region commercially. But someone might just as well be interested in preserving it, planning to limit or entirely prohibit commercial use. Whatever the projected use, an individual, cooperate, partnership, non-profit, or business firm with ownership rights can be expected to care for the owned space.

To be sure, there's no guarantee that the allocation of rights to, say, the Gulf (on the basis of active homesteading or prior customary possession or something similar—certainly not on the basis of allocation by the state, which has no title to anything and is all too likely to favor its cronies) will result in its being put to the predetermined use preferred by any group, noncommercial or commercial. There is good reason to believe that, as a general rule, if people own things, they will care for those things, but their objectives may vary (though of course there may be a general consensus that can be enforced through ordinary social norm maintenance mechanisms).

Just as groups like the Nature Conservancy buy up currently privately held property in the U.S., they would likely be willing to homestead unowned property in the Gulf. I'd expect a fair amount of this sort of thing, though it would obviously be important to figure out ways of preventing title from being established just by announcement while also not requiring commercial cultivation if that's not what someone wants.

And commercial homesteading certainly could and would occur, too. A stateless society would doubtless feature a mixture of both. But, in any case, if there were specific property owners to whom liability would be owed in the case of spills, rather than politicians often indebted precisely to the entities doing the spilling, things would surely be different to some extent, whatever the nature of the property-owners' interests in the property.

* Mechanisms for Protecting the Interests of Nonhuman Sentients

If your goal is protecting, not geographically fixed spaces, but rather mobile organisms, say, within those spaces (sea turtles, for instance), then enabling anyone to take on a case (for, e.g., a sea turtle) and recoup salary and expenses when successful in court (thus functioning as something like what is today called a "private attorney general") would do the trick. Whether this option would or should be available would depend, obviously, on the existence of a social consensus regarding non-humans. If most people don't think sea turtles—individually or collectively—ought to be protected, they won't be. If they are to be protected, though, it's easy to envision the kinds of mechanisms a stateless society could use to protect them.

∗ Protection of Ecosystems by Property Owners

Whether individual owners were responsible, or whether those—for instance—along the shoreline controlled the Gulf (or any other ecosystem) as common property, or whatever, specific owners not in the pockets of oil companies would have to decide to allow drilling to take place, and they could obviously take whatever preventive measures they wanted, including prohibiting drilling, requiring performance bonds, requiring on-site inspections, etc.

∗ Is the State a Desirable Alternative, Even Absent Optimal Protection by Private Owners?

If particular individuals or groups didn't control a particular ecosystem, the alternative would seem to be some sort of state-like entity. Any institution capable of forcibly implementing ex ante environmental regulations on unowned property or on the property of others (however property ought to be handled in this and other cases) would seem to be altogether too much like a state, and its creation and maintenance highly dangerous, and likely unjust.

∗ Regulating Ecosystems Without the State

If there is a property regime in a given ecosystem, specific owners—individuals, for-profit firms, or non-profits—could preempt or regulate conduct that might be environmentally harmful as they liked (and would be liable if spills moved beyond their property to that of others). And if there is no such regime, one is likely to emerge. The alternative is a state, or something like it; we have no good reason to want that, and a regime of voluntary cooperation in which people use their individual or group property interests to protect ecosystems seems perfectly workable. Environmental challenges can be satisfactorily addressed by a combination of voluntary, peaceful cooperation and robust tort liability. Statist and quasi-statist alternatives are neither necessary nor appealing.

AUTHORS

Dawie Coetzee. An architect based in Cape Town, South Africa. I discovered C4SS through Kevin Carson's participation in the Distributist Yahoo Group, and found that I agreed with virtually everything he was saying. My peculiar fields of interest are urban design and automobiles, though each of those is linked to a broader underlying philosophy.

Gary Chartier. Professor of Law and Business Ethics and Associate Dean of the Tom and Vi Zapara School of Business at La Sierra University and a left-wing market anarchist. I take anarchism to be the project of doing without the state. I'm a leftist because I support inclusion and oppose subordination, deprivation, and aggressive and preventive war. I'm happy to identify as both, in something not unlike the sense suggested by Benjamin Tucker's work, a socialist and a libertarian. Recent books: *Anarchy and Legal Order* (Cambridge 2013); *Economic Justice and Natural Law* (Cambridge 2009); *Radicalizing Rawls* (Palgrave 2014); *The Conscience of an Anarchist* (Cobden 2011); and *Markets Not Capitalism* (Minor Compositions-Autonomedia 2011) (co-edited with Charles W. Johnson). Next, among others: *Libertarian Theories of Class* (co-edited with Ross Kenyon and Roderick T. Long).

Kevin Carson. Kevin Carson is a senior fellow of the Center for a Stateless Society (c4ss.org) and holds the Center's Karl Hess Chair in Social Theory. He is a mutualist and individualist anarchist whose written work includes *Studies in Mutualist Political Economy*, *Organization Theory: A Libertarian Perspective*, and *The Homebrew Industrial Revolution: A Low-Overhead Manifesto*, all of which are freely available online. Carson has also written for such print publications as *The Freeman: Ideas on Liberty* and a variety of internet-based journals and blogs, including *Just Things, The Art of the Possible*, the P2P Foundation, and his own Mutualist Blog. Website: http://desktopregulatorystate.wordpress.com/

M. George van der Meer. A mutualist and decentralist. Formerly a curator of fine art, his interests include social philosophy, antiquing, and film.

Grant Mincy. Grant A. Mincy is a senior fellow at the Center for a Stateless Society (C4SS.org), where he holds the Elinor Ostrom Chair in Environmental Studies and Commons Governance. He also blogs at appalachianson.wordpress.com. In addition, Mincy is an associate editor of the *Molinari Review* and an Energy & Environment Advisory Council Member for the Our America Initiative. He earned his Master's degree in Earth and Planetary Science from the University of Tennessee in the summer of 2012. He lives in Knoxville, Tennessee, where he teaches both Biology and Geology at area colleges. Feel free to contact him at grant.mincy@c4ss.org. Website: http://appalachianson.wordpress.com/

Roderick T. Long. Roderick T. Long (A.B. Harvard, 1985; Ph.D. Cornell, 1992) is professor of philosophy at Auburn University, president of the Molinari Institute and Molinari Society, editor of *The Industrial Radical* and *Molinari Review*, and co-editor of *The Journal of Ayn Rand Studies*. A founding member of the Alliance of the Libertarian Left and senior fellow at the Center for a Stateless Society, Long blogs at *Austro-Athenian Empire* and *Bleeding Heart Libertarians*. Website: http://aaeblog.com

Thom Holterman. Thom Holterman is emeritus professor of Constitutional and Administrative Law at Erasmus

University, Rotterdam. He holds a Ph.D. in the science of law with the thesis *Law and Political Organization: A Study of Convergence in Views on Law and Political Organization of Some Anarchists and Some Legal Scholars* (Rotterdam, 1986). Besides having written a number of books on law and anarchism in Dutch, together with Henc van Maarseveen he published the anthology *Law and Anarchism* (Montreal, 1984). Recently he published his first book in French, *L'Anarchisme, c'est réglé! Un exposé anarchiste sur le droit* (Lyon, 2013). Holterman has been an editor of the Dutch anarchist quarterly *De AS* since the early 1970s.

C4SS's
MISSION STATEMENT

The Center for a Stateless Society (C4SS) is an anarchist think-tank and media center. Its mission is to explain and defend the idea of vibrant social cooperation without aggression, oppression, or centralized authority.

In particular, it seeks to enlarge public understanding and transform public perceptions of anarchism, while reshaping academic and movement debate, through the production and distribution of market anarchist media content, both scholarly and popular, the organization of events, and the development of networks and communities, and to serve, along with the Alliance of the Libertarian Left and the Molinari Institute, as an institutional home for left market anarchists.

MOLINARI INSTITUTE
MISSION STATEMENT

The form of social organization known as the State, an increasingly virulent parasite on civil society, is entering the final stages of an unsustainable growth that threatens the existence of civilisation itself.

The mission of the Molinari Institute is to promote understanding of the philosophy of Market Anarchism as a sane, consensual alternative to the hypertrophic violence of the State.

The Institute takes its name from Gustave de Molinari (1819-1912), originator of the theory of Market Anarchism.

The Molinari Institute is a 501(c)(3) tax-exempt organisation.

ALLIANCE
OF THE
LIBERTARIAN LEFT
PREAMBLE

The Alliance of the Libertarian Left is a multi-tendency coalition of mutualists, agorists, voluntaryists, geolibertarians, left-Rothbardians, green libertarians, dialectical anarchists, radical minarchists, and others on the libertarian left, united by an opposition to statism and militarism, to cultural intolerance (including sexism, racism, and homophobia), and to the prevailing corporatist capitalism falsely called a free market; as well as by an emphasis on education, direct action, and building alternative institutions, rather than on electoral politics, as our chief strategy for achieving liberation.

C4SS's
EDITORIAL POLICY

The Center for a Stateless Society (C4SS) commissions and distributes media content designed to challenge the state: to undermine the false perception of its legitimacy, demonstrate its irrelevance to truly solving social and economic problems, and encourage its abolition. At no time will any C4SS publication implicitly or explicitly support the state's continuation or augmentation.

C4SS's publications will convey a positive vision of voluntary, peaceful cooperation as the basis for a flourishing life in society; they will seek to foster not only the free exchange of goods and services but also the many other kinds of voluntary interaction that help to make social existence viable and attractive. Thus, they will urge the abolition of all those privileges that impede peaceful cooperation, while unequivocally rejecting the privilege-riddled capitalism so frequently mistaken for a genuinely freed market. And they will help to realize a culture free from authoritarianism, exclusion, submission, and deprivation—whether effected and sustained violently or non-violently—as well as aggressive violence.

C4SS emphasizes education, direct action, and the construction of alternative institutions, rather than electoral politics, as strategies for achieving liberation.

While its basic commitments will be consistently embodied in C4SS's publications, not every C4SS author will embrace all of them, and the C4SS's core values are reflected in part in its willingness to publish the work of a broad range of thinkers who oppose the state and who value economic and cultural freedom.

Donate Today!

The Center for a Stateless Society (C4SS.ORG) functions on the enthusiasm of writers and volunteers, but it is the continued donations of supporters that keeps us going and growing. We have big plans and even bigger dreams for C4SS, and we need your help.

Fundraising is not begging or charity. It is a barometer of success, support, and professionalism. It is about offering an opportunity to participate in the project, the task at hand. So we ask you, dear supporters, let us know how we are doing and play a crucial part in our success by giving to C4SS.

C4SS's parent institution, the Molinari Institute, is a tax-exempt 501(c)(3) nonprofit organization; hence donations to the Molinari Institute—and thus to the Center for a Stateless Society—are tax-deductible. The Molinari Institute's tax identification number is 20-3731375.

Made in the USA
Columbia, SC
01 April 2019